50 Years of Chrysler's Hottest Cars

Hottest Cars

TEXT AND PHOTOGRAPHS BY

NICKY WRIGHT

GRAMERCY BOOKS

NEW YORK

For the Little Rascals:
    Ambre, Britainy, David, Julian, Sharon, Ian, Ben, Lee and Sam . . .
    I love you all.

And to Ducky,
    whose flights of fancy merit a special thank you.

This edition is published by Gramercy Books,™
a division of Random House Value Publishing, Inc., 201 East 50th Street, New York, New York 10022.

Gramercy Books™ and colophon are trademarks of Random House Value Publishing, Inc.

Random House
New York • Toronto • London • Sydney • Auckland
http://www.randomhouse.com/

Printed and bound in Singapore

Project editor: Gregory Suriano
Book design: Helene Wald Berinsky

A CIP catalog record for this book is available from the Library of Congress.

50 Years of Chrysler's Hottest Cars / text and photographs by Nicky Wright
ISBN 0-517-18734-5

8 7 6 5 4 3 2 1

Acknowledgments

The author would like to thank the following for allowing their cars to be photographed, and all those without whose help this book would not have been possible: David Arent, Rick Cain, Brownie Mascow, Door Prairie Museum (La Porte, Indiana), Bob Schmidt, Glen Patch, Tony Lengacher, Robert A. Lutz, Dave Jones, Mel Atkins, Merle Begley, Randy Renbarger, Otto Rosenbusch, Richard Carpenter, Jacquelyn and Michael Krug, Classic Heaven Museum (Mesa, Arizona), Milt Jenks, Gary Disney, Chrysler Corporation, Steve Witmer, Larry Bell, Joe Bortz, Russell Beckett, Gilmore Classic Car Museum (Kalamazoo, Michigan), Dick Braun, Classic Car Center (Warsaw, Indiana), Frank Kleptz, Virgil and Dorothy Meyer, John Mitchell, Stuart Cole, David Long, Mike Sturgeon, and all the others whose cars are shown but whose names aren't.

A special thanks to Chrysler Corporation. This great motor company helped above and beyond the call of duty. Here are a few of the people whose assistance will always be remembered: Brian Wallace, Larry Rathgeb, John Herlitz, John Pointer, Dave Cummins (rtd.), Chris Preuss, John Thompson, Brant Rosenbusch, Art Pound, Rita McKay, Gary Romberg, R. L. Lajoie, Frank Chianese Jr., Louis Patane, John P. Wehrly, Dick Myers, and James Kenyon. My thanks to you all. Neon, Dodge Trucks, Chrysler 300M, and Viper racing photography courtesy Chrysler Corporation.

The author would also like to acknowledge the various books and magazines that unknowingly helped in the preparation of this work: *Motor Trend, Car & Driver, High Performance Mopar, Collectible Automobile, Automobile Quarterly, Cars & Parts, Chrysler Power, Special Interest Autos;* Brooklands Books' series of magazine reprint books such as *Mopar Muscle Cars, Dodge Charger, Muscle Cars Compared, Chrysler 300, Plymouth Barracuda, Plymouth Muscle Cars,* and *Dodge Muscle Cars;* Publications International's indispensable books *The Complete History of Chrysler, Encyclopedia of American Cars, 1930–1980, Viper: Pure Performance by Dodge,* and the *Consumer Guide Auto and Auto Test* series. Other significant books include *Chrysler 300: A Source Book,* edited by Thomas E. Bonsall, Robert Ackerson's *Chrysler 300: America's Most Powerful Car,* and, from *Cars & Parts,* its *Legend Series: Muscle Cars of the '60s & '70s.*

Advertising copy and period advertisements contained in this book have been reproduced by kind permission of Chrysler Corporation. A majority of the photographs were taken using Fuji slide film and photographed with the Pentax 6 x 7, Pentax 645, and Nikon cameras.

Contents

Former Chrysler vice chairman Robert Lutz with three of his blazing-red classic collector cars: the Chrysler 300, the Viper, and the Cunningham C2.

Foreword

Thirty-five years in the auto business has taught me that there are basically two types of people in the world: motorists and *driving enthusiasts.*

To the former, driving is nothing more than a mind-numbing exercise in getting from one place on a map to another.

For those of us in the latter group, driving—at its best—is an affair between the open road, the five senses, and the intellect. It is an emotional experience, capable of providing everything from unbridled exhilaration to something bordering on bliss. For us, drama on wheels is not only desirable but necessary.

As *50 Years of Chrysler's Hottest Cars* so ably chronicles, Chrysler's history is bursting with the kind of "hot" cars that driving enthusiasts love. Looking back, it is clear that the 300 Letter Series cars, the Dodge Charger, the Plymouth Road Runner, and many others laid down the genetic code at Chrysler that made possible the Dodge Viper.

Hot cars like the Viper and the Plymouth Prowler were not born from logical, left-brain thinking. Instead, they owe their existence to intuition, gut feeling, and imagination.

Case in point: The instantaneous success of the Viper prompted more than a few Japanese auto executives to ask me a question that went something like this: "What kind of market research did you do to convince yourself to produce an outrageously designed, 400-horsepower V-10 sports car that goes from 0 to 60 in four seconds?" My answer was always the same: "None. We built it because we *wanted* to." I suspect that the same thing could have happened the first time a Max Wedge Plymouth Sport Fury roared across the pavement.

Which is not to say that we didn't perform market research during my twelve years at Chrysler as a way to get into the consumer's head, because we did. On the other hand, the company is no longer—as are all to many auto companies—a slave to science, or to overly analytical thinking, just for the sake of being analytical. As I used to explain to the uninitiated: At the end of the day, the thing that gives us the most satisfaction is knowing that we design and build the kinds of vehicles that are as much fun to look at as they are to drive—great cars and great trucks that give back more than they promise, because they are designed, engineered, and manufactured by people with a proud heritage to uphold.

That declaration of independence from mundane motoring goes a long way toward explaining the motivation behind the creation of the vehicles featured in *50 Years of Chrysler's Hottest Cars.* In recounting Chrysler's hot-car heritage and passion for driving, this book is meat to the driving enthusiasts in all of us.

ROBERT A. LUTZ
Former Vice Chairman, Chrysler Corporation

50 Years of Chrysler's Hottest Cars

*Out with the Old,
In with the New*

CHAPTER 1

September 1945. With two devastating strikes against Japan, America had become the world's first atomic power, believing the use of the bomb would save a million American lives. World War II was finally over. The world rejoiced and the soldiers came home.

Americans stateside hadn't suffered as badly as their European and British allies. Nobody occupied them, nobody bombed them, but they still had to make sacrifices for the war effort. There was rationing, there were shortages, and a nation's youth was spirited away to battlefields far from home, far from the sounds and the smells of the dusty little towns they grew up in. And there were no new cars.

Automobile production stopped in the early part of 1942 when Detroit turned its factories to tanks, trucks, and airplanes. As soon as the conflict drew to a close, Motown switched back to car production faster than Superman can fly. Car makers knew, and rightly so, that the returning military personnel would want new wheels, as would those awaiting their return.

Such was the desire for new cars that anything would do. The manufacturers happily obliged by dragging out 1942 designs, changing a grille or two, and advertising them as "all new." Met by glossy and colorful *Saturday Evening Post* double-page spreads,

Chrysler, like other companies, dredged up 1942 models, changed grilles and trim, and offered them for sale as "all-new cars." This is a 1946 Chrysler New Yorker Club Coupe, of which 10,735 units were built between 1946 and 1948.

the public hardly noticed their rusting 1942 cars were virtually the same; instead, they rushed down to the more-than-happy dealerships, plonked down their savings—or more likely a deposit—and drove away in a shiny new/old automobile.

Chrysler, like the rest of the motor industry, had turned over its assembly lines to the making of military machines during the war. When Japan's surrender came, Chrysler stopped churning out Sherman tanks powered by five six-cylinder engines lumped together and returned to car manufacture. And like all its competitors, Chrysler offered warmed-over 1942 models. Nonetheless, Chrysler made

enough styling modifications to ensure a 1946 model would not be confused with a 1942.

One car Chrysler put out in 1946 could almost be described as new. This was the Town & Country, a beautiful machine that began life in 1941 as a wood-trimmed station wagon. In 1946 it blossomed from its lowly beginnings to emerge as a very stylish personal luxury car heavily trimmed in white ash, replete with mahogany paneling. There was a sedan and a convertible, the latter of which became a favorite of Tinseltown. (Leo Carillo, who played the Cisco Kid's pal, Pancho, in the movies, had one adorned with the stuffed head of an unfortunate steer.) The Town & Country is now regarded as a true classic, and deservedly so.

At this time little thought was given to fast and sporty cars. It was all Detroit could do to keep up with demand for regular cars. Anything with an engine, transmission, and four wheels

Cadillac's first postwar design appeared in 1948. The Coupe de Ville has attractive good looks and was streets ahead of Chrysler styling. This is the 1949 model, which had the added advantage of a brand-new 331-cid OHV V-8.

Chrysler's smart, personal car, the 1948 Town & Country, became a cult with the Hollywood set. This is the sedan version. Note the hand-crafted real wood on doors and body.

sold. It wasn't until 1947 that the first truly postwar design came about from Studebaker, who beat everybody to the punch. The design was a complete departure from the accepted norm—with its low profile, flow-through fenders, larger glass area—and was obviously the shape of things to come. It was also designed by the man who would soon recreate Chrysler Corporation's styling image.

Virgil Exner, after a stint at General Motors, joined Raymond Loewy Studios around 1937 and was soon handed the Studebaker account. During the war Exner turned to military vehicles and was responsible for such famous machines as the amphibious Weazel half-track and legendary DUKW, or "Duck." He couldn't keep away from cars, though, using his spare time to work on ideas that eventually resulted in the 1947 Studebaker.

Due to its revolutionary design Studebaker enjoyed a banner year. A year later, the Indiana-based (South Bend) company was somewhat eclipsed by Hudson's slab-sided, unit-bodied step-down beauty that gave the small

independent its best year ever. Packard launched the first of many radical facelifts to produce a smooth but overweight-looking car soon labeled the Pregnant Elephant. Meanwhile, over at General Motors, Cadillac, under the watchful eyes of design guru Harley Earl, introduced a classic beauty whose stubby little rear fins became a talking point in country clubs and bars.

Over at Dearborn a coup had taken place. Worried lest old Henry's mental state might seriously affect Ford war production, the government arranged for Henry's grandson, Henry Ford II, to take over. Young Henry was fired with ideas the old man would not have tolerated had he remained in charge, but once he had been safely removed, the new Henry on the block brought in fresh young faces who enthusiastically promoted major changes to improve Ford's market share.

Chrysler, however, remained solidly with its old guard. Walter Chrysler's designated successor, K. T. Keller, had been president since 1935 and a man steadfastly committed to practicality over style. His philosophy had proven merit for Chrysler, which had ousted Ford from the number-two spot in 1936, a position Highland Park still enjoyed in 1948. Chrysler knew Ford had something up its sleeve for 1949, but K. T. wasn't worried. A conservative individual, Keller was a true mid-westerner who deemed flashy styling would not sell cars. Good, solid, upright automobiles high enough to allow the driver to wear his homburg or stetson was what people wanted. Practical cars, K. T. continually drummed into his staff, would always sell.

If one looked at what used to be, K. T. was right. Chrysler's main claim to fame was engineering, not style. Reliable engines and transmissions, solid workmanship, and comfortable interiors were what Chrysler had built its name upon—and what helped it keep ahead of Ford. But Harley Earl, the ingenious styling wizard over at GM, changed the public's perception of what a car was supposed to be. By the late forties, it was not how a car should run, but how it looked.

Henry Ford's young turks followed Earl's philosophy that styling was the thing. They got their chance to show their colors with all-new designs in 1949. Nobody, with perhaps the exception of K. T. Keller, disputed that Ford had pulled a masterstroke. Slab-sided, lower, and very exciting, the new Ford was a complete break with the past; only the V-8 engine remained the same. Likewise with Mercury and Lincoln: the former became the darling of the customizing set and later a piece of James Dean memorabilia (he used a '49 or '50 Mercury in the classic film *Rebel without a Cause*). Ford had correctly gauged the times: the war had been over for four years, and a generation that had found its feet in the Depression and had fought in the fields of Europe and Asia now wanted to erase bitter memories of yesterday. As the bells pealed for 1950, they pealed for a brave new world.

New cars had been launched by Chrysler in 1949 and while they were quite handsome, they did not have the pizzazz of Ford, Studebaker, Cadillac, or Hudson. Still, in Chrysler's time-honored tradition, the cars were solid, well built, and—following Keller's doctrine—a driver could wear his/her hat in comfort. Not that Chrysler even lost any sales: 1949 was the highest production year in the company's history. It was still very much a seller's market.

Considering the radical designs Virgil Exner was capable of, it seems strange that K. T. would offer him twenty-five thousand dollars a year to head a new Advanced Styling Studio at Chrysler. Even though he may not have admitted it publicly, Keller probably saw the writing on the wall for boxy, practical cars. Whatever he may have thought in private, Keller didn't give Exner free rein when he hired him in 1949. That would come a year later, after K. T. became chairman and Lester Lum "Tex" Colbert took over the presidency in November 1950. Colbert belonged to the Henry Ford II school; he believed in change, in fresh, young expression. As the old order retired, Colbert replaced them with the new.

Remembering that production lead times for a new design can take three years, Exner had his work cut out to try and improve the dowdy styles Chrysler already had in the can, and the first results were the 1953–54 models. Exner took the 1949 models, softened the bodies, added more glass area and one-piece curved windshields, and got rid of the separate rear fenders. Not that it was much, but what he was able to do was a great improvement. It wouldn't be until 1955 that Exner's *designs* would reach full bloom; earlier, 1951 to be exact, Chrysler showed its

Although quite regal, the all-new 1949 Chrysler Windsor is more practical than stylish. One could, as the Chrysler president insisted, wear one's hat in it!

mechanical prowess by launching an engine to end all engines at the time.

As already noted, Chrysler was first and foremost an engineering concern. Not content with a conventional overhead-valve, wedge-shaped V-8 similar to the one Cadillac introduced a couple of years earlier, Chrysler came up with a V-8 possessing a hemispherical combustion chamber.

The Hemi had been in the works for a long time, since 1937 in fact. In those days Chrysler had in-line, L-head six- and eight-cylinder engines, which, although durable, trouble-free units, were crushingly boring. If these engines were ever to be replaced, Chrysler management said they wanted something superior to what everyone else would have. So, under the auspices of Chrysler development engineering chief R. K. (Ken) Lee, the team looked at various engine configurations that had come and gone before eventually settling on the hemispherical design.

Not that an engine with hemispherical combustion chambers was new: Jaguar had had an in-line six with a hemispherical combustion chamber since 1948. Even earlier were the engines powering Duesenberg, Stutz, and racing cars like Indy 500 Offenhausers and Millers.

After the initial research had been completed, Chrysler decided the advantages of a Hemi far outweighed the disadvantages. Further engineering research and development became the responsibility of W. E. Drinkard, supervisor of Chrysler's engine-development laboratories, and M. L. Carpentier, then assistant chief engineer in charge of engine design. Carpentier had been with Chrysler ever since the company began and was associated with three of the greatest engineers of all time, Carl Breer, Fred Zeder, and Owen Skelton. These three, incidentally, were the creators of the advanced Airflow.

Although more complex than a conventional V-8, the design, Carpentier and Drinkard found, had a lot of merit. It had more versatility, ran cooler, and was far more durable. The engineers decided on a short-stroke, big-bore configuration for the Hemi, which had two sets of rocker shafts, arms, and pushrods. Large, unobstructed ports allowed for better breathing and cooler running, and the smaller hemispherical combustion chambers increased efficiency and held the heat better. Inclined valves and centrally located spark plugs resulted in more even power and more complete burning of fuel. Not only that, the design allowed a greater percentage of horsepower over conventional engines, an advantage not lost on hot rodders when the Hemi finally appeared in 1951.

Cadillac thought itself the bee's knees with its excellent 331-cubic-inch V-8 introduced in 1949, but the design was eclipsed by Chrysler's Hemi in 1951. Sporting the same 331-cubic-inch capacity as Cadillac's 1951 engine, the Hemi packed 12 percent more horsepower—180 versus 160—and was definitely peppier. Talk of Chrysler's top speed was the sort of stuff men would prop up bars with; 106 mph was unheard of in those days when 90 was considered as fast as a Super Sabre jet fighter. So compared to the Cadillac's 99.6 mph, Chrysler's heavy old dowager heralded the new jet age, if not in looks, certainly under the hood in terms of get-up-and-go.

Speaking of looks, the Chrysler was quite short on style compared to the fleet proportions the Cadillac boasted. But perhaps that was not so noticeable a deficit in 1951, when folks were still used to rather square, upright designs that reminded one of the grim Victorian aunt who lived in the gabled house in Wisconsin . . . the

one mother always talked about! Chrysler, DeSoto, Dodge, and Plymouth all sold well despite automobile shortages caused by the Korean War.

Naturally Chrysler played up its radical new engine to the hilt: "The sensational new FirePower V-8 is the most powerful, the most efficient, and the most economical engine ever developed in this country for a motor car," boasted the copy in Chrysler's *Events* magazine. To prove the point, Chrysler entered fourteen Saratoga models in the brutal, two-thousand-mile Mexican Road Race guaranteed to floor most cars. Of all Chrysler's entries, six actually finished, which was more than could be said for many other makes; and one of the Saratogas, driven by race ace Bill Sterling, finished first in class and third overall, just eight minutes behind the winning Ferrari. Not bad for a first time out.

Chrysler also made hay and lots of publicity points much nearer home when Chrysler was chosen, for the fourth time in its twenty-eight-year history, to pace the legendary Indianapolis 500 race. D. A. Wallace, then president of the Chrysler Division, drove the handsome New Yorker convertible around the two-and-a-half-mile brick and asphalt course. With him was glamorous movie star Loretta Young, who assuredly kept spectators' and the media's eyes and minds on her and the car.

Chrysler enjoyed a 1951 calendar year production of 1,233,294 units, keeping the company solidly in second place, though Ford was catching up. Korea, which America seemed to have adopted as its own war, even though it was a "United Nations police action" with many other nations involved, was beginning to take its toll on car production. Anticommunist hysteria had reached its peak, ably fueled by the alcoholic senator from Wisconsin, Joseph McCarthy, and continued to spark unconstitutional witch-hunts for activities and persons some zealot might decide was "un-American." Even childrens' comic books were put to the test. But nobody bothered to go after organized crime, perhaps the most un-American activity of all.

Together, the Korean conflict and the political hate-mongering probably helped to quell car sales in 1952. But the main problem for Chrysler, which suffered a drop to 950,000 units produced for the calendar year, was style. Even the fact that well-known driver Brewster Shaw posted a speed of 76.44 mph to win the Standing Start Mile at Daytona Speed Week in a stock Chrysler Saratoga, failed to encourage Chrysler showroom traffic. What people wanted

Compare Ford's new 1949 shape with Chrysler's and ask yourself which one would you rather have had. Clean, uninterrupted lines devoid of trim are graceful. More than 51,000 Custom Convertibles were produced in 1949.

was style. Something to make them feel good in the brand-new postwar age. Ford gained mightily because it had new styling, a look of tomorrow and Aldous Huxley's *Brave New World*. Because Ford was so new, it recaptured its long-lost second place, a position it has held to this day. Hardly anything was done to Chrysler's divisions; all Chrysler got were new taillights; Plymouth, a new hood badge and slightly altered decklid. At least DeSoto was given a smaller, 276.1-cubic-inch Hemi V-8 christened Firedome.

Briggs Cunningham, a native of Cincinnati, Ohio, was wealthy. Very, very wealthy. He had inherited a fortune that would sustain him for the rest of his life. He went to Yale, then decided to remain in Connecticut to participate in sailboat racing on the Atlantic. He often won the Atlantic Class Sloop events before the war. Always interested in cars, Cunningham used to race regularly. After the war, friends persuaded him he should return to car racing. Which he did. On October 2, 1948, Cunningham made history of sorts by entering his "Bu-Merc"—a Buick-engined, Mercedes-bodied hybrid—in the first Sports Car Club of America race, which helped christen the brand-new track of Watkins Glen, New York. Cunningham finished second in that historic race.

In the same year in Italy, an event took place of monumental automotive importance. The first Ferrari was born. In 1949 Briggs Cunningham imported a 166 Spyder Corsa, the first Ferrari to come to America, and only the fourth one ever built. Cunningham raced the car extensively between 1949 and 1950, until good friend Sam Collier was killed racing the Ferrari at Watkins Glen in 1950.

Nothing would deter Cunningham's adventurous spirit. With a fortune at his elbow, he was able to make almost anything possible. He decided to enter a car in the 1950 Le Mans twenty-four-hour endurance race in France.

Le Mans is the most prestigious, most famous road race in the world. A win there and you are king!

Because Le Mans had become known as the mecca for thoroughbred European cars, Cunningham wanted American know-how to compete. He had seen racing mechanic Bill Frick's "Fordillac" in operation and realized a high-performance American racer could be made. The trouble was that the Le Mans organizers had made it a rule that only recognized car manufacturers were allowed to race. Out went the idea of some sort of sporty hybrid; instead, Briggs Cunningham entered two Cadillacs.

One of the Caddies was a stock coupe, the other an incredible machine with an ugly body that was flat and low to the ground. When the French saw it they dubbed the car "Le Monstre"—and "Le Monstre" it has remained to this day. Anyway, the Cadillacs actually did surprisingly well. They finished tenth and eleventh overall, and were given an ovation by the spectators along the route. Shortly after this race, Cunningham formed the B. S. Cunningham Company to create a sports car that would race at Le Mans, Daytona Beach, and Watkins Glen.

Initially Cunningham meant to build a sportscar using the peppy new Cadillac V-8. Then he got wind of Chrysler's radical Hemi, which was to power 1951 Chrysler models. The more Cunningham heard about the engine, the more he knew this was what was needed. Now, to get a brand-new engine hardly off the drawing board is not exactly easy. Unless you know someone. Cunningham knew somebody: the son of Chrysler chairman, K. T. Keller. Suffice it to say, he got his engines.

The first Cunningham had been the C-1. It had a tube frame, inboard brakes, and de Dion rear suspension; under the hood, Cadillac's 331-cid V-8. Now he had the Hemi engine, and Cunningham built the C-2. Its transmission was Cadillac's three-speed. The C-2 was entered at

Watkins Glen and at Elkhart Lake; it finished first in both races. A pretty good beginning and proof that Chrysler's engine had what it takes. Everybody had high hopes of a good showing at the 1951 Le Mans race.

It was not to be. The C-2 finished a disappointing eighteenth overall, even though it had been in second place behind the winning C-Type Jaguar at one period during the marathon race. The trouble was the low-octane French gasoline, which caused the high-compression Hemi to have detonation problems. With superior, high-octane gasoline available in America, Chrysler hadn't given much thought to how the engine would run on poor-quality fuel, so they had a drum of the French gas shipped to the U.S. to be used in further engine development. It is

worth noting that European gas was of poor quality in the immediate years after the war, but by the mid-fifties it was on a par with American petroleum. Today European and British gas are of a higher octane than the fuel available at American pumps.

Some years before he built cars to take on the might of Europe on their own turf, Cunningham had befriended American midget-car racing champion Phil Walters. Walters was an accomplished engineer besides being a good driver and worked closely with Chrysler on developing the Hemi. He made several improvements to the engine, such as reducing cam scuffing with the introduction of a roller-tappet design borrowed from Harley Davidson. To reduce friction, Walters placed needle bearings in the rocker arms and Chrysler improved the crankshaft using materials that were kept under wraps. Several of these engines were made for Cunningham's new C-4R competition car, each engine developing 325 bhp. They also cost a cool sixty thousand dollars each, a lot of money almost half a century ago.

While the C-4R was been readied for the 1952 season, Cunningham began producing road cars for sale to the general public . . . or the few able to afford one of the Vignale-of-Italy-bodied machines. The road cars were designated C-3 and cost ten thousand dollars. What the buyer got was Italian flair on an American chassis—a modified C-2 chassis, actually. Vignale shipped the bodies to Cunningham's West Palm Beach factory for twenty-seven hundred dollars. Under the hood lay the heart of the matter, a 331-cid Chrysler Hemi V-8. Just like the race cars!

Profits from the sales of the C-3 road cars were sunk into Cunningham's racing endeavors, which included the development of the C-4R. The car dominated American road racing, beating all comers from Europe with aplomb. As the Cunningham team set out for the 1952 Le Mans race, there were high hopes for victory. Unfortunately that would not be the case. The C-4R driven by Phil Walters and John Fitch developed valve trouble, but the Briggs Cunningham/Bill Spear car came in a very creditable fourth place overall, and first in class.

A new Cunningham, the C-5R, was entered, along with a couple of C-4Rs, in the twenty-four-hour race in 1953. Racing fans all over the world sensed there would be a battle royal between the snooty Europeans and upstart Americans; the cars would be driven to their limits of endurance. Many backed the American underdog, but Cunningham had to face stiff opposition from the race-winning Jaguar and new Ferraris.

It was a terrific race, one of the best. Although Cunningham didn't win, his cars put the wind up the likes of Jaguar as they thundered easily around the circuit. The C-4R driven by John Gordon Benett and Charles Moran finished tenth overall, the Cunningham/Spear car came in seventh, and the new C-5R, driven by Fitch and Walters, crossed the line in third place. This was a tremendous performance from a private team without the huge backing factory-supported cars were getting.

The big 5.4-liter Chrysler Hemis performed perfectly throughout the race. Then, why didn't they win? Several factors come to mind. The cars were generally bigger and heavier than the opposition, the engines considerably so when compared to the 3- or 3.5-liter motors of Jaguar, Ferrari, and Aston Martin. So, overall weight difference was considerable. Then there were the brakes. Jaguar had the huge advantage of disc brakes compared to the seventeen-inch drums employed by Cunningham. Even large drum brakes tend to fade when used repeatedly, a problem not encountered on disc-braked cars. Even so, with all these disadvantages, the C-5R's drums held. As Walters said in a feature about Briggs Cunningham in *Automobile Quarterly* a few years ago, the C-5R might have won. "We really didn't know what we had in the C-5. We didn't know the brakes would last as long." In other words, the drivers would slow down appreciably before applying the brakes because they weren't sure they would last.

As can be seen from the rear, the 1951 Ford was very appealing, very modern. A 95-horsepower L-6 was the standard engine for all but three models, which had the L-head V-8 under their hoods. The V-8 was an option on all others.

For 1954 Cunningham fielded two C-4R cars at Le Mans. There would have been the C-5R but it had not yet been rebuilt following an acrobatic somersault John Fitch had with the car in a race at Rheims. Fitch, incidentally, only suffered a cut ear. But the C-4R driven by Spear and back-up driver Sherwood Johnston posted a third overall and first in class.

That was the final year Cunningham would enter Chrysler-powered cars at Le Mans. Jaguar founder and boss Sir William Lyons approached Cunningham with an offer to supply him with a team of D-Type Jaguars . . . if he would stop building cars. Surprisingly Cunningham said yes, and in 1955 he was racing Jaguars. Cunningham continued to race for several more

years, and very successfully. Even though his cars carried the blue and white American colors, they were built in England or Italy.

Whether Chrysler was disappointed that Cunningham had thrown in the towel as regards his own Hemi-powered cars is not known. The cooperation between the two parties since 1951 had been beneficial to both; Cunningham got the engines, Chrysler all the performance data it needed from the practical application of its engines in real-world situations. From the word go Chrysler was interested in how far the engine could be pushed. In 1952 a Kurtis Kraft Indy car turned up at the famed Indianapolis track powered by a Chrysler Hemi. The car had been loaned to Firestone by a local businessman, ostensibly to conduct high-speed tire tests. The tests could have been carried out equally well using an Offenhauser racing engine. There is no doubt that Chrysler had a lot to do with its engine being used. It

Briggs Cunningham, wealthy sportsman, built a racing car using his name, and equipped it with Chrysler's powerhouse Hemi V-8. This was in 1951. Shortly after, Cunningham produced a road car, the 1952 Cunningham C-3, shown here.

was a specially prepared motor developing 404 bhp thanks to its Hilborn-Travers fuel-injection system and a Vertex Scintilla magneto ignition. Over a five-hundred-mile distance the Kurtis/Chrysler posted speeds well in excess of the 1951 Indy 500 winning car, with an average of 134.35 mph. The car's fastest lap was 137 mph.

Chrysler kept up the performance pressure at all the racing venues where the cars would receive maximum exposure. A New Yorker won NASCAR's Grand National race in 1953, and again in 1954. At the Daytona National Speed Trials, a four-door New Yorker sedan set a new record of 117.06 mph. Returning to Indianapolis, another New Yorker sedan ran for twenty-four hours nonstop to cover a distance of 2,157 miles at an average speed of 89.89 mph. Over at Chrysler, the engineers were delighted with the results, which justified their faith in the hemispherical head layout. Now

Chrysler, instead of letting others have all the glory with its engine, needed to develop and produce a car capable of winning races and be available to the public as a form of street rod. The year 1955 promised to be historic for the American automobile: Chevrolet already had the Corvette, Ford was rumored to be bringing out a two-passenger sporty vehicle. Chrysler had nothing but the great engine.

Enter Bob Rodger, Chrysler's chief engineer. He, more than anybody, put Chrysler at the top of the sporting heap with one of the greatest cars of all time. The almighty 300 was about to be born.

"As Solid as Grant's Tomb and 130 Times as Fast"
—Tom McCahill

A great year: 1955. There were no wars, Americans found that the Reds-under-the-Beds scare was a myth, and the man mostly responsible for the terror was yesterday's news. That President Eisenhower spent much of his time on the golf course told a prosperous nation there was little to worry about. Except the teenagers. They were sporting ducktails and quiffs and jiving to a new noise called rock 'n' roll. Every day "the sun was out, the sky was blue." Or it appeared to be the way Buddy Holly said it was.

For the car-buying public, 1955 was a year to remember. Almost every make was genuinely "all new." The cars reflected the holiday mood of America: bright two- and three-tone color schemes, flashy good looks, new OHV V-8s, and bags of power. After two years of limping around like an anemic turtle, the pretty Corvette got itself Chevrolet's terrific new V-8. Ford introduced its sporty car, the very attractive two-passenger Thunderbird that had a V-8 as standard. All cars were lower, longer, had wraparound windshields, and were much faster than Aunt Emily would have liked for her cruise to the Bingo parlor. Happy days were here again. And how!

Virgil Exner's superb styling is reflected in the 1955 Dodge Lancer. Note the unusual but attractive two-tone paint scheme. Top engine was the 270.1-cid V-8, pushing out 193 bhp. Midprice and midsize, the 1955 Dodge Royal Lancer continued Chrysler's rebirth with handsome Exner styling. Like the Chrysler, the Dodge has an embryonic fin atop the rear fender.

After one of Chrysler's worst sales years on record—only eight hundred thousand units in 1954—the company could hardly wait for 1955. Finally Chrysler would have all-new models designed by Virgil Exner, new V-8 engines across the board, and the elevation of Chrysler's luxury Imperial as a separate make in its own right. Exner's designs couldn't have been bettered. The cars were fleet and graceful and had an Italian flavor. Chrysler advertised the cars as the Forward Look, and that they were. At long last another company was pulling the plug on GM's styling leadership; a couple of years more and GM would be trying to catch up.

Not all of Chrysler's cars had the Hemi V-8. Both the Chrysler and Imperial did, and DeSoto had a bored-out, slightly smaller version called the Firedome that was rated at 291

A platinum knight to the rescue! Any damsel would have felt honored to be whisked away in this beauty. The 300 belongs to Richard Carpenter of musical fame, and is part of his collection of Chrysler cars. Interior restoration was done by Gary Goers.

Perhaps one of the finest cars ever made, the 1955 Chrysler C-300 had the advantage of race-winning performance and beautiful lines. Small wonder it was quickly christened The Beautiful Brute. The C-300, powered by Chrysler's race-winning 331-cubic-inch Hemi V-8, won both NASCAR and AAA championships. It also took Daytona Speed Weeks in its stride, the 300 winning everything in sight. From whichever angle the C-300 is observed, it looks just right. A styling tour de force in every way, thanks to the artistry of Virgil Exner.

Here is the C-300's fabulous, mystical 331-cid hemispherical V-8 that made history on road and track.

Quite tasteful interior of C-300 smacks of class and of European Grand Touring sedans. The C-300 was at home with the Bentley Continental, Mercedes, Aston Martin, and the wonderful Spanish Pegaso.

Classy dashboard avoided the headlong rush into chrome almost all other car makers thought was right for their cars.

cubic inches. Besides the Hemi, there was a smaller V-8 featuring a polyspherical head: that meant the intake and exhaust valves were placed diagonally across from each other instead of being directly opposite, as in the Hemi. This allowed for a single rocker shaft for each bank of cylinders instead of two. Although simpler and cheaper to make, the polyhead engine retained the Hemi's admirable breathing qualities.

An obviously posed publicity shot showing the assembly of a 1955 C-300. Apart from Rolls-Royce and Aston Martin, where would one see this sort of assembly these days? The heart of the matter is the Hemi V-8 sitting in the chassis.

The new engine replaced the old six-cylinder unit in the low-priced Chrysler Windsor series, and was the major power in Dodge and Plymouth. The six was still standard in the latter cars, the V-8 a desirable option. A smaller cubic-inch-displacement Hemi was offered in the Dodge Custom Royal. It developed 193 bhp in what was known as the Power Pack D-500 trim. It was an exciting time at Chrysler; since L. L. Colbert had become president, the company had done a complete turnaround. Chrysler was well and truly back on track.

Even with the vibrant Forward Look bringing accolades and customers back to the

Daytona Speed Weeks, February 1955: The C-300s walked away with the whole event, setting a couple of records in the process. After a triumphant season, Carl Kiekhaufer's main driver, Tim Flock, receives the NASCAR Championship Trophy.

showrooms, Chrysler lacked the sort of car both GM and Ford had—a sports-type car. After spending most of its resources retooling for the new models, there wasn't enough left in the piggy bank to develop a two-seater sports car to compete with the Corvette and Thunderbird. But something had to be done. Enter Bob Rodger.

Robert M. Rodger, as already stated, was Chrysler's chief engineer. He was born in 1917 and from an early age became interested in mechanical things. Graduating from Clarkston College of Technology in Pottsdam, New York, Rodger immediately joined Chrysler Corporation in 1939. He went to the Chrysler Institute of Engineering and received a master's degree in automotive engineering in 1941. His first ten years at Chrysler were spent in the engine-development laboratory where the hemispheri-

cal power plant was born. In fact, Rodger was one of the engineers involved with the Hemi.

In 1951, the year the Hemi first appeared before the public, Rodger was promoted to assistant chief engineer. A year later he became chief engineer. He closely watched all phases of the Hemi's adventures on road and track, often being present when the engine was trying for a record-breaking run. Rodger was mindful of the fact that many Chrysler enthusiasts were following the Hemi's fortunes and writing letters asking for a true high-performance machine. The usual corporate meetings took place, and there were no dissenters.

Chrysler Division manager Ed C. Quinn was enthusiastic about the idea, and so were the boys upstairs.

Money was a problem; so was time. It would take at least three years to develop and produce a sports car, by which time it might be too late. To bring a high-performance car out in 1955 would mean using existing components and modifying them to fit. Which is exactly how the 300 came about.

What the engineers and designers came up with was arguably the prettiest Grand Touring car in the world, and also the fastest and most powerful. It was a sensation. It was based upon the Windsor body because the 300 would have the Windsor's single trim line. Exner wanted the least embellishments on the car, so a single rubbing strip would be ideal. And because the Windsor had the right mounting holes for the trim, it would save money—as opposed to adapting the New Yorker body, which had different trim holes.

At the front, the Windsor grille was replaced by the elegant but simple Imperial one. The Imperial grille came as two separate units, and between the units was an attractive checkered-flag medallion with the numerals *300* set above it. Front and rear bumpers and bumper guards were adopted from the Windsor. Imperial wheel covers had a checkered flag and gold *300* numerals at the center; but most buyers would choose the beautiful wire wheels measuring 15 x 5.5 inches that were manufactured for Chrysler by Motor Wheel as an option on other Chrysler models. The set of forty-eight-spoke wires added $617.60 to the base price of $4,055.25, quite a lot of money in 1955.

Although the dashboard was the same as that in the normal Chrysler and Imperial models, a recalibrated speedometer reading up to 150 mph was installed in place of the stock 120 mph unit. Interior trim was New Yorker, though

the leather seats and leather and vinyl trim were hand-stitched. All C-300 (the *C* presumably stood for *Chrysler*) interiors were beige in color, but the steering wheel was two-tone black and white.

Under the hood? What else but the Hemi. Still displacing 331 cubic inches, the engine developed 300 bhp. This made it the most powerful automobile engine in the world, news not welcome in the boardrooms of rival manufacturers. They knew that the Hemi was so versatile that Chrysler would be able to up the horsepower whenever it felt like it. And, as time went on, they did.

If one produces a limited-edition Grand Touring car that is capable of high top speeds, it needs suspension to match. This was a time when few cars had independent rear suspension, and there was no manufacturer in the United States that would consider it until it was cost effective. So the C-300, like its brethren, had a live rear axle. Only the suspension was made considerably stiffer to cope with the extra performance the car was capable of. American cars at the time were not known for their road handling prowess, which was dismal to say the least, and the C-300 would redress the balance a little.

Heavy-duty shock absorbers mounted within the front coil springs, and a rear suspension consisting of seven-leaf semielliptical springs rated at 160 pounds per inch was considerably higher than the standard and somewhat slushy suspension found on the New Yorker. The late, great automobile road tester Tom McCahill said that the 300 was not a car for "henpecked Oscar and his seven kids to use touring the suburbs with an occasional trip to the seashore." McCahill was right. The C-300 was too damn good for that. Soon, very soon, it would show just how good it was on the ovals, and on the beaches, and on the racing tracks of America.

When the 300 was announced, every car-magazine writer worth his salt wanted to road-test it. They fell over themselves to be first in line for the first feel behind the wheel. "You're not in an ordinary vehicle when you're in the 300," wrote Walt Woron in *Motor Trend*. Although Karl Ludvigsen inclined to side with those who said the 300 was not a sports car, he said in *Sports Car Illustrated* that the 300 "is just as much a sports car as is a Bentley Continental or a 300S Mercedes Benz." High praise indeed. But the best came from the irreverent but humorous pen of Tom McCahill. Writing in the May 1955 issue of *Mechanix Illustrated*, Uncle Tom, as he was known to his faithful

"Beautiful Brute," as the 300s became known, is a fitting description for the forward-looking Chrysler 300B. It repeated the 1955 C-300's success on road and track. Its 331-cid Hemi grew to 354 cubic inches. Standard power was 340, but the optional 355 horsepower was available. This car was a real scorcher at Daytona and elsewhere. The embryonic "fins" became full-fledged in 1956, but wouldn't reach their peak for another year. Otherwise, the 300B was identical to the 1955 model.

readers, said: "This is a hard-boiled magnificent piece of semicompetition transportation, built for the real automotive connoisseur." He criticized the lack of power steering; the car he had tried out was the Daytona Beach Flying Mile winner, but that car was specifically set up for competition; power steering was a $113 option. Later, in the same article, McCahill said that he "was greatly impressed by the 300 as a car for the sports-car-minded man who wants the sureness of sports-car suspension and the pride of owning the fastest full-size sedan in this or any other country." And he said the suspension "was as severe as a New Hampshire winter."

There was one oddity with the car, and that was its transmission. All 300s came standard with a two-speed PowerFlite automatic operated by a small lever sticking out of the dash. You would have thought that a car of this nature would have had at least a three-speed box, best of all a four-speed manual. None were available at the time; even the competition rigs had PowerFlite. A more sporty transmission would probably have helped shave at least a couple of seconds off the 300's 0–60 times of between 9.5 to 10 seconds. Considering the engine's power, the 0–60 times were a little disappointing, especially when a lowly V-8-powered Chevrolet could better those times. However, it is important to understand that the Hemi engine only came into its own after 60 mph. Then the car took off like a berserk space probe and could easily rattle up to 130 mph-plus.

In the first three days after the 300's introduction, over a thousand orders were taken in by Chrysler dealers. Yet only 1,725 units were actually built in 1955, to keep it a very special limited-edition automobile. It had an expensive base price, and once the few desirable options such as wire wheels, power steering, power windows, Touch-Tone radio, and antenna were added, the buyer was digging deep to find five thousand dollars. But what a buy!

Perhaps taking a hint from European specialty vehicles such as the beautiful Bentley Continental, Chrysler offered only three one-color choices, which certainly helped give the

car class. The colors were Platinum, Tango Red, and Black. Black was the least favored of the three colors, Tango Red the most preferred. All C-300s were built on the Imperial assembly line, where more care was given to assembly and workmanship. Production of the C-300 ended on June 24, 1955, by which time it was already a legend and one of the best public-relations exercises any auto manufacturer could have conceived.

England in 1955 was a smaller version of the United States. It had a strong economy and little to worry about in the world. The young were heavily influenced by American movies and culture, particularly music. "Rock Around the Clock" had been a major hit, and Elvis's rock 'n' roll was knocking 'em dead. American cars were not popular at the time; they were regarded as too big, too chrome laden, too gas hungry, and poor on handling. Some people

All Chrysler Corporation cars displayed true fins in 1956. Fins were Exner's passion at first; later they were to be his nemesis. They looked great on the 1956 DeSoto Fireflite shown here.

were exceptions, however, and thought they were the best thing since sliced bread.

A young English boy thought the C-300 was the most beautiful automobile in the world. He had read Tom McCahill's report in *Mechanix Illustrated* and vowed one day he would own one. Sometimes the lad would day-dream about driving around in a platinum-colored 300 when traveling home on the bus . . . and miss his stop.

One long, hot day in July, when school was out and time was one's own, the suntanned youngster had been to see friends and had missed his bus home. He took to the road, plan-ning to hitch a ride if he could. In those days, hitching rides was still a safe occupation.

After hitching unsuccessfully for over a mile and a half, the road started to climb. At the crest the road veered to the right through a small village called Wrecclesham. On the left, at the corner, an ancient ivy-covered cottage rose into view. It was beautiful, with wrought-iron gates, a gravel entranceway, and a typical English country garden. What was not typical was what was sitting in the driveway. And it was what was sitting in the driveway that attracted the boy and made his heart go "boom-ba-de-boom," like the Peter Sellers/Sophia Loren song. It was platinum white and only the rear could be seen. There was an emblem with a checkered flag on it. The boy's legs began to give way—he was looking at his icon, his dream. A Chrysler C-300.

Whatever it took, the youth had to get closer to his valhalla; it really did not matter what trouble he got into. He opened the wrought-iron gates and walked onto the gravel path. The gravel crunched beneath his feet as he approached the car. Now he could see the taste-ful, slender taillights, the stainless-steel side strip extending the length of the car. He saw the elegant interior, the 150-mph speedometer, the heavily chromed twin grilles at the front. He thought that his father absolutely had to see this car. Before he knew it, the boy was knocking on the cottage's front door.

Commander Kribs was a short, fair-haired man with a nice disposition. He was in the U.S. Navy and a military exchange had brought him to study in Britain. He hadn't had the C-300 long, and as the navy took care of the shipping, he brought the car as well. He smiled at the youngster's enthusiasm as he raised the hood. Then he told the boy to jump into the car and took him home.

One can imagine the boy's expression as he was driven home in what was the only 300 in Britain. There were no others. There are a few now, different models from different years, in collectors' hands. But in 1955 there were none. Only the one an excited youngster was lucky enough to be driven home in. His lifelong ambition has been to one day own one.

If you haven't already guessed, that small boy was me. I don't know where a by-now-retired Commander Kribs is, but if he sees this book I should like to thank him for giving me the chance to realize a dream. I still don't own a C-300, but the time to start looking is getting ever closer.

Karl Kiekhaufer owned Mercury Outboard Motors up in Fond du Lac, Wisconsin. Partly to promote his business, but mostly because he liked it, Kiekhaufer raced cars at NASCAR's big oval tracks. When he heard of the C-300 he knew this was the car to win races with, so he sponsored a team of 300s, which were to be driven by the best drivers money could buy. He had Tim Flock, Buck Baker, Speedy Thompson, and Lee Petty, the racing father of the legendary idol, Richard Petty.

One of the major events on the racing/competition calendar is the Daytona Speed Week

held in February. Of course the Kiekhaufer team was there in full force to make motoring history. As was to be expected, Florida's weather was glorious and by the end of the week the sun's warmth had cast its glow on Chrysler's 300s. They had won virtually everything on the golden sands of Daytona. Kiekhaufer's team won the 160-mile Grand National, though not without incident. The incident occurred when veteran race driver Glenn (Fireball) Roberts apparently took the NASCAR Grand National in his 1955 Buick Century.

From the word go, Roberts screamed past the two 300s, driven by Flock and Petty. They were unable to catch him, suffering the disadvantage of a two- speed automatic transmission in the cars. Roberts had a manual three-speed box, which allowed him to change down when he barreled into a turn, change to second as he came out, then take off like a Saturn rocket. In its report of the event, *Speed Age* magazine noted the Chryslers cornered and handled better than anything else, but didn't have the backup of a good three-speed, much to Flock and Petty's chagrin.

Even with the lack of a decent transmission to race with, the 300s beat everything else but Fireball's Buick. NASCAR rules stated that the top three cars had to be thoroughly checked to ensure no fiddling with any mechanical parts had taken place. The next day, NASCAR commissioner "Cannonball" Baker announced Fireball Roberts and his Buick had been disqualified because the Buick engine's push rods had been altered. This alone would have helped the Buick maintain the high rate of acceleration it possessed. In its altered state the Buick averaged 93.158 mph, which was a new record. Or would have been. Instead, Tim Flock was declared winner, his 300 averaging 92.05 mph for the 160-mile course. Lee Petty's 300 was second.

Other victories during the week included

airline pilot Warren Koechling's two-way average of 127.580 mph in the American Stock Car Flying Mile Class. C-300s took second and third places as well. The second-place win was with a factory-prepared car driven by Brewster Shaw, who averaged 126.542 mph. A Detroit housewife, Vicki Woods, came in third with a speed of 125.838 mph. Another 300 took the Standing Start Mile with a speed of 76.84 mph. At the end of the week, C-300s had broken just about every record there was to break. The only event they didn't win was the *Mechanix Illustrated* Acceleration Trophy. This was won by a Cadillac, the nearest 300 placing fifth.

Chrysler didn't design the Hemi engine to out-accelerate everything else, yet it was able to hold its own against most other makes. The engine was designed to show its real power when it reached 60–65 mph. Then there was nothing in this world at the time that could compete. For a car that weighed forty-four hundred pounds, it is remarkable what it was capable of.

An interesting fact emerged during the 1955 Daytona Speed Weeks. Kiekhaufer's team found that running the C-300s at high speed across the sands would sometimes cause the engines to balk. This was put down to sand grains getting into the system. An Italian engineer working for Kiekhaufer designed a paper filter that immediately cured the problem. Later he perfected his design, which became the basis for all paper air filters used in the air cleaners of all carbureted automobiles. Now, who says racing doesn't improve the breed?

After Daytona there was nothing to stop the 300s. Kiekhaufer's Mercury Outboard Motors were becoming associated with the winner's circle time after time. Entered into the NASCAR and AAA stock car championships, Chrysler 300s won both with consummate ease. All in all, Kiekhaufer's 300s won 37 races, Tim Flock winning 18 on the NASCAR circuits, another

Kiekhaufer driver, Frank Mundy, winning 10 AAA races. The other 9 races were won by Speedy Thompson, Buck Baker, Norm Nelson, Tony Bettenhausen, and Fonty Flock. All in all, C-300s won 23 out of 40 NASCAR races, far ahead of its nearest rival, Oldsmobile, which won 10. Once again Chrysler made history with the 300, for nobody else had ever won both the AAA and NASCAR National Championships in the same year.

For a car that won races on Sunday, Chrysler didn't sell that many on Monday. Only 1,725 C-300s were built in 1955, and 33 of them for export. Granted, it was a limited-edition car not meant to be produced in quantity; what was important to Chrysler was the prestige and publicity attained. And the C-300's racing program helped improve the breed. Carl Kiekhaufer virtually had a hotline to Chrysler, which allowed him to call any time of the day or night with suggestions for improvements and how the cars fared at each race. By the time 1956 rolled around, some of those improvements had made their way into the new cars.

In 1956, there was the long, drawn-out process of hand shaking, baby kissing, and meaningless speeches by politicians: it was an American election year. Hungary rose against its Communist masters, only to be swiftly crushed by Soviet tanks. Britain, France, and Israel embarked on a foolhardy military expedition against Egypt. Marilyn Monroe wed playwright Arthur Miller, Grace Kelley married Prince Rainier of Monaco, and Elvis Presley topped the charts with a string of hits. These 1956 events served as a backdrop to Chrysler's second coming, the 300B.

While the first 300 was the Chrysler C-300, the C as we know standing for Chrysler, it was decided the 1956 model should have a letter after 300. Henceforth the 300 series would be known as the Letter Series, which gave the car a touch of extra class in the European mode. Although the car was virtually the same in the looks department, Exner had added fins. It is debatable whether the fins improved the looks of what was perhaps the most beautiful car in the world in 1955, but it was still a classy thoroughbred whatever one may say.

Mechanically the 300B was much improved—and also more powerful. The 331 Hemi engine had been bored out to 354 cubic inches with the resultant increase in horsepower. Now a buyer had two choices of engine power: standard was 340 bhp with a 9.0:1 compression ratio, or an even wilder 10.0:1 compression and 355 bhp. The auto's standard axle ratio was 3.36:1, but there were eleven,

yes, eleven, other ratios to choose from, going all the way up to a heady 6.17.

As far as the controversial two-speed PowerFlite went, it didn't. It stayed. At least for a short time. Mindful of the discontent among racing drivers, Chrysler tried to redress the balance by offering a three-speed manual with a Borg and Beck heavy-duty clutch. The transmission came from the Dodge Division of Chrysler, and it really was something of a stopgap measure that didn't meet a favorable response from anybody. Tom McCahill, in his own inimitable way, complained that "if you miss a shift in one of these lumpy box deals when trying to beat your iceman down to the corner you stand a good chance of creating a hailstorm of gear teeth." Remembering that the manual was intended for a Dodge with a far more docile engine with less torque, it was not meant to take on the power the ferocious 300B ladled out, and certainly would have

Three engine versions were available in the 1956 T-Bird. Design was virtually the same as the 1955 models. Hardtop roof had a porthole window, which added a classic-car look. Top engine was the 312-cubic-inch V-8, which churned out 225 horses.

crumbled to dust if used in endurance races.

Mechanix Illustrated estimated the top speed to be 140 mph-plus, but other testers weren't quite so generous. Probably in stock-road tune the car would easily make 130, a speed that was pretty good in anybody's book in 1956. The 0–60 times were a considerable improvement over 1955 when using the three-speed manual tranny. Two journals recorded 8.2 seconds from 0 to 60, while others trying the car with the disagreeable two-speed Power-Flite varied widely between 9 and 10.5 seconds.

For the second year in a row, the 300s swept the competition field. At Daytona, Tim Flock, once again driving for Carl Kiekhaufer's Mercury Outboard Team, smashed Warren Koechling's American Stock Car Flying Mile record of the previous year with a two-way average speed of 139.373 mph. Obviously remembering his disenchantment with the two-speed PowerFlite automatic the year before, Flock chose the three-speed manual as he knew, being the professional he was, exactly when to shift for maximum effect. Whether Vicki Wood had a manual, I am not sure, but whatever the transmission was she set a new women's record of 136.081 mph. Flock also went on to win the 160-mile Grand National event at an average speed of 90.836 mph. Even though Flock again used the manual transmission, he was over a mile and a half slower than in 1955's race. Weather conditions that weren't the best for high-speed runs probably were to blame for the lower average; at least it was an outright win not complicated by rule-breaking cars of any make.

Once again the 300s scored by winning the 1956 NASCAR championship. For reasons not abundantly clear Kiekhaufer pulled his team out of the AAA racing. Out of fifty-six NASCAR races, 300Bs won twenty-two of them, Buck Baker winning the driver's championship. Then Kiekhaufer surprised the racing world by withdrawing his team from any more involvement

with NASCAR, claiming unfair favoritism to other teams, notably Chevrolet. NASCAR tends to chop and change rules as it suits them. America's leading oval-track authority doesn't like successful cars or teams winning too often, considering the same cars winning all the time to be bad for business. So they change the rules when they deem it necessary. There has been much controversy over the years, with teams withdrawing from the competition in protest against one or another rule change. There haven't been any changes of late—hardly surprising considering the cars are all alike.

As in 1955, the 300B created a lot of column inches in the motoring media. Tom McCahill loved the car, thinking it an improvement, though he didn't care for the manual transmission. *Hot Rod* magazine's test found the car to be completely stable, even on the roughest roads. There was no wallow or pitching, or nose-dive in severe braking, the magazine's tester discovered. The tester for *Speed Age* considered the 300B to be the "best handling car I've ever driven from a dealer's showroom." And so on it went. The only criticism any tester offered had to do with the brakes. For some unexplained reason, stock showroom 300Bs shared the same twelve-inch drums with the less powerful New Yorker. One magazine made three emergency stops from 100 mph; and while there was no pull to the left or right or nose-dive, the brakes had faded to the point of no return by the third stop. Kiekhaufer's racing 300Bs were equipped with metallic linings to ensure good stopping power. It was going to be a few years more before the American auto industry built brakes equal to those of England, France, Germany, and Italy.

Base price of the 1956 300B rose 8 percent over 1955 to $4,419; yet, perhaps responding to customer complaints, the 300B offered all the options to be had on the New Yorker. Even air conditioning and the natty Highway Hi-Fi built by RCA. The latter had a fixed armature and played 16 2/3 rpm records. Very few 300Bs had the Highway Hi-Fi fitted; even so, it was a nice idea that didn't last.

As can be expected in any industry, if someone comes out with a good idea, everyone else follows suit. The same with the 300. It was on its own for only a year before others began to copy: not so much a Grand Tourer, but rather the power the 300 had. That the 300 was the first true muscle car cannot be denied. Nor the fact that it was responsible for an accelerated horsepower race. In 1954 Buick's most powerful engine developed 200 bhp; by 1957 this had gone up to 300. Cadillac had jumped to 325 bhp, Ford to 300, and Chevrolet had a 283 cid V-8 pumping out 283 bhp. And as sure as Wurlitzers are Wurlitzers, Ford and Chevy seemed to have less horsepower, though it was all relative. After all, the low-price cars weighed nine hundred to a thousand pounds less than a 300.

If the competition were playing catch-up, so were Chrysler's other divisions. Both Plymouth and DeSoto premiered special editions in 1956. Plymouth's car was the Fury, DeSoto's the Adventurer. They came painted only in white and gold, and had enough gold anodized trim to make a drunk think he had discovered a goldmine! As for Dodge, it didn't do much other than drop in a big engine under the hood and place a *D-500* emblem at the rear. Maybe this was one of the reasons for only 1,102 300Bs being built. After all, the limited-production Plymouth Fury cost $2,866, almost half the 300B's price, was limited to only 4,485 being sold, and had a very sporty 303-cid engine developing 240 bhp, 9.25:1 compression heads, and a solid lifter cam. At Daytona Beach, test results recorded the car doing almost 145 mph, though in stock road trim, top speed would have been a lot less.

The engine in the Fury was not a Hemi; that

was deemed far too expensive for a low-priced car. But it was the closest design to the Hemi and featured a polyspherical combustion chamber. Instead of the costly double-rocker arm used in the Hemi, a single-rocker shaft above the cylinders was employed. The engine did feature the expensive self-adjusting tappets, though.

Like Plymouth, DeSoto bowed in with a limited-edition model, midyear 1956. Color choices were limited to gold, black, or white and featured gold anodized wheel covers and side trim. Although flashier than the 300, the Adventurer was strictly a Grand Touring car with beefed-up suspension, a 341 cid, and a 320-horse Hemi V-8. It went like the clappers and was quite capable of 130 mph-plus once the Hemi unwound. Only 996 units were built for 1956.

For some reason Dodge didn't go for gold anodized trim and white paint to identify a limited-edition performance model. A special hemispherical head V-8 developing 260 bhp, identified as the D-500 package, was offered on any model the buyer cared to name. The only recognition was the letter and numerals spelling out *D-500* at the rear of the car. As this wasn't normally seen unless you were directly behind a car with the performance option, a 1956 Dodge looked just that at a traffic light—a 1956 Dodge Coronet, or whatever. Until the light changed. The guy looking smug in the 225 bhp Chevrolet thought he had it made. Until he found himself reading *D-500* as the Dodge disappeared over the horizon.

After the record-breaking 1955 sales year, 1956 was something of an anticlimax for the entire motor industry, and Chrysler Corporation, having moved from a 13 percent to a 17 percent market share in 1955, dropped back a bit in 1956. Not that Chrysler's range was any less handsome; in some cases models were better looking than in 1955. Now all Chrysler products carried rudimentary fins at the rear.

Exner had been waiting for the day he could apply fins to his designs in the same way the Italians put fins on their more exotic cars.

Fins or no fins, rumors were flying around Motown regarding Chrysler's 1957 season.

Extensive retooling had been going on at all Chrysler factories and outsiders were not allowed behind the many closed doors. Something really big was up that would turn the entire industry on its proverbial head.

Power of the Hour

unny how things never change on the world's political front. Look at 1957 for instance. President Eisenhower took the Oath of Office for a second term with a promise to axe the growing budget deficit. The Mideast was causing problems, cigarette smokers were advised to quit, man-made satellites were sent into space, and favorite film stars died (Humphrey Bogart was one, Oliver Hardy of Laurel and Hardy fame, another). In Europe, the European Common Market became a reality without Britain joining; the great island nation joined later, but to this day begs to differ on various issues. Before and since then, these events retain familiarity.

Over at Highland Park, home of America's third-largest auto maker, Chrysler Corporation, there was change. Radical change. Heart-stopping change. Beautiful, wondrous change. There had been nothing like it since Gordon Buehrig's artistic Cord took to the road in 1935. Through Virgil Exner's design creativity, Chrysler's 1957 models literally made everything else look like past tense, especially General Motors' cars: compared to Chrysler's, they were dumpy to a fault. Ford was somewhat better, as in the case of Mercury (though perhaps a little overcrowded with bumps and bulges and sculpturing).

Those must have been fun years when it came to new automobiles. It was an annual event almost as

The 1957 Plymouth Belvedere Convertible, with its sharklike tailfins, was a sensation to look at, great to drive. Torsion-bar suspension, shared with other Chrysler products, toned up handling and ride no end. Standard engine was L-head six, but the most-opted-for engine was the 235-hp V-8. More than 655,000 Plymouths were built in 1957, putting it firmly in the number-three spot.

popular as Thanksgiving. In September big car haulers dropped off new cars under wraps to dealers across the nation. To excite public interest the wraps were kept on the cars until announcement day. More often than not, small boys would see the cars before their parents did by climbing fences, sneaking through doors while their parents were occupied elsewhere in the dealership, and getting under, or lifting, the sheets covering the new models. Kids had to have some excitement, didn't they? Their comic books had been sanitized to boredom since the Comics Code came into being a couple of years earlier, and they weren't into rock 'n' roll like their bigger brothers and sisters. So for a large number of little boys, and girls too, discovering the new models before the grownups held the allure, the mystery, and the excitement children crave. Even if they were discovered and chased by angry dealers, it was all part of the fun.

Although handsome, Chevrolet's 1957 Bel-Air was behind the times compared with the Plymouth. About 1.5 million Chevies were built in 1957—proof that most Americans preferred more conservative lines.

"Newest new cars in 20 years," glowed Chrysler's copy in full-page color advertisements in all the national magazines. How right the ad writer was; there hadn't been such a radical change in car design since GM's all-steel, turret-top automobiles of the mid-1930s. General Motors had taken it for granted that it would always lead in design, so what a rude shock it must have been to wake up to "Suddenly It's 1960," as Chrysler happily crowed. GM executives were probably reaching for the Kaopectate in record numbers that day! And with good reason. From Plymouth to Imperial, five inches had been hacked off the height of the cars, the windshields were forward facing rather than the awkward dog-leg design favored by other makers, and most newsworthy of all, there were graceful fins that soared to the sky. In other words, a wedge-shaped design.

The man responsible for these incredible-looking cars was Virgil Exner. They were the fulfillment of a dream. Exner had always admired Italian design, how they dared to experiment with fins, not only as a styling

The 1957 Chrysler New Yorker hardtop is fleet, looks like it is moving when standing still. Fender skirts were an aftermarket option favored by many. Exactly 8,863 units were built of this model in 1957.

INSET: The '57 New Yorker's TorqueFlite transmission had radical push-button selector. Note that there's no *Park*: people were encouraged to use the parking brake in those days.

exercise but using them to provide aerodynamic stability. Moreover, it was the overall concept that tickled Exner's fancy, the elegance, the tongue-in-cheek flamboyance that only the Italians appeared to get away with. It was sometime during the very early fifties, when he was trying to do something with Chrysler's stodgy designs, that Exner made up his mind that the future 1957 Chrysler Corporation cars would possess the same flair the Italians exercised.

It is hard, on hindsight, to make the choice of which Chrysler product one prefers. They are all so dramatic. Back in 1957, although wallets dictated how much could be afforded on a new car, driving a new Plymouth probably turned as many heads as Marilyn Monroe walking down the street. And if the beautiful

Imperial convertible was on the cards as the family's country-club conveyance, the Plymouth was no less beautiful. Especially in a Fury suit!

"It's a rare car that rates a toast!" So said the Plymouth Fury copy accompanying the painted advertisement of three men raising their glasses to the picture of the white and gold beauty on the wall. This was the sporty Fury's second season, a humdinger of a car that made the first one look old hat. A 318-cubic-inch engine developing 290 horsepower gave the Fury rapid acceleration and speed that would have blistered Daytona's Speed Weeks had the car been introduced earlier instead of midyear. Actually, Plymouth was on the sands for the famed event; a Plymouth Belvedere was chosen to pace Daytona.

With the exception of the Imperial, which accompanied Jayne Mansfield as she wriggled her more-than-generous anatomy in the rock 'n' roll film *The Girl Can't Help It!*, all Chrysler divisions had a hotter-than-hot car to offer. DeSoto's 1957 Adventurer cranked out 345 horses, and any Dodge in D-500 trim got a 354-cid Hemi producing 340 bhp. These were exceptionally fast cars giving 0–60 times in the eight-second range, and for the first time the engineers had come up with a suspension system consisting of torsion bars. Chrysler used torsion bars combined with ball joints for the front suspension in every make and model across the board, calling it Torsion-Aire. At the rear were outrigger-mounted leaf springs. It should be noted that the 1955 Packard also had torsion bars, though not quite like Chrysler's. Packard's stretched from front to rear and had automatic leveling to boot.

Unlike coil or leaf springs, which transmit road shock into the car's structure, the idea behind torsion bars is for them to absorb most of the shock by winding up against their anchor points in a twisting motion. The result for Chrysler Corporation cars was the best handling in America: there was absolutely nothing to beat them. In the limited-edition sporty cars

the torsion bars were thicker and the rear springs had an extra leaf.

Chrysler engineering didn't end there for 1957. There was a superior new automatic transmission as well. It was called TorqueFlite and was available in all models, standard in some, optional in others at $220 extra. TorqueFlite was a three-speed unit that had been introduced on the 1956 Imperial, no doubt as a test. Instead of the conventional shift lever on the steering column, TorqueFlite was shifted by way of push-buttons set on the dash to the left of the driver out of the way of inquisitive children. It was a delight to use: push a button and your gear is selected. Push the Drive button and the transmission took care of all the shifts.

There were also a couple of not-so-good points. According to *Motor Trend* and other car magazines, Chrysler's full-time power steering, the fastest at three and three-quarter turns lock to lock, required constant vigilance. It made the cars effortless to drive, but was so quick and light, it took some getting used to. If one lost control on a slippery road, there was no feel to help the driver correct the slide. But it was the braking system that was the major problem. Chrysler used total-contact brakes, which were attacked in no uncertain manner by the motoring press. They complained the brakes would fade very rapidly, cars would rarely stop in a straight line, and wheel lock-up was another evil. American cars were bigger, heavier, and more powerful in the fifties, but there was little thought given to safer brakes.

At least it can be said Chrysler went a long way to curing another American ailment, and that was handling. Yank tanks would fly in a

Fabulous Chrysler 300C Letter car was a sensation in convertible form. What is surprising is that only three hundred were made of this 140-mph-plus 1957 convertible. Note the beautiful Ferrari-inspired grille, which worked well with the body shape.

The 1957 Chrysler 300C was a stunner. The car was exceptionally fast, one of the fastest production cars in the world. Once again Exner got everything right, with nothing out of place in the design. Grille was unique to the 300C. This is the hardtop version of the 300C that belonged to Richard Carpenter. Paucity of chrome showed just how good the design was.

straight line; give them a corner and almost any European car would leave them standing . . . or more likely in a ditch! Experienced drivers could take a Dodge Custom Royal D-500 at high speed on a straight road before barreling into a moderate corner at a rate of knots usually the preserve of Ferraris and Jaguars. Naturally the tail would hang out before responsive steering correction and pliant suspension would whip the car back into shape.

In grateful recognition of the leap forward in handling and ride qualities, *Motor Trend* magazine handed its prestigious annual achievement award to Chrysler Corporation. It was the second year for the award (which has by now become the Oscar of the motoring world). In its road test of a Chrysler New Yorker in the same May 1957 issue, *Motor Trend* said the car's cornering ability was comparable to "that of a sports car. The lean in sharp, fast

turns is held to a minimum, especially for a car of its size, weight, and nose heaviness." This was a pretty fair comment on what was ostensibly a luxury automobile. However, Chrysler saved the jewel in its crown until last. When the 1957 300C made its bow a little later in the season, Kaopectate reappeared on the coffee trays of the opposition.

Of all Virgil Exner's 1957 designs, the 300C was without doubt the most handsome. From its Ferrari-inspired grille, sleek, unadorned profile, and upswept tail, the 300C was poetry in motion. And for the first time in its existence, the 300 was offered as a convertible.

The engine had been bored out to 392 cubic inches and developed 375 bhp. Optional was a high-lift cam version rated at 390 horses. According to *Motor Trend*, the 300C could do 0–60 in eight seconds, though the magazine felt in the right state of tune, the 300 would do it in just seven seconds.

As a looker the 300C had no peer. It was elegant, it had class, and it looked and behaved like a thoroughbred. There were other full-size Grand Touring automobiles dotted about the globe: the Bentley Continental for one, Lagonda Rapide for another. It was also the fastest by far. Now an obligatory ritual, the 300C made its way to Daytona Beach, where it again set the fastest two-way average through the measured mile of 134.108 mph. This was over 5 mph slower than the time set by a 300B a year earlier, though it is worth noting that the beach surface was very poor compared to when the 300B made its run. Nonetheless Vicki Wood, our intrepid housewife from Detroit, had a one-way run of 138.985 mph. After Daytona, nothing—

apart from acceleration tests conducted by Chrysler Corporation at its Chelsea (Michigan) Proving Grounds, where the car posted a top speed of 145.7 mph. As Little Richard would have said: "Good Golly, Miss Molly!"

Chrysler Dart Diablo by Ghia. Designed by Virgil Exner and built by Ghia of Italy, the Dart Diablo was powered by the Hemi V-8. It was a one-off show car that should have made production.

Due to the Automobile Manufacturers' Association, a powerful independent body to which all American automobile companies belonged, factory participation in stock-car competition was banned. The AMA, mindful of the growing public disquiet over the accelerating horsepower race and lack of any positive safety measures coming out of Detroit, banned all forms of motor sport. This was a bitter pill for the manufacturers to swallow because they knew that racing improves the breed. Not only that, people loyal to one make or another tended to go and watch their favorite cars race. Without manufacturer involvement, NASCAR would have as much excitement as a boxload of fireworks doused in water.

Despite the racing ban it wasn't to be long before the manufacturers came roaring back. AMA was unable to do anything about privately entered cars, which increased in number

The 1957 DeSoto Adventurer was a limited-production, high-performance car following Chrysler's lead with the 300. Everyone talks about Chevrolet's 1 hp per cubic inch; the Adventurer had a 345-cid engine developing 345 bhp, yet there was no fuss about it. Only 1,650 units were made of this stunning car, which cost a basic $3,997. There were three hundred convertibles made in addition to the hardtop coupe.

INSET: The 1957 DeSoto Adventurer engine was 345 cubic inches and developed 345 bhp—in other words, one cubic inch for every horse. Nobody blew any trumpets at Chrysler over this little mechanical miracle, while Chevrolet pushed its 283/283 for all it was worth.

ABOVE, RIGHT: The '57 DeSoto's trio of taillights was simple, tasteful design. Not so good was the exhaust exiting from the bumper.

once the controversial ban took affect. What nobody said, nor were they supposed to say, was that the manufacturers started supplying this or that team with parts and advice under the table. Initially Chrysler didn't bother, hence the disappearance of 300Cs from the racetrack. Chevrolet and Pontiac obviously did, if their success in NASCAR racing was anything to go by. It has to be said that Chrysler had other things on its mind: a certain amount of shadiness involving outside suppliers and a questionable quality of workmanship, including inferior parts from suppliers, sloppy assembly, and even file marks under the paint of cars like the expensive Imperial.

Of course Chrysler would suffer greatly. Having reached a market share of more than 19 percent in 1957, it was all thrown away as

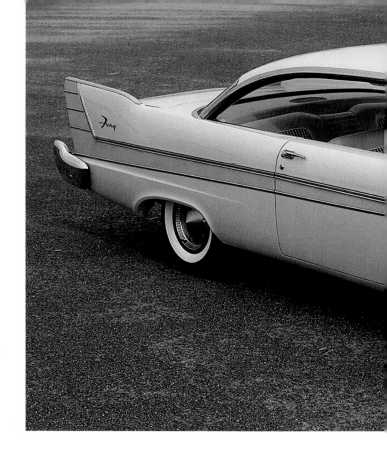

Chrysler knocked 'em dead in 1957. Would the highly touted Edsel from Ford do the same in 1958? No, it didn't; the car was an almighty flop. Vertical grille partly hid otherwise standard shaped body. Big 410-cid engine ensured lots of power in Corsair and Citation models.

buyers became disenchanted with their cars. Truly magnificent-looking cars, too. According to John Herlitz, Chrysler's president of design, it took twenty-five years before the company lost its reputation for poor quality. For Virgil

Exner to see his designs suffer from such inattentive workmanship must have been very disappointing.

Quality was improved on the 1958 models, but apart from the Plymouth, the looks weren't. In those days moderate facelifts were the norm in a three-year cycle, and seldom did they improve upon the first year of the design. So the compulsory facelift resulted in busier grilles, complicated trim, and less appealing taillights.

After the successful sales years of 1955 and 1957, the economy performed one of its habitual downturns in 1958. That is the nature of the capitalist beast: have a few good years, then bang! you're dead. Very few Presidents escape minirecessions, and now it was Ike's turn. Turning up like the proverbial bad penny, the minirecession went for the jugular when it came to the auto industry. An instant casualty was Packard, one of the nation's all-time great cars: Hudson and Nash bowed out at the end of 1957.

Nobody in car manufacturing escaped. Sales were down, way down, across the board. Ford caught a cold, partly of its own making, when it launched the Edsel. Market research

One of the prettiest cars to come out of Chrysler in 1957 was the high-performance, limited-production Fury. Standard mill was a 318-cid V-8 rated at 290 bhp. Gold anodized trim and white was the only color combination for the Fury. Exactly 7,438 Furys were built in 1957, but due to terrible workmanship and rust problems, there are few surviving today.

INSET, TOP: Taillight and fin treatment of the '57 Fury could not have been bettered. Heavy-duty torsion-bar suspension gave the Fury the best handling and ride in its class.

INSET, BOTTOM: All Chrysler dashboards were works of art in 1957, as witness the '57 Fury's. Speedometer goes to 150 mph, a figure that might have been an optimistic dream rather than reality.

proved as bad as the opinion polls in the 1948 presidential election. They forecast a landslide victory for Thomas Dewey; it was the other way around—Truman won. Saying the market was ripe for a new midprice car, Ford's market analysts were taken at their word and the Edsel was slated for a 1958 launch.

Not that the Edsel was bad. It looked a little strange, what with its odd grille, descriptions of which bordered on the amusing to the pornographic. Apart from the controversial grille, the Edsel looked fairly ordinary and followed the fashion dictates of the time. What it did have, though, were a pair of engines that alluded to the horsepower race, big time—303 bhp in the lesser model, 345 in top car. Not that any of this mattered; the public was unimpressed and the Edsel sank faster than the *Titanic*.

GM wasn't doing too well, either. The world's largest corporation had been truly caught with its pants down when Chrysler brought out the "Suddenly It's 1960 / Forward Look" designs a year earlier. With the exception of Buick and Oldsmobile, GM's divisions rustled together quite palatable designs such as an attractive Chevrolet and Pontiac. Cadillac was so-so, but Buick and Oldsmobile looked as though they'd fallen into a vat of chrome plate. One wonders what on earth Harley Earl and his team must have been thinking of; nobody liked the cars and they didn't sell as they should have. Part of the lack of sales can be put down to the recession, they tell us. Well, Chevrolet managed to produce 1.1 million cars of a completely new model. So it wasn't all recession.

As for Chrysler, the darling of the industry in 1957, the company almost sank out of sight. Mostly Chrysler could only blame itself. While the award-winning designs of 1957 were a

Here's the 1957 Dodge Coronet D-500 convertible in front of the Door Prairie Auto Museum in La Porte, Indiana. Chrysler pioneered the wrap-around, wrap-over windshield that was first used on 1957 convertibles. This Dodge resides at the museum.

INSET: Massive bumper/grille was actually attractive on the 1957 Dodge Coronet D-500. It only lasted one year and was replaced by a mesh grille.

The 1958 Pontiac Bonneville was a handsome albeit chrome-laden car. Concave rocket-type side spear echoed space race. Engine was optional 370 fuel-injected V-8, developing 310 bhp. Pontiac would become GM's performance division in the same way Dodge eventually did for Chrysler.

great step forward, quality, as noted earlier, took a back seat. In the rush to put the stunning designs into production, somebody forgot about quality of workmanship. Minirecession or no, Chrysler suffered a major downturn in sales, losing almost all the market gains accomplished between 1955 and 1957.

It was a great shame, really. Some of the corporate hot cars were as appealing as ever, particularly the new Plymouth Fury. *Motor Trend* had criticized all Plymouths for having verticals and horizontals clashing in the grille area. Above the bumper the grille was horizontal; beneath it, there were verticals. In 1958, Plymouth switched to horizontals beneath the grille, and this small change made a world of difference to the look of the car.

"The Fantastic '58 Fury" was the heading for the January 1958 issue of *Hot Rod* magazine's road test on the Plymouth. Staff drivers picked the car up from Detroit and drove it to

L.A., a distance of twenty-six hundred miles. After putting the Fury through some pretty grueling tests, *Hot Rod* said that in their opinion the Fury was the "number-one full-size road car in this country."

And well they might; the car was equipped with limited-slip differential, stiff suspension, and a brand-new engine. Dubbed the Golden Commando, the new engine displaced 350 cubic inches, had a 10.0:1 compression, Carter twin four-barrel carburetors, and hydraulic lifters, and developed 305 bhp at 5,000 rpm. Of conventional design, technical improvements allowed stamped-steel rocker arms instead of cast-iron manufacture, thus enabling significant weight saving. Rearranged coring in the cast-iron heads allowed the intake ports to be unobstructed by the water jackets, thus saving more weight. Standard transmission was a heavy-duty three-speed manual.

An interesting, if not the most reliable, option was Bendix fuel injection, pushing horsepower to 315. Not that anybody really needed it; the Fury equipped with the 305-horse engine could blast from 0 to 60 in 7.7 seconds using the manual transmission, while *Hot Rod* averaged about eight seconds. Not bad for a big car weighing 3,590 pounds. There is no doubt that had there not been the AMA racing ban, company-prepared Furys would have been hard to catch on sands or track. *Sports Car Illustrated* magazine found it difficult to believe that here was a Detroit full-size car "that can easily outcorner many 'bona-fide' sports cars."

A little busier grille and new side trim identified the 1958 DeSoto range, including the high-performance Adventurer. Due to the expense involved with building the Hemi, DeSoto had a new wedge-shaped V-8 rated at 361 cubic inches. Horsepower was the same, at 345, but there was a considerable gain in torque.

A privately entered 1958 DeSoto Adventurer raced through Daytona Beach's Flying Mile at 119.7 mph and 81.15 mph in the standing-start quarter-mile. This compared to a 1958 Chrysler 300D, which did the same at 126 mph and 87.48 respectively. The 300D was little changed from 1957 and still retained the hemispherical V-8. *Road & Track* magazine accelerated from 0 to 60 in 8.4 seconds and estimated the top speed at about 135 mph.

Giving the 300D its heart and its phenomenal power were 392 cubic inches and 380 horsepower. With the horsepower race still going full blast despite the AMA racing ban, the 300D still comfortably kept its title as the most powerful production car in the world. Don't forget, those were the days when the

In 1958 there was a minirecession, and midpriced cars suffered most. Only 432 DeSoto Adventurers were built, 82 of them convertibles. Standard engine was the 345-hp V-8. A 361-cubic-inch, 355-hp V-8 was an option. Anodized gold trim and a gold roof distinguish the long, low DeSoto Adventurer. The fins are just the right height, proportionately correct.

philosophy "There's no substitute for cubic inches" was the American Way. It was simple, it was direct, and it spawned a number of rock 'n' roll songs devoted to the idea that life is incomplete without a set of wheels able to beat all else.

The 1958 300D's engine had mechanical tappets instead of hydraulic as in the New Yorker, there were larger intake and exhaust valve lifts (.435 inch compared to .389, and .442 inch compared to .389, respectively), and valve-lift opening was increased from 252 degrees to 276. The 300D engine was highly tuned to minimize roughness, give 30 percent better idle speed, and perform with greater efficiency than its lesser brethren. Which it did!

Odd trim design was supposed to emphasize fin of 1958 DeSoto Adventurer but was a poor idea that failed.

Dual headlights were all the rage in 1958. Only the T-Bird, Studebaker Silver, and Golden Hawks didn't have them.

All Chrysler Corporation cars had beautifully designed taillights in 1957/58, and the DeSoto is no exception. Exhaust exits through bumper . . . not a practical idea because they rusted out!

Adventurer used functional dials which were necessary in performance cars capable of swift acceleration and high speeds.

Adventurer's attractive hubcap used gold anodized trim to complete the design.

Even *Road & Track*, a magazine that considered the majority of Detroit iron the pits, gave praise to the 300D. The worldly journal still thought the car too big (at 220 inches long and nearly 80 inches wide, they might have had a point), though, they admitted, the 300D was twenty-six inches shorter than the smallest Bugatti Royale. However, *Road & Track* declared without hesitation that the 300D "is an American prestige car, whose sports-car-derived features and characteristics make it outstanding." The testers made the observation that the car's capabilities would be appreciated by "above-average drivers" though overconfidence in the 300's "gentle competence could be a real threat to others."

Motor Trend described the 300D as "a true sportsman's car" and one designed to "go, and go, and keep right on going until you run out of road." Unlike *Road & Track, Motor Trend* considered the 300 a sports car and said so. "One of the two (Corvette's the other)," the magazine began, "honest-to-goodness sports cars built in Detroit, this Chrysler is a hard-riding and handsome high-performance traveler." High plaudits indeed, but let's go one better. The 300D might have been twenty-six inches shorter than some Bugatti Royales, yet it could have been considered a pretty close American substitute of the fifties, and at least one that was clearly more practical. And undoubtedly more fun.

Because 1958 was such a miserable year for the auto industry, there were only 801 300Ds built, of which 191 were convertibles. Exterior color choices were changed and increased, the only original shade being Raven Black. The other colors were Ermine White, Mesa Tan (must have been like the Arizona desert), Tahitian Coral, Matador Red, and Aztec Turquoise. Poor old DeSoto was even worse; only 432 Adventurers came down the line, 82 of them convertibles. There were

5,303 Plymouth Furys. As Dodge insisted on having its D-500 as an option package across the model range, there's no telling there—except to say the total number of cars with the D-500 option was obviously much less.

"Here Comes Summer" by Jerry Keller was the big song hit of summer 1959. It was the end of a decade of small-town innocence and Washington paranoia, the space race had begun, raunchy rock 'n' roll was being replaced by heavenly choirs, organs, and orchestras . . . and Fabian. Revolutionary Fidel Castro got Cuba and a warm bed after years sleeping in the hills, and America rushed to recognize his new government; this was a honeymoon that ended in one of quickest divorces ever known. Back to rock, and Elvis was in the army, and Buddy Holly, the Big Bopper, and Richie Valens all died, victims of a plane crash.

As for the 1959 cars, they were wild, surreal, spaced out on cloud nine. Especially the cars from GM. It looked as though management had contracted surrealist painter Salvador Dali to design them. Cadillac had a grille filled with row upon row of tiny chrome blocks and tail fins that rivaled the Empire State in height. One might suppose that Chevrolet read too many Batman comics if its extraordinary rear was anything to go by; still, it was quite handsome. Best-looking car out of GM's crop was the Buick. It had canted fins and front fenders and had shed 1958's chrome.

Ford was the most conservative style on the block, winning a prestigious international design award as a result. The same couldn't be said for Lincoln, whose length told us it really wanted to be an aircraft carrier, while Mercury wasn't sure about anything. As for Edsel . . . well, it tried to make amends but lacked in subtlety. And sales.

Racing was a dead issue as far as the manufacturers were concerned. Of course they sneaked bits and pieces out to private teams

Fins reached their peak on 1959 Cadillac Series 62 special convertible. This was pure surrealism crafted in steel. Design was meant to eclipse anything Chrysler had.

and everybody knew it. They were never caught, that's all. More on Motown's mind was the public's burgeoning interest in small cars. Volkswagens were selling like hot cakes, Opels, Vauxhalls, small cars with small engines that couldn't blaze across the sands like a Super Sabre. They were economical, practical, and weighed less than half what an average full-size American car topped out at. AMC's Rambler had gotten the message a decade earlier when it was still Nash. It was called the American and had a hundred-inch wheelbase. Even more extreme in downsizing was the Nash-designed, Austin-of-England-built Nash Metropolitan. It was quite popular. Then, in 1959, Studebaker introduced the smart little Lark, which was really a big Studebaker abridged in

size. When the Big Three saw the interest Studebaker and AMC were getting with their small offerings, they decided to follow suit. But their little ones were still a year away from birth when 1959 began, and they were left to watch the independents make hay while the sun shone ever so briefly in their corners.

Perhaps due to the continuous cries against more horsepower, Chrysler didn't increase it in the new 300E. What they did, though, was to dump the fabled Hemi as being too costly, and gave the 300 a new 413-cubic-inch conventional wedge-shaped engine. Called the Golden

Lion, the new engine was 101 pounds lighter than the Hemi, and for the sake of smoothness, hydraulic tappets were used instead of the mechanical type employed before. Horsepower remained the same, at 380. It may not have been a Hemi, but boy, the Golden Lion sure roared!

All Chrysler Corporation cars were heavily facelifted in 1959 with the single exception of the 300E. It shared the standard Chrysler's new, sharp-pointed taillights and heavy bumper assembly, which spoiled the overall good looks of the car. More optional creature comforts such as Chrysler's new swivel bucket seats, automatic headlight dimmer, a novel new gimmick introduced the year before on Imperials and New Yorkers called Auto-Pilot (actually an early form of cruise control), air conditioning, power this and power that—all scared performance addicts that perhaps the 300 had gone soft. Yes it had, to a point. The 300E was still one of the most powerful cars around, but it was losing its edge to lighter, fleeter machines being put together by its rivals. Nevertheless, *Speed Age* clocked a 0–60 time of 8.3 seconds while *Sports Car Illustrated* managed 8.7 seconds. This was faster than the 300D but not as quick as the 300C.

Even though Chrysler products had new (and in the case of Dodge, very attractive) styling, sales were stagnant compared to the resurgence being enjoyed by everyone else. Peoples' memories of 1957 quality was one reason; the astonishing new styling offered by GM was another. As for the 300E, only 690 were built, making it the lowest production figure for any 300 thus far. Of the 690 built, 140 were convertibles. And as usual with anything coming out of Detroit, prices were hiked once again, this time to a base $5,318.50 for the hardtop, $5,745.50 for the convertible. That's base price and does not include air conditioning, Sure-Grip limited-slip differential,

The 1959 Dodge Custom Royal D-500 was, if anything, better looking than the previous year's model. Outrageous taillights were very vulnerable to rear-end shunts of even a minor nature. Generous use of chrome did not mar '59 Dodge's handsome looks. Notice "eyebrows" over headlights. They evoke the looks of a 1940s Hollywood film star like Betty Grable! Car was extremely quick, with D-500 package consisting of 383 engine rated at 320/345 bhp.

radio, power windows, and other options. In those days one got a very basic car for the base price . . . even a paltry heater was an extra. Therefore, the addition of air, radio, limited slip, power windows, and outside rear-view mirror would add more than a thousand dollars—a lot of money in 1959.

One item that seemed quite nice was what Chrysler referred to as living leather. The result of an ingenious manufacturing process, living leather had the ability to "breathe." In other words it was porous and therefore able to remain cool because of efficient air circulation. Whatever the claims, the seats certainly looked classy, with their basket-weave effect. The only

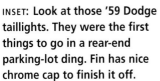

INSET: Look at those '59 Dodge taillights. They were the first things to go in a rear-end parking-lot ding. Fin has nice chrome cap to finish it off.

The D-500 engine was the 383, developing either 320 or 345 horsepower; 0–60 came up in the seven-second range. Note dual air cleaners for the dual carburetors.

Tell-tale sign this particular Custom Royal was something special.

Unique in the industry was Chrysler's swivel front seats. They were optional on top-line Chryslers, DeSotos, and Dodges. They allowed women attired in dresses or skirts to exit gracefully from low-slung cars.

Glittery gold-anodized hubcap seemed par for DeSoto's course in 1959. Sales actually went up a little that year.

disadvantage, according to some, was that living leather had a short life span. If the owner lived in Arizona, living leather was similar to Dracula once the sun hit. And horror movie buffs will remember what happened to Christopher Lee's Dracula when the sun blasted through the basement windows—he shriveled and turned to dust. More or less what happened to these attractive seats if exposed to too much sunshine. Ah, well. At least the living leather was standard . . . as was the deterioration.

Interesting "eyebrows" and a wide oval, opened-mouth grille gave the new Dodge the semblance of a Hollywood caricature depicting an aging (but trying desperately hard not to show it) actress. In the potent D-500 form, Dodge had a new 383-cubic-inch V-8 shared with other divisions. The engine had twin four-barrel carburetors and was definitely no slouch off the line. Overall it was an attractive car that begged, like all other Chrysler Corporation "sporty" cars, to be raced.

Plymouth notched up fifteen thousand more sales with a heavily reworked redesign and stayed in third place. Fifteen thousand

wasn't much compared to Chevrolet and Ford, who racked up nearly half a million; maybe it would have been less if they had not had all-new bodies. The new Plymouth had a bold egg-crate grille and strange, sculpted headlamp brows. A curious decision was made when it was decided the 1959 Fury would no longer be a limited high-performance machine but a regular series instead. Above the Fury came the high-performance Sport Fury in hardtop and convertible form. Standard engine was a 260 bhp 318, and above that, a 361 cubic-incher that developed 305 bhp. Both engines were optional on all other Plymouths though, and with almost twenty-four thousand units produced in all colors, the Sport Fury was far from something special like the Furys of old. As with all Chrysler products, one could order the new swivel seats that spun out when the doors were opened.

Times were hard over in the DeSoto camp . . . and getting harder. Medium-priced cars were taking a beating across the board. Model-year production was down to a mere forty-six thousand units. Besides which, DeSoto's facelift consisted of a busier, heavier looking front end, clumsy side trim, and an ungainly bumper at the rear. The Adventurer suffered the same indignities, even losing its Hemi, which was replaced by the 383 Wedge-head developing 350 horses. Mind you, the 383 was standard in other DeSotos as well, and an option on the lower-priced Firesweep model, though horsepower was less than in the Adventurer.

Like all Chrysler cars in 1959, DeSoto had the optional Torsion-Aire suspension system with Level-Cruise ride. Air suspension was a new fad that was probably influenced by the air-suspension system introduced on the 1955 Citroen DS-19. While the Citroen's system worked, most American ones didn't . . . or certainly not too well, anyway. GM had a shot and gave up; Chrysler's was no better. Many customers got so fed up with the troublesome nature of air suspension that they took their cars back to be converted to conventional systems. American air suspension might have worked had the manufacturers given it time to work the bugs out. They didn't, and got into trouble for not spending more time on development.

As before, the DeSoto was a powerful, well-handling auto that could keep up with the best of them on the performance front. As DeSoto's catalogue said: "The Adventurer is an exclusive car . . . made for a discriminating few." It certainly was; just 590 hardtops and 97 convertibles were made. Never mind. That was 255 more than in 1958.

Model year 1959 rolled to a close, and the small boys were back at harassed dealers' lots to try and catch a glimpse of the 1960 models. With sales of midprice cars falling, and big cars getting a lot of stick from all and sundry, small-car sales were gaining momentum. AMC's Rambler almost passed Plymouth, just behind the third-place finisher, so the Big Three had their compacts ready for a 1960 launch.

The Fabulous Fifties had been an innocent, but careful, decade. It had begun the youth revolution and rock 'n' roll. Little did anybody realize what the sixties would bring, what incredible cars would hit the streets, and how four young men would help change the course of the world.

Muscle A-Go-Go

I f the fifties was a memorable, important decade, then the sixties was like a great movie one never forgets. This decade, more than any other, remains a series of picture shows that play and replay in the minds of those who were teenagers or in their early twenties when this extraordinary period unfolded. So strong were the influences of the time that many today find it hard to wrest themselves away and move on. The common man still had a say, then; now only the lobbyists, good or evil, tell the nation's guardians how it is going to be.

January 1960 saw the rebirth of a nation—a rebirth that heralded a series of events destined to give a jolt to our precious planet, a jolt so severe it would destroy the comfortable path upon which history seemed to be taking us. It was the month that a wealthy, handsome young man from Massachusetts decided to enter America's presidential race. The heat was on, the die was cast, and John F. Kennedy and his beautiful wife, Jacqueline, became the sweethearts of the tabloids, the darlings of the nation.

While history took a turn off the straight and narrow, America's car industry entered the new decade with its own ideas of change. The year 1960 gave birth to three smart, much smaller cars. One had European flair, another was a technical wonder, and

Introduced a year ahead of the Big Three compacts, the 1959 Studebaker Lark temporarily saved the company. Riding a 108.5-inch wheelbase, the Lark used an old L-head six rated at 90 bhp and a 259-cubic-inch V-8 developing 180 bhp. A four-barrel version was good for 195 horses. This is the 1960 Lark Regal convertible, which was virtually identical to the '59s.

the third was utterly conventional in every way. Three new cars and they were all different from each other, so different that they were instantly recognizable when they came over the hill. Chevrolet's rear-engined Corvair, Ford's utterly conventional Falcon, and the attractive-looking Plymouth Valiant had come to town.

There was nothing muscular about any of them. None had any more than six cylinders. They were the result of a public move to smaller, less powerful cars, retaining the comforts of the behemoths in a compact package. Of the three, the Chevrolet Corvair was the most advanced, following the engineering designs of Porsche and VW. The engine was an air-cooled, opposed-cylinder, aluminum-alloy six located where the trunk would be in an ordinary car. Four-wheel independent suspension—a first for a production American car—consisted of a completely unitized front-suspension subassembly and a swing axle arrangement at the rear. It measured a mere 180 inches overall on a 108-inch wheelbase, a midget compared to the 210 inches of a full-size Impala. The Corvair was shorter than the other pair of compacts: the Falcon was a little over 181 inches, the Valiant slightly more than 183 inches.

Of the three, the Corvair was the only one that was entirely new and built from the ground up. The Falcon and Valiant were big cars put on a diet. From the word go, Corvair was advertised to appeal to the young at heart. It was given more of a sports car image when the pretty two-door Monza Club Coupe was introduced in February 1960. About 250,000 Corvairs of all types were built for 1960.

That sounds like a healthy total for a new, untried automobile, though the very ordinary Ford Falcon produced 435,676 units, a production record for a new car at the time (Mustang would beat the record four years later), which left the Corvair gasping in second place. As for the Valiant, the prettiest of the bunch, it came in third with a healthy 194,202 produced.

As the whole world knows, the Corvair would shortly come in for a lot of stick, especially from consumer advocate Ralph Nader. After studying a number of disturbing flip-over crashes concerning the Corvair, Nader went public and declared the car unsafe. So, at a later date, did flawed but ingenious motoring whiz kid, John Z. DeLorean. In his eye-opening book *On a Clear Day You Can See General Motors*, DeLorean alleges corruption in high places within the GM warrens during the fifties and early sixties. DeLorean claims the making of the Corvair with swing-axle rear suspension was irresponsible: it had been proved, even by GM engineers, to be unsafe and unstable. Mercedes, DeLorean says, threw out the idea of a rear-engined car with swing-axle suspension as unsafe. The late Ed Cole, then general manager at Chevrolet, believed the Corvair to be safe, and refused to put any more money into the car to make it safer. This decision would come to haunt him in the very near future. Especially when those close to home were killed in Corvairs. Like the son of Cadillac general manager Cal Werner, who claimed the Corvair had a design defect. The Pontiac general manager's niece was horribly injured in a Corvair, and famous comedian Ernie Kovacs died when his Corvair flipped over. General Motors would pay dearly for a foolhardy decision to save a few bucks.

Apart from the very handsome body design, Chrysler's Valiant was fairly conventional. Initially it was referred to simply as the Valiant, for it was considered to be a distinct model on its own. A year later Plymouth took the little waif under its wheels and it became a Plymouth Valiant. Like all Chrysler products in 1960, the Valiant featured unitized body construction, seven-dip rust proofing—in an attempt by the company to do something to erase the problems

The 1960 Plymouth Fury's biggest engine option was the 361 V-8 developing 330 horsepower. It was obvious nobody knew quite what to do with the styling other than make it more garish with larger fins. Oddly shaped wheel-arch openings and painted front section distinguished the 1960 Fury. Compared to earlier Plymouths, quality control was a little better.

(especially rusting) encountered since 1957. For the sake of survival, Chrysler was doing everything it could to improve the quality of its cars.

Torsion-bar front suspension and a three-speed manual transmission were standard, although the two-speed PowerFlite automatic was an option. Not TorqueFlite though. Recognized as the world's finest automatic, Torque-Flite was only available on V-8 engined cars. The Valiant had the new OHV Slant Six engine that had been introduced as a replacement for the weary old in-line, 230-cid six in use since it propelled Noah's Ark!

By 1960, most manufacturers were beginning to openly defy the nonracing rule set by the AMA a couple of years earlier. Pontiac had become the car to beat on the track, and showed just how good they were at Daytona. Speeds of over 150 mph were set by both Pontiac and Chevrolet in the five-hundred-mile race, which was eventually won by the Chevy, with Pontiac second. A very creditable third and fourth placing went to father/son team Lee and Richard Petty driving 1960 Plymouths. Here was the makings of a racetrack legend. By the end of the decade, young Richard would become the hero of the NASCAR circuits, driving for Chrysler.

What was particularly interesting at the 1960 Daytona event was the team of Valiants that wiped out all other compact competition with ease. The cars were sent to dealers with factory-modified, 148-horsepower engines (these were the stock 170-cubic-inch mills rated at 101 bhp in standard form); they had tougher suspension rates, and the bodies had as much removed from them as rules permitted, to lighten weight. Then, as was clearly meant to be, they were sent to the racetrack. And how those Valiants ran! They beat everything in sight. On the 2.5-mile oval and the 3.8 road course and oval, the Valiants averaged speeds of 122 mph-plus and 88.154 mph respectively. Sizzling stuff for a car not even meant to be for racing. Similarly treated and modified Falcons and Corvairs joined in the fray but came up short.

Even if Chrysler had quality-control problems, it still could come up trumps when it came to engineering. The Slant Six engine is a case in point. It did what its name implied; it slanted 30 degrees to the right and was built that way to allow Chrysler to take advantage of lower hoodlines. The engine had lighter, stronger cast-iron block castings, aluminum oil pump and intake manifold, tubular pushrods, a single-throat, down-draft carburetor, pressed-steel rocker arms, and a flat-bottomed crankcase. As noted earlier, the engine displaced 170 cubic inches and pushed out 101 horses.

It wasn't long before Bob Rodger's engineering team realized that the new engine was capable of much more than carting Grandma down to the bingo hall. Its design was versatile enough to allow a degree of power input. Hence the special racing engines used in the successful Daytona Valiants, which were then offered as a performance option to the public. Called the Hyper Pack option, the engine developed 148 bhp at 5,200 rpm, had a four-barrel carburetor and a compression ratio of 10.5:1. Now if this didn't smack of Europe (small engine, high compression, high speed), what did?

After ten years in the hot seat, ten years of groundbreaking innovation, Tex Colbert handed over the Chrysler president's baton to old pal William C. Newberg. Colbert now became chairman of the board, but not for very long. In what could only be described as a Night of the Long

Knives with a touch of "et tu Brute?" thrown in, Chrysler's hierarchy went into a tailspin.

It all began when word got out that Newberg had financial fingers in a number of Chrysler's outside suppliers. Conflict of interest charges were dumped on Newberg's doorstep, forcing him to resign sixty-four days after assuming office. Colbert took over the presidency again, this time with his embittered friend turning against him. On top of the internal unrest came bad marketplace news; it had been a poor year for Chrysler Corporation despite new innovations and better-produced cars. The war of words and a continuing downward turn in sales left nobody very happy.

All the political unrest was a shame because the product was decent. Perhaps the original Exner designs had been messed with a little too much, but the cars were good. Especially the new Chrysler 300F. Not since the 300C had there been such a promising new 300. It was extremely handsome and now featured four bucket seats in a beautifully designed interior. In common with other Chryslers, the 300F had the new unit-construction body, the advantage of which was more structural rigidity. Squeaks and rattles were a thing of the past it was claimed, and certainly the 300F felt more solid than previous editions from 1957 on.

Ram induction was the big thing for all Chrysler makes in 1960, and standard on the 300F. Not that ram-induction manifolding was new; it had been used on Chrysler's 1952/53 Indy cars but not again until 1960, by which time it had reached its maximum potential. Some called ram induction a poor man's supercharger; whatever, the system worked to great effect.

What ram induction did was to ram air and fuel into the engine when the accelerator was pressed. The air and fuel mixture is carried from the twin carburetors through thirty-inch-long tubes leading to each combustion chamber.

Unlike a supercharger there were no moving parts or adjustments necessary to maintain optimum performance, although shorter tubes fifteen inches long were available, thus moving the maximum torque output to 3,600 rpm. The longer tubes maximum was 2,800 rpm.

Anyone would be able to tell Chrysler's ram-inducted engine by the four tubes running across the top. Each tube has two channels within. They feed the fuel directly to each intake port. This form of delivery is similar to supercharging, but is less costly and less complicated. As for the carburetors, they were removed from their central location to the outboard ends of the tubing.

Under the layer of tubes lay the same 413-cubic-inch engine used in the 300E. Horsepower was down from 380 to 375, but performance levels were superior to the E. All 300Fs were equipped with TorqueFlite automatics, except nine. The nine were the odd cars about town—if they were ever seen about town. Called the 300F Special, the cars differed inasmuch as they had 400-horsepower engines and four-speed manual transmissions. Motoring journalists, professional drivers, and enthusiasts of real driving machines had been asking for a manual transmission since the first 300 in 1955. Now it was here . . . but in only nine of them?

A press release dated January 8, 1960, told of these special 300F models and the kind of transmission they would be using. It was the French-built Pont-a-Mousson four-speed box normally used in the Facel-Vega, a French luxury-class automobile that employed Chrysler's hemispherical V-8. The Pont-a-Mousson was a heavy-duty unit perfectly matched to handle the power and torque of Chrysler's big engines—hence the decision by Bob Rodger to use it in the special racing editions being prepared for Daytona.

Of the nine specials built, six went to Daytona, one was an experimental "mule," and two others were specially built for good Chrysler customers. Interestingly, one of these cars was supposed to have been broken up in Phoenix, Arizona, but the author has actually seen and photographed this car, which still resides in Phoenix. The car belongs to Don Petty, who also owns examples of every 300 Letter Series model. Don, by the way, is the cousin of racing hero Richard Petty.

Once news got out about this special 300, the Chrysler phones didn't stop ringing. People wanted the car and orders poured in. But Chrysler, for some extraordinary reason, wouldn't budge. In a letter written on February 25, 1960, G. J. McCarthy, divisional distribution manager for Chrysler and Imperial divisions, wrote a letter to all Chrysler dealerships in an attempt to stop the steady flow of orders for the car. His letter said the order book "far exceeded our expectations and we are already sold out of them." Then he went on to plug the standard 375-bhp version with TorqueFlite transmission, claiming it would out-perform the manual transmission version "within legal driving ranges."

Daytona Speed Week came in February as usual, and there were a lot of cars from different manufacturers eager to put their names in lights. When it came to the NASCAR Flying Mile, each 300F shattered the original record set in 1955 by a C-300. The top car was driven by Gregg Ziegler, who posted a new record of 144.927 mph. Daytona Beach fixture Brewster Shaw came in second with a speed of 143.369 mph. Harry Faubel Jr. was third at 143.198 mph. Of the six cars, the lowest timed speed was 141.509 mph. Sand being what sand is, surface slippage occurred, so the 300F's potential speed was considerably reduced.

Following the 300F's Daytona successes, inquires persisted on the availability of this special model. On March 7, 1960, Bob Rodger was moved to write to one individual explaining why no more would be made. Conceding that Chrysler was taken aback by the car's popularity, Rodger made the case that it would perform badly under normal city dri-

General Motors introduced three new compacts in 1961—one, the Pontiac Tempest, came with a four-cylinder 195-cid engine, an innovative flexible driveshaft, and a rear transaxle.

ving conditions because of the "use of a race-type camshaft and headers which provide no carburetor heat. With this in mind no mass-production tooling was contracted for the trans-mission or engine parts." And like McCarthy before him, Rodger suggested the interested party should try the standard 300F because it was a better performer.

There was no doubt the 300F Special was an outstanding machine and one that should have been put into limited production of say five hundred or a thousand units. Of course the special tooling required would have been very costly, and the car would have certainly needed vastly improved brakes. Unfortunately—and nobody ventured to say this at the time—Chrysler was in the financial doldrums follow-ing a succession of bad sales years since 1958. And bearing in mind the cost to produce the special 300F, the market might have balked at paying a premium price to own one. For Chrysler to have made anything at all on the car, it would have had to cost at least $1,000 more than the base $4,952 for the standard automatic-equipped model. Add the necessary extras and buyers could have looking at figures approaching $7,000. While the 300F's interior was outstanding, the dashboard was given the Flash Gordon treatment meted out to New Yorkers and Saratogas. There was more chrome and the not-entirely-round steering wheel was made of transparent materials. The infuriating dashboard-mounted rear-view mir-ror, the bane of all Chrysler products since 1957, continued to be used. Even though Chrysler's year wasn't all that good, 300F pro-duction jumped 75 percent to 964 hardtops and 248 convertibles. Only four colors were available: Terra Cotta, Toreador Red, Formal Black, and Alaskan White.

That Chrysler would not produce the 300F Special in some way says a lot about the com-pany at that time. Financial difficulties or no,

Chrysler was not prepared to be adventurous, to take a gamble and try something really unique. Which was extremely frustrating to designers and engineers trying to better their products.

Larry Rathgeb was one of those gifted engineers. He joined Chrysler in September of 1958. Larry had been a mechanic before he went into the service, where he continued as a mechanic for the military. When his time was up Larry went to college in Missouri to take a course in engineering. He applied for a position at Chrysler, studied at the Chrysler Institute, graduated in 1960, and went into engineering operations preparing monthly books that cov-ered various designs, which went to different people within the company. "Late in 1960 there was a big layoff," said Larry, "but I was kept on and was moved to a position where I was a design cost analyst. . . . I did that for a short time."

While employed as a cost analyst, Larry noted that the Imperial's emergency brake was a complex and costly design and set to work with an idea of his own that would ultimately reduce the cost of the hand brake.

"I realized the job could be done a lot cheaper, so I drew up my little plan," chuckled Larry. "It was just a cable that was hooked to the parking-brake release lever so that when you took the parking brake out of park posi-tion, it pulled . . . on the emergency brake, and the emergency brake released. I wrote the whole thing up and wrote the pros and cons, added drawings and presented it to my leader, who was Jack Gilmore. He looked at it rather doubt-fully, then told me to take it to Jim McCormick who was the man in charge of cables. 'He'll pass on it,' Gilmore said to me.

"Well, I took it to McCormick and I said: 'Mr. McCormick, I have a design here that involves a cable. Would you take a look at it?' He took it and said: 'Did you do it?' I said

'Yes.' To which he replied: 'Well, if you did it, it won't work. What is it, anyway? Oh, forget about it. It won't work.'

"So I went back to my boss and he said: 'Let me talk to McCormick.' Which he did, and after a while he said to me that McCormick told him it wouldn't work and for me to stay away from the idea."

Rathgeb's design didn't end there. He took his design to the person in charge of safety: here he received an entirely different reception. "He looked at it," related Larry, "and said, 'My goodness, this is exactly what we have been looking for! This will get us off the hook in New York State because they have these laws, etc., etc.'" Immediately the vehicle-safety executive called the then head of Product Planning, Burt Bowcamp, and told him about Larry's design. Bowcamp asked to see the design and Larry was asked whether he had any car with his brake modification attached. Larry had a friend's car to which he had added his design. The safety man told Bowcamp they had an engineering car with Larry's brake attached and they set off to see him.

"Bowcamp jumped into the car," said Larry, "went around it, and said: 'By golly! This is great, really great. This is exactly what I want on next year's Chrysler.' So at the next big engineers' meeting, Bowcamp told the assembled about my brake and how fabulous it was and that he wanted it on the next year's Chrysler models.

"All the chief engineers looked at one another," continued Larry, "looking back and forth, and you could see they didn't have the remotest idea what he (Bowcamp) was talking about. They had absolutely no idea what he was on about. Nobody said anything.

"After the meeting was over, the engineers all huddled together, and my boss, Gilmore said, 'I think it's that S.O.B. Rathgeb who went over my head to show Bowcamp his idea.

. . .' Shortly after, Gilmore called me into his office and read me the riot act. He yelled at me: 'By golly, I'll have you in the street for this. I told you not to do anything with that: you've made me look like a fool.' And he went on and on.

"I was feeling really down when I returned to my desk. I hadn't been back long when I got a call. I figured it was probably another chief engineer who wanted to chew my ass!

" 'My name's Dave Dillman,' the caller said. 'Are you the young gentleman who designed that brake release?'

"I said, 'Yes, I am.'

" 'Well, I want to shake your hand. Gosh, I've been looking for somebody who is not afraid to step out of line and do what they think is right. Will you work for me?' "

Not believing his luck, Larry said he would love to, but he would have to talk to Gilmore first, to which Dillman replied he would take care of everything. He told Larry to go and collect all his belongings and bring them to Dillman's workplace (Dillman was in charge of suspension at the time). Larry mentioned that he was due to go on a two-week vacation and Dillman said he would have his office ready upon his return.

Rested and refreshed, Larry returned from

Picture shows the lithe shape of the 1961 Chrysler 300G. The 413 engine and ram-induction remained, but performance was down ever so slightly. More luxury was coming to be the name of the game. Dark, dismal day doesn't hide the fact that even the lesser performing 300G was still a thoroughbred. But 1961 was the last year of Chrysler's controversial but world famous fins.

his vacation, eager to begin his new job. He went to Dillman's design section . . . but no Dillman. While he was away, Dillman had accepted a position at Ford and his replacement was . . . Jack Gilmore! Talk about a twist ending!

Larry chuckled. "I walked into Gilmore's office rather sheepishly and I looked at him and he looked at me, smiled, and said: 'No hard feelings?' 'No hard feelings.' 'Fine,' he said. 'Then back to your desk and go to work!'"

Although Larry Rathgeb admits there would be many other times he would step out of line, it was always over ideas that would improve the breed. Corporate rules and regulations were very stiff, almost as if they had been set up to challenge the designers and engineers on staff to break them in the interests of a better overall product. Still, there appears to have been a certain amount of lackadaisical thought in the upper echelons of the corporate structure, which drifted down to those immediately in charge of the product. Like the 300F, for example.

Although there would be five more 300 Letter Series models, the 300F was the last really great driving, handling, and performance car. Arguably it was the best of the whole bunch. Perhaps not as attractive as some of the earlier cars, the 300F scored in every

other way. One Ferrari driver was quoted in *Sports Car Graphic* as saying he was amazed at how fast the 300F was and how well it handled very tight bends. Sure, there were other fast cars around in 1960, but the 300F was number one in a field of one. Of that there is no doubt.

Plymouth sold ten thousand units fewer than in 1959 but managed to hold onto third place. Styling was awkward, with curiously styled color contrast panels ahead of the front-wheel arches. The Fury range was extended with the inclusion of a convertible, and the big 361-cid V-8 was optional on all Plymouth models. No longer was the Fury an exciting, limited-edition automobile; now it was just another Plymouth that cost a couple of hundred dollars more than the Belvedere. What was quite interesting was Plymouth's XNR show car. It was named after Virgil Exner, who designed the two-seater sports car sporting a Jaguar D-Type fin at the rear. Obviously casting an eye in the direction of Chevrolet's successful Corvette, the XNR had the potential to take on America's only sports car. As it was only what Chrysler liked to call an "idea car," the XNR's heart was the Slant Six engine, probably the modified 148-horsepower version used in the Daytona Valiants. But, like so many good automotive ideas, the XNR remained just that . . . an idea car.

All new series names identified the oddly finned Dodge lines for 1960. Gone were Royal and Coronet, to be replaced by Matador, Seneca, Polara, and Dart. As before, there was no special Dodge performance car, only the D-500 option package available on all models. DeSoto had the Adventurer, but this had been turned into a model series. There were no convertibles in the much depleted DeSoto lineup, which only managed to produce little more than 25,500 in 1960. A year later DeSoto would be gone, a victim of the shrinking medium-price market. Another casualty was the sickly Edsel. Less than 2,300 Edsels, now just a Ford with a different grille, were produced for 1960, and it was gone, alone and forgotten, a far cry from all the hoopla of two years earlier.

America had a new president in 1961. John F. Kennedy, despite his popularity, just managed to eke out a narrow victory over his Republican rival, Richard M. Nixon. Kennedy won 303 electoral votes to Nixon's 219, and

Kennedy's share of the popular vote was only 120,000 more than his disgruntled opponent. It would not be long before Kennedy would be treated like royalty, an instant icon beloved by his people. Yuri Gagarin became the first man in space in April 1961; less than a month later, America sent up Alan B. Shepherd for fifteen minutes and Kennedy asked Congress to approve a program to send men to the moon. Gary Cooper, star of the films *High Noon* and *Sergeant York*, died, the Berlin Wall went up, and Jackie Kennedy wowed the French. These were some of the events that took place in 1961. The political and social dies were cast, the stage was set, and the rumblings of change began to be felt around the world.

On the 1961 car front, GM introduced a new bunch of compacts. Buick had the Special, Olds the F-85, and Pontiac came up with the Tempest. All had the same 112-inch wheelbase and shared the compact Buick, Oldsmobile, Pontiac platform. Even so, each car had a distinct character of its own, especially the Pontiac Tempest. This was a very revolutionary car that was years ahead of anything else on the road. It had a flexible driveshaft and transaxle that incorporated independent link-type rear suspension. The transaxle was completely

Chevrolet had woken up to the fact that Plymouth was stealing its thunder on the track and its sales in the showroom. So along it came with the awesome 1962 Impala SS 409, an out-and-out performance car if ever there was one.

Pontiac's: nobody else had ever used such a system before and wouldn't until the Porsche 928 some eighteen years later. Unfortunately, as with many innovative and radical ideas that have come from Detroit, the Tempest's advanced technology was dropped in favor of a conventional drive train in 1964.

Over at Highland Park dreadful things had happened to many of the cars' designs. Chrysler bodies were unchanged with the exception of the front, which was given canted headlights and 1960's grille in reverse. Taillights were different—they were moved from the fins to just above the rear bumper—and the trunk lid restyled. These changes were shared by the new 300G, which still managed to look elegant despite the desperate need to make the car look "new."

On the mechanical side, nothing was changed; the 300G still had the 375/ 413-cid V-8 as standard with the 400-horse version offered as an option. There was no Pont-a-Moussin gearbox to be had, so Chrysler tried offering a heavy-duty three-speed manual transmission to placate all those still clamoring for something like the French box. In the interests of better brake cooling and road handling, the 300G reverted to fifteen-inch wheels; for the sake of an ultra-low profile, fourteen-inch wheels had been the order of the day since 1957. The classy interior was much the same but the little seat perforations perforated in a different pattern.

"Uncle" Tom McCahill had described the 300F as the "hottest sedan ever built in the history of the world" (why he called it a sedan when the car was a two-door hardtop is beyond me), but it is unlikely that he would have enthused so much about the 300G. It was fast, yes, very fast, but not quite as rapid as the F. At the 1961 Daytona Speed Week competition, Gregg Ziegler drove a 300G to victory in the famed Flying Mile event, posting a speed of

143 mph—which was only one mile an hour shorter than Ziegler's winning speed in 1960. Another 300G driven by Bud Faubel won the NASCAR Standing Mile acceleration run with an average speed of 90.7 mph. Road testers driving stock 300Gs for their respective journals found 0 to 60 times almost a full second less than in 1960. Part of the reason may have been the bigger wheels, which tended to slow the car in acceleration runs but helped when the 300G was pouring it on past 80.

The 300Gs built numbered 1,617 (1,280 hardtops and 337 convertibles), making it one of the most popular 300 Letter cars in the seven-year series. There is no question that it still held the mystique accorded to fine, thoroughbred machinery, and deservedly so. Four exterior hues were available and they were Formal Black, Alaskan White, Mardi Gras Red, and Cinnamon. Base price was now $5,413 for the hardtop, $5,843 for the convertible—actually only a couple of dollars more than the 300F.

Dodge gave birth to a Valiant lookalike called the Lancer, and it was quite a handsome machine. It shared almost everything with the Valiant, including the efficient alternator pioneered by the 1960 Valiant and now on all Chrysler products. Unfortunately the same could not be said about the rest of Chrysler Corporation's cars, which were akin to the misfits in the *Star Wars* bar. Plymouth's Fury, which had been so spectacularly beautiful, was about the ugliest car on the block, the sort of thing nightmares are made of. *Motor Trend* said in retrospect that it "sparked a whole generation of Japanese sci-fi monsters." It made the unfortunate Edsel look like the belle of the ball by comparison. The Plymouth's front end looked very similar to one of Marvel Comics' monster covers of the same time, the rear was devoid of fins, and the taillights were curious pods that were slapped on the sides of the rear fenders. Nevertheless, this sad styling spectacle is so awful that one becomes fascinated by it, almost motherly toward it. Which is perhaps why these awkward Plymouths are snatched up when they come up for sale on the collectors' market.

As for Dodge, it retained some semblance of restraint in its styling—well, at the front, anyway, which had a fairly conventional concave mesh grille. It was in the rear where Exner went psychedelic: he reversed the fins. The high point started at the C-pillar, then tapered down and around to finish up as the car's side trim. There was a range of engine options, the big 383-cid V-8 rated at 330 bhp being the top dog in Polara and Dart models.

There was a funeral at Chrysler this year, actually at the end of 1960, with the passing of DeSoto to the Great Gas Station in the Sky. Only 3,034 units were produced of what once was a proud name, albeit a car priced too close to Chrysler for comfort. And as such, it had always come in second best in sales. Not that the final DeSoto was very memorable: it had 1960 styling with one of those awful grilles that compared favorably with early Toyotas. And to end Chrysler's 1960 horror story, there is the Imperial. Even though not a performance car, its *Star Wars* design needs mentioning. Exner gave the Imperial a smaller grille with dual free-standing headlights on either side. The fins, hand-me-downs from 1960, took the crown for being the biggest since Cadillac tried to scrape the stars in 1959. But the free-standing lights up front were a conversational curiosity if nothing else.

Obviously due to its unfortunate design, Plymouth sales sagged to fourth place behind little Rambler, which was having a field day on the economy front. Small cars were selling briskly yet Chrysler managed a reasonably healthy 96,454 sales for the season, rising 34 percent over 1960. Otherwise the rest of the corporation didn't fair well. Something urgently needed to be done to bring the public back to Chrysler show-rooms in 1962. It was not entirely a good omen for Lynn A. Townsend, who succeeded Tex Colbert as president on July 27, 1961.

After a pretty disastrous year in 1961, Valiant sales rose almost 50 percent in 1962. Unfortunately the newly restyled Plymouth went down like a lead balloon. It really wasn't such a bad-looking car, either; the trouble was it had been downsized, and compared to the big new Ford and Chevrolet, the Plymouth was a nonstarter.

Actually, the new Plymouth/Dodge designs were not Virgil Exner's fault. Design work for the '62 cars had begun in 1958–59, and Exner wanted them to share a family resemblance to the Valiant with its long hood / short deck theme. Exner liked his Valiant because it incorporated many design features he had done for various Chrysler show cars. Fins were out as far as Exner was concerned; they had run their course, especially after being lampooned by the 1959 Cadillac.

Exner's original designs for the Dodge/Plymouth bodies were for the long hood / short deck, echoing classic shapes of old but done in the modern manner. He asked William Brownlie, Cliff Voss, and others who worked for him to design a completely new car in utmost secrecy. They were to be full-size cars—until executive vice-president Bill Newberg saw them. Playing on a hunch that Chevrolet was downsizing its cars for 1962, Newberg blitzed the team's designs and demanded the cars be shorter. Exner was disappointed with the decision, referring to the eventual (and shorter) Dodge and Plymouth as "plucked chickens."

In retrospect, the 1962 Dodge and Plymouth weren't that terrible to look at. Take the resurrected Sport Fury (it had last appeared in 1959), for example. Certainly it is controversial and not at all conventional, but one would have thought that would have been its appeal. Trouble is, the general public was rather

conservative, especially in the early sixties, after years of three-tone color schemes, fins, and fishbowl glass areas. It may not have been one of Exner's best efforts, but given the time in which the cars had to be designed, the Plymouth, especially the Sport Fury, came out looking far more appealing than given credit for. In fact, the car magazines of the day came down on the side of Plymouth/Dodge styling, and said so. Whatever was said didn't sway the buyers; although small cars were in, the customers still wanted the "big is better" look to impress the neighbors with.

There must have been a trillion engine variations to choose from in 1962, the smallest being the Slant Six. For those who wanted husky, he-man stuff, there was the 361-cubic-inch V-8 pumping out either 305 or 310 bhp. Later in the season, after having been dropped as an option, the 383 returned along with a brutish 413-cubic-incher. The 383 developed 330 horsepower while the 413 came in four states of tune, the smallest being 365 bhp at 4,600 rpm, the largest a whopping 415 bhp at 5,200 rpm.

Even if the public was leery of buying Ply-

mouths, they did extremely well in all forms of motor sports. Plymouth won the Mobilgas Economy Run on one hand, and the Daytona 500 with the other. There was nothing to touch these Plymouths in NASCAR or USAC short-track competition; the much-vaunted and sizzling Chevrolet 409s, Ford's 406s, and Pontiac's barnstorming 421 Super Duty cars generally were outclassed by the smaller, lighter Highland Park sensations. Much of Plymouth's success was due to the lightning-quick short-ram V-8 equipped with dual carburetors.

Despite its good fortune in competition, the "win on Sunday, sell on Monday" didn't materialize the way the pundits expected. Plymouth had one of its worst sales years ever in 1962, dropping to eighth place overall. Dodge fared a little better, retaining its ninth place due partly to a hastily thrown-together full-size Dodge that appeared in mid-1962. In essence the car was a 1962 Chrysler Newport with a 1961

Dodge Polara front end. Called the Custom 880, this Chrysler/Dodge transplant realized 17,505 units in the short time left for the 1962 model year.

One of the nicest-looking cars to come out of Highland Park in 1962 was the Chrysler. Time didn't allow a complete redesign so the 1961 body was given a major facelift starting with the complete removal of the fins. The front remained much like the 1961 car but the entire rear was new. Of course the new 300H was an even more attractive alternative to the standard Chryslers but was delivered an insulting body blow by its corporate parent who, in a desire to cash in on the 300 Letter cars' sporting image, replaced the Windsor with a mass-produced 300 series consisting of hardtops, sedans, and convertibles. To add insult to injury, the 300 series even had the Letter car's red, white, and blue emblem. Even worse for Letter Series enthusiasts was the erosion of the great car's exclusivity; many of the 300H options and standard fittings were available on the upstart 300. Options like the big 413 engine, heavy-duty suspension, even the manual transmission. And the grille. The upstart had the temerity to steal the 300H's blacked-out grille fronted by a crossbar with the 300 emblem in the center. Was nothing sacred?

In a somewhat tacky way, Chrysler did themselves a favor with the mass-produced 300. In its first model year, the 300 realized a healthy 25,020 sales. That was quite a bit higher than its Windsor ancestor managed the year before. Compare that to the more expensive 300H, which struggled to produce a mere 558 units (123 of them convertibles), and it is easy to see why Chrysler chose to make a cheaper, mass-produced clone.

Although some magazine editors chose to cough and sputter shocked indignation, most decided the clone wasn't such a bad car. *Hot*

Rod magazine had a 300 specially prepared to compete in the NHRA Winternationals event. The drags were delayed a week by rain, which meant the *Hot Rod* staffers who were going to drive the 300 had to fly down to cover the Daytona Speed Week competition. They asked a friend to drive the 300 at the Winternationals, and he happily complied: Gary Nichols put up some pretty shattering times like 108.40 mph in 12.88 seconds, but an unfamiliarity with a temperamental starting technique allowed a big 421 Pontiac to just pip him at the post.

An excellent magazine no longer with us was *Car Life*. It tested a stock 300 with a 413 V-8 rated at 340 bhp. The magazine noted the 300 was on the shorter 122-inch wheelbase as compared to the 126 inches of the New Yorker. In 1962 the 300H was also on the 122-inch wheelbase instead of the New Yorker's. A comparison between the 1961 300G acceleration figures and the mass market 300 found there was little difference: the 300G covered 0 to 60 in 8.4 seconds, the 300 in 8.7 seconds; and 0 to 30 actually found the clone to be fractionally quicker— 2.9 seconds compared to 3.2. There was a difference in top speed between the 300H and 300. The magazine claimed the 300 topped 112 mph while the 300H was good for 131 mph.

After what seemed like ages, the 1962 Chryslers were bereft of fins. Up front there was no change; the canted lights and reversible grille were still there, but at the rear the fins were gone. Exner had done a good job restyling the 300-H.

INSET: Heavy, concave sculpturing highlights finless rear of the 300H . . . and all other Chrysler models. Circular emblem was identical to regular 300, but didn't have letter suffix.

Car Life also described the 300 as a car "not for the faint of heart." If one took all the insignia off the car, the testers said, one would have no idea of the "monster dormant within." The power is such, *Car Life* went on, that it "doesn't just push you back into the seat, it slams you there."

Remember, Chrysler was getting back into racing (starting with the 1962 Plymouth). Dodge was out there on the track as well. John DeLorean's Pontiac GTO was still two years off, so the 300 clone was perhaps a precursor for all the excitement that was just around the corner.

Then before anyone realized it, in roared 1963. Over at Chrysler, Elwood Engel was beginning to make his presence felt. Engel, by the way, was a Lincoln designer spirited away by Townsend to replace the unfortunate Virgil Exner, who had been given his walking papers in November 1961.

Exner's influence wasn't entirely out of the picture with the 1963 designs, but Engel certainly made his mark. The new Chryslers were

Interior of the 300H is handsome, even if the steering wheel is a bit too glitzy for a car of the 300's nature. The steering wheel is transparent, the instruments covered by a large "shroud."

The 300H engine is 413 rated at 380 bhp, 5 more horses than the 300G. Standard 300 shared the same engine but was 40 horsepower lighter and could do 0–60 in 8.7 seconds.

a far cry from anything that had gone before, and apart from the windshields, which hadn't changed since 1957, the cars were a complete change around. Available only as a two-door hardtop coupe, the 300J's Exner-cum-Engel styling smacks of the crisp, elegant lines that were favored in British upper-crust cars of the late forties and early fifties. The squared design was also similar to Bill Mitchell's beautiful Buick Riviera, which made its first appearance in 1963.

Perhaps because it was so different, everybody heaped much praise on the new Chrysler 300J. "We particularly admired the interplay of light and shadow on the sharp-edged planes of the Chrysler, and the retention of the traditional 300 grille work." So said *Car Life* magazine in its test of the 300J. The same magazine was quick to point out it didn't like what it termed a retrogression "to a level of being just a sedan with station wagon springs." In other words, Chrysler lessened the 300J's ride rate over other models from 165 lbs./in. for the 300G to 125 lbs./in. for the 300J at the front wheels. This reduced roll stiffness considerably but didn't give a controllable, yet softer ride in the European tradition. According to road testers at the time, what was required were larger, compatible shock absorbers, which would have resulted in a better ride with handling to match.

There was a great improvement in the brakes, which had been a bone of contention with critics and professional drivers ever since the first Letter Series car. They never were up to the job of hauling the heavyweight 300s down to safe, secure stops as they should have been. On the 300J, Chrysler had dumped its own center-plane drums and switched to the Bendix Duo-Servo system entirely. Now Bendix brakes were used throughout the U.S. auto industry—in GM, Ford, and Chrysler products anyway. The Bendix units were far superior

and much more in keeping with a car of the 300J's performance potential. Mind you, disc brakes would have been the real answer, as GM found out when they put them on the new Corvette; a year later, Ford would offer front discs on the Thunderbird. One well-known car collector owns a 1955 C-300 and he has had the braking system converted to discs. He says the car now feels safe with a braking system vastly superior to what was offered in the mid-fifties and into the sixties.

For 1963, Chrysler returned to the ram-induction system offered on the potent engines until 1962. It had been dropped for what was called a double-runner type of four-barrel manifold for better throttle response. Improvements with sonic-tuning at the torque peak range of 3,600 rpm or around 90 mph, which is where the 300J operated at its maximum, gave better acceleration at higher speeds. The engine, by the way, was the 413, now rated at 390 bhp and which did 0–60 in 7.9 seconds (*Car Life*) and 8.0 seconds in both *Motor Trend* and *Car & Driver* magazine road tests. Which was not bad for a car weighing 4,412 pounds and capable of speeds over 130 mph.

Base price of the 300J was $5,184, but adding air conditioning, power windows, Sure-Grip differential, radio, power antenna, and tinted glass raised the price to $6,134. Only four hundred 300Js were produced, making even Rolls-Royce and Aston Martin seem like mass-production cars. The 300 Letter Series was on its way out as Chrysler began to pay more interest in giving power to the people through its Plymouth and Dodge divisions.

As we have already seen, Chrysler was really getting it together in NASCAR, USAC, and drag competition. Plymouths and Dodges loaded with the Max Wedge 413 were giving 409 and 421 Chevies and Pontiacs a run for their money—and winning, too! If the 413 was good, then the awesome 425-horse, 426-cubic-inch Max Wedge V-8 engine was pure get-up-and-go rocket performance. The year 1963 started out with the 413 Max Wedge, which proved very successful. But not successful enough, as far as Chrysler was concerned. Taking the 383 block, the engineers bored it out to 426 cubic inches and added aluminum pistons, high-lift camshaft, and of course dual four-barrels. Instead of letting the 300J have it, the 426 Ram Charger was shoveled into the new Dodge. Lighter and shorter than the 300J, the Dodge weighed a little over 3,200 pounds, or 1,200 pounds less than the 300J.

The new Dodge 330 so equipped was the terror of the track. In terms of styling the '63 Dodge was squarer, more conventional than the disastrous '62 models. Considering what he was up against, Elwood Engel did a good restyle of Exner's controversial, truncated 1962 design. With the exception of the Custom 880 and the pretty new Dart compact (it replaced the short-lived Lancer), the numerous Dodge models had increased wheelbase length from 1962's 116 to 119 inches. Dart had been a full-size model through 1962 and in 1963 adopted a 111-inch wheelbase, which it shared with no one else.

A highly tuned Dart was capable of 0–60 in a phenomenal 4.2 seconds. This was with the big 426/425 engine, and the quarter-mile zoomed up in 12.5 seconds. There could have been hardly anything out there to compare with these rip-roaring figures in 1963. Naturally the 426/425 became the engine of choice for the stock-car fraternity and helped Richard Petty on his way to the top of the racing league. With engines as versatile as the 426, it could be had with compression ratios up to 13.5:1. And the other engine that met with great favor from the dragster boys was the 413. Mounted in the lightweight Plymouth Super Stock and the Dodge Ram Charger, the 413 had short ram tubes and developed 410 bhp.

Motor Trend's M/T Road Test in the January 1963 issue evaluated the Plymouth Sport Fury: "Dust-kicking Fury models carry Plymouth's performance banner into the biggest, most extravagant sales year in Detroit history," the feature claimed in its secondary heading.

Another '62 Dodge funny car (*funny car* is a popular term for dragsters). Bigger, fatter slicks adorn rear wheels for more grab. Cars can do 150 mph-plus in a quarter-mile and have to use parachutes to assist in braking. (Courtesy Tom DeMauro)

"If records are broken, this car's clean looks and clean heels should help break them," the heading continued. Perhaps the heading was a little premature, for while 1963 was a good sales year, Plymouth didn't break any records. Certainly it was one of Plymouth's best years; Chrysler's economy-priced division built almost half a million cars for the model year, which put it well and truly back on the road to recovery, helped no doubt by its racing successes, its performance street cars, and an appreciable return to decent quality. Of these, 15,319 were the top-line Sport Fury models.

High-speed cruising combined with the best handling and ride of the low-priced three made the Sport Fury an excellent buy in its day. The car achieved 0–60 in 7.2 seconds if it used the 330-horse, 383-cubic-inch engine. Top speed was about 118 to 120 mph. Compare yesterday's technology with today's, and one can see how far the motor industry has advanced. Many four-cylinder engines have faster acceleration and more top speed than the V-8s of old.

Almost all Chrysler products relied on the TorqueFlite three-speed automatic transmission for gear changing. This automatic was a world beater in its day, and was versatile enough to make leisurely changes if it was in a Slant Six–powered Valiant or could be modified to make true racing shifts with the right engine combinations. TorqueFlite was indeed a phenomenal shifter, which was why many European car makers picked it instead of the highly touted (and very good) GM Hydra-Matic. Chrysler engineers adapted the TorqueFlite to such an extent that it could change faster than a person shifting a manual.

As noted earlier, Chrysler Corporation has always been known for its fine engineering. Since before World War II, Chrysler had been interested in gas turbine engines and designed and built an aircraft powerplant that had economy equal to that of a standard piston engine. The idea that a gas turbine engine might be a good replacement for the normal piston powerplant in automobiles intrigued Chrysler engineers. In the fifties, they set to work to develop a gas turbine engine for automobile use.

In 1963, the result of all their work was unveiled to the public. It was a beautiful car nicknamed the Engelbird because Elwood Engel designed it and because it had similarities to the 1961 Thunderbird, a design Engel had been more than involved with.

Chrysler contracted Ghia of Italy to build fifty Engelbirds, which were then given to carefully selected members of the public to drive for three months at a time. About two hundred people ages twenty-one through seventy drove the cars from 1963 to 1966, and the drivers' experiences were evaluated. Almost all the drivers loved the sharp styling and smooth running of the turbine Engelbird and the 0–60 acceleration in ten seconds, but didn't care for the 11.5 mpg even though the engine was forgiving enough to run on kerosene, diesel, or jet fuel.

Despite the colossal expense undertaken by Chrysler to build the fifty cars, the fact that they were built overseas would have found America's dour customs and excise wanting a large hunk of change from Highland Park. Chrysler wasn't prepared to sink any more money into cars that had fulfilled their purpose. Under the gimlet eyes of U.S. customs officials, forty of the cars were destroyed; the remaining ten were paid for and went to various auto museums around the country. Harrah's in Reno, has one, for instance, and two are kept at Chrysler Corporation's Chelsea, Michigan, proving ground. Unfortunately, Chrysler shelved the project when it found one in four drivers complained about the gas mileage.

It was in 1963 that Larry Rathgeb joined Chrysler's racing program under Ronnie Householder. "He was a midget racing champion right after the war," said Larry. Householder was in planning before being switched to manage some of the performance program in the mid-fifties and was involved with the 300s' runs at Daytona.

When Chrysler decided they wanted to go into NASCAR racing, they needed a car. Householder hired Ray Nichols from Griffin, Indiana. "Griffin was running Pontiacs at the time," said Larry. "When he came to Chrysler he brought over a bunch of Pontiac front-suspension pieces with him. He got together a bunch of engineers . . . Jack Gilmore was one of them . . . , and dumped all these Pontiac pieces on the table and said, 'What I want to do is hire your drafting skills and put these pieces into a Plymouth.' Of course nobody in our organization wanted that kind of task, so since I was low man on the totem pole, they said, 'Rathgeb, here's a new job for you. Put these pieces on the Plymouth.'"

Larry was as surprised and as shocked as the rest of the engineers and told Nichols the Pontiac pieces wouldn't work but they would design something that would. Nichols replied, "No, no, no. I'm not hiring your engineering talent, I'm hiring your drafting talent. I just want these things put into a Plymouth car and I'll take care of the rest of it."

To ensure everything would fit correctly, Larry designed similar front-suspension parts. "I put these things through our computer program," Larry continued, "and called Nichols and said the work had been completed. I also told him that as a functional piece from a geometry standpoint, it wasn't satisfactory. It wasn't any good from a structural standpoint, either. All he did was to repeat what he'd said before . . . that he wasn't hiring me for my engineering skills but for my design and drafting abilities. 'The rest I'll take care of,' he said.

"We handed over the design; the parts were built and put on several Plymouths. And we won! The Plymouths came in 1, 2, 3, 4 at Daytona Beach."

Shortly after the Daytona triumph, Nichols, much elated, took the cars to a race at Atlanta. There, the cars wouldn't perform and were withdrawn due to tires and suspension problems. "It was a very poor design," said Larry. "Nichols came back and said we had screwed him with the design. I said, 'Now wait a minute. You told us you didn't need our engineering skills and we gave you exactly what you wanted.' Nichols was angry. He said, 'You'd better get to the racetrack and fix the problem.' 'No,' I replied. 'I don't need to go to the racetrack. I'll fix it from here.' Nichols's rejoinder was, 'No. You go to the racetrack.' So they forced me to go to the racetrack and look at all this stuff, and I went back and did a proper design. We showed him what we had done and told him that this was what it would take to fix the car. And that is what we did."

All told, Chrysler had a very profitable sales year after the dreadful 1962 season. The Grim Reaper had been put to flight at Chrysler, but chose instead to help himself to the world's most popular leader. On November 22, 1963, President John F. Kennedy was shot and killed in his open-topped limousine while on a visit to Dallas, Texas. A couple of days later, through incredible police bungling, Lee Harvey Oswald, the alleged assassin, was shot by nightclub owner Jack Ruby. Vice-President Lyndon B. Johnson was sworn in as the new President.

The world was devastated by Kennedy's death and mourned openly with his family. Nobody could quite believe it; I can remember my father, normally a calm man, breaking down in tears. This was a tragedy that anyone old enough to know what was going on would never, ever forget.

Earlier in 1963, May to be exact, Britain's government was shaken to its foundations by a sex scandal involving the minister of defense, John Profumo, and a pretty, high-class call girl named Christine Keeler, who also was on more than friendly terms with a Russian diplomat based at the Soviet Embassy. Rumors and innuendoes surfaced, implicating everyone from Prince Philip to show-business personalities. It shook the Establishment and the tabloids had a field day.

On a more cheerful note, and ten months before the November tragedy, a quartet of smartly dressed, long-haired young men rose to number one on the British pop charts with a single entitled "Please Please Me." John, Paul, George, and Ringo were the Beatles, Britain's new singing sensation. Evolved from the 1957 skiffle group, the Quarrymen, the band had for years played clubs in Hamburg, and were then spotted by record-store owner Brian Epstein at Liverpool's Cavern Club. Epstein became the Beatles' manager; their first Parlophone disc, "Love Me Do," was recorded in September 1962. The Beatles became the lads to love, their music was a delight, and they opened the floodgates to a wealth of British musical talent like the Rolling Stones, Gerry and the Pacemakers, the Kinks, and many, many more groups. The world stopped and listened . . . and changed course.

February 1964, and the Beatles come to America for the first time. They were the beginning of a mighty British musical invasion of the United States, an invasion everyone gladly accepted. Though the British pop groups had little effect on the 1964 cars, later in the sixties their undeniable influence became obvious. In the meantime people drove their handsome new 1964 cars designed when Elvis lopped his sideburns and sold out to Hollywood. Most of Chrysler's various cars were facelifts, with the exception of the Imperial, which was all new and very much Elwood Engel's design. In fact it looked very similar to Engel's 1961 Lincoln

Continental and followed that car's square-edged design with its stainless-steel-tipped fender line running front to rear, its fake spare tire bulge, and clean body sides. It was the most impressive-looking Imperial since 1957 and gained almost 65 percent in sales over 1963.

The 1964 Imperials were swift, silent, and sure, but hardly what one would term performance cars. Only one engine was available and that was the 413 rated at 340 bhp. This is a big engine in anybody's book, and one capable of exciting things in the right state of tune and housed in the right sort of car. In the Imperial the block was toned down; after all, it wouldn't be fitting to see Uncle Elmer driving the luxury car he wanted all his life like a dragster.

Performance machinery there was in abundance in 1964. The full-size cars especially. Chevrolet had its 409, Ford its whopping 427, Plymouth a 426. Pontiac was right up there with a 421, while staid old Buick had a big 425 powering its hot Wildcat. Can you imagine? A Buick called Wildcat? A full-size two-door car first introduced in 1962, and one that kept up with the best of them.

Oldsmobile had a 394-cubic-inch V-8, and Mercury shared Ford's brutal 427. Olds was the only super car with an engine less than 400 cubic inches, though the engine was enlarged to 425 cid in 1965. Super stocks all measured between 205 and 219 inches, so they weren't exactly small. Another disadvantage was weight. None of them were less than 3,300 pounds and most weighed over 4,000—some, like the Wildcat convertible, as much as 4,590 pounds. Then there were the brakes. All insisted on sticking with drums. Here were cars capable of earth-shattering acceleration, high top speed, and brakes generally not safe enough to halt a kiddie bicycle after a couple of emergency stops. Strange, isn't it? Crown Imperials had disc brakes back in 1950 through 1954, yet development ceased as they were deemed too costly. Disc brakes wouldn't turn up again until 1963 on the Corvette, and 1964 on the Thunderbird.

It was odd that most manufacturers concentrated on full-size cars for performance. John DeLorean saw it differently. Whatever one says about DeLorean, there is no doubt the man was a genius. Flawed perhaps, but a genius nonetheless. He was a man so completely in tune with the sixties that he could have invented the decade.

DeLorean had joined Pontiac Motor Division of General Motors on September 1, 1956. It didn't take long for DeLorean to become recognized as a true engineering talent, with good ideas to boot. As the muscle-car race blossomed, DeLorean saw the logic in producing a powerhouse out of one of the lighter-weight intermediates or the cars a little larger than the original 1960 compacts. Although the faceless, dark-suited bigshots at the top didn't care for the idea of creating an intermediate muscle car, DeLorean went ahead without telling anyone. He took a Tempest Le Mans coupe as the base and created a special $300 sporty option package for it. The option would be suffixed "GTO."

Turning a mild-mannered Clark Kent–type car into a black-top stormer was quite something. DeLorean's team gave the car a three-speed floor shift, responsive steering, dual exhausts, better tires, stiffer shocks, dual exhaust—and a 389-cubic-inch engine. More expensive but even better was a four-speed manual shift at $188 and metallic brake linings for $75; plus, you could have a 360 bhp version of the 389 for $115 more. And there was limited slip and a heavy-duty radiator to complete the picture.

Nobody in GM's top echelons seemed to realize what was going on in Pontiac's division until it was too late. The GTO option was offered in mid-1964 and did better than any-

one at Pontiac expected. Over 32,000 GTO LeManses were produced, and an entirely new car was born. GM executives suddenly didn't mind, anymore; the GTO was making money, wasn't it?

Lee Iacocca was another man in tune with the sixties. At the beginning of the decade he began to think about a small, sporty, four-seater car that would have a low base price, yet the customer could spend what he/she wanted to build a personal car from a huge list of options. The car came out on April 17, 1964, and was, of course, the Mustang. It was another first, another car that exerted a tremendous influence on the world's motor industry.

Now, what was Chrysler doing while all this was going on? As has already been said, apart from the Imperial, it was a matter of refinement and improvement. All new cars would come along in 1965. Not that Chrysler was inactive on the sporting front. Far from it. Dodge and Plymouth still were top dogs with the 426 Wedge-head at the drag strips. For NASCAR stockers Chrysler pulled a masterstroke: it reintroduced the Hemi, or a new version of the old that was lighter in weight, had a great many improvements, and displaced 426 cubic inches. Horsepower was a colossal 425.

"We had the B-body car and we threw the Hemi into that thing," reminisced Larry Rathgeb. "We needed bigger brakes for it so we developed them at the time. We also developed what was called the A-8-33 transmission, which was superb. A good set of gears in it. At first we had a few problems with gears that wouldn't work so we had to go back and do a lot of additional work on all the gear sets. It was a four speed and it was a fine transmission." The new Hemi was not offered to the public, only to stock-car racers. Dodge and Plymouth dominated NASCAR and came in first, second, and third at the Daytona 500,

In 1963–64 Dodge/Plymouth ruled the roost in what is known as quarter-mile drag racing. Equipped with either the 413 or 426 Max Wedge V-8, these cars were capable of speeds touching 165 mph. The car shown is not one of the Max Wedge cars, though similar. Chrysler built two Plymouths and a pair of Dodges equipped with the second-generation Hemi. This car is the very first second-generation, Hemi-powered Chrysler product, built late in 1963 as a 1964 model. In 1965 Chrysler produced a few altered-wheelbase cars for the drag strip. A wealthy individual had acquired the above Dodge but wanted a 1965 model. Chrysler wouldn't sell one to him so he converted his 1964 by altering the wheelbase and tacking on 1965 body parts. Mike Guffy, who lives in Indiana, now owns the car and—due to its rarity and the fact that it is the first Hemi—is going to restore it back to its original 1964 specifications.

the winning driver being Richard Petty in a Plymouth. It was Petty's first win on a NASCAR track, the first of many that would make him the racing fans' favorite son and top NASCAR driver of all time.

While Plymouth and Dodge were writing their names in lights, Chrysler didn't disappoint with the 1964 300K. Base engine was a Firepower 360 bhp, single four-barrel version of the 413 with a 10.1:1 compression ratio. In this

guise, the 300K ran to 60 in 8.8 seconds. Which wasn't bad, and was certainly comparable with others of the same ilk.

Standard in 1963, but an option in 1964, was the Firepower 390. Fitted with a dual-throat Carter carburetor and short ram tubes, the 390 horse mill could still accelerate to 60 in a fraction over eight seconds. One item missing from the 300K's dashboard was a 150-mph speedometer. This had been exclusive to 300 Letter cars from the beginning; now an ordinary Chrysler 120 mph unit was used instead. Another insult to the Letter Series was the 300K's upholstery. Leather had been standard since the first 300 in 1955; now it was optional. Standard interior trim was vinyl. More and more the Letter cars were losing their exclusivity, their long-standing Grand Touring tradition of being the Beautiful American among Europe's finest. Now all it was an ordinary non-Letter 300 with knobs on. Bob Rodger, the father of the original 300, must have been appalled.

Although it was lost amid the hysteria

surrounding the Mustang, Plymouth actually introduced its pony car—as Mustang-type cars became known—a few days earlier than Mustang's April 17 debut. Built on the Valiant platform (1963 saw the introduction of a new, somewhat more conventional Valiant that was certainly not pretty compared to the 1960–62 models), the new car had a radical fastback shape and was called the Barracuda.

It was smart, it was stylish, and it could be had with a new 273-cid V-8 (the new engine was derived from the venerable 318) pumping out 180 bhp. The same engine was available in the Dodge Dart as well. The Valiant/Barracuda cars had a 106-inch wheelbase; the attractive and sporty-looking Dodge Darts had a 111-inch wheelbase, except for the Dart wagons, which shared Valiant's 106 incher. Returning to the Barracuda, while the Mustang took most pony-car sales, the Barracuda still managed a respectable 23,443 units for a very shortened calendar year.

Full-size Plymouths and Dodges commanded the drag strips and fought it out with Ford on the NASCAR circuits, with assistance from the new Hemi engine. Out of the 62 races, Ford won 30, Dodge/Plymouth 24, and Mercury 6. There was hardly ever a Dodge or Plymouth that didn't finish in the top three places, and it was almost always a Chrysler product that broke the fastest qualifying lap records at nearly all the tracks. Richard Petty came home as Grand National champion with 40,252 points over second-place Ford driver Ned Jarrett with 34,950.

While Ford's 427 engine was tops in Dearborn's Total Performance program, they knew they had their work cut out when Dodge and Plymouth roared onto the NASCAR circuits with the new generation Hemi under their hoods. This was not available to the public, but the successful 426 Wedge-head was. A Plymouth Sport Fury equipped with this engine was the one to beat in a traffic-light Grand Prix. With the exception of the compacts, the 426 was available across the board, even in lowly cars like the Plymouth Savoy. Sleek looking GTOs might well have been shocked into oblivion by a full-size Savoy looking all sweetness and light until the accelerator pedal was pressed.

Returning to NASCAR's Grand National Championship for a moment, it is worth mentioning the 1962 Chrysler driven in all but a couple of the events by Neil Castles. Although he suffered many indignities, such as blown engines, transmission failure, and sundry other mechanical problems, Neil piloted his faithful Chrysler to seventeenth place in the final driver points standing. And it has to be said the Chrysler finished more often than it did not. The Chrysler didn't race again after 1964; in 1965, Neil Castles had a brand new Plymouth to play with.

America was being turned on by the British pop groups that seemed to be there all the time. In September the Rolling Stones arrived. Long-haired, scruffy, revolutionary, the Stones possessed everything America's frustrated youth wanted. They had charisma and they reached out in spirit to the rebellious young. Times were a-changin' and they were a-changin' fast.

On the political front there were problems. There was Vietnam, for instance. It had been a pain ever since 1954 when the French occupiers of the country were defeated. Now America was becoming more and more involved with protecting South Vietnam. On the home front, LBJ signed the Civil Rights Act, and in Tokyo, the world competed in the Olympics. In Detroit and in Dearborn, the car makers watched the market swing more to performance, more to the intermediates. If Pontiac could score a success with its intermediate GTO, then, by golly, so could everyone else.

Soft Breezes, Hurricane Alley; or, The Beat Goes On

There's not very much one can say about the 1965 Chrysler 300L, not very much at all. Not when it came to performance, anyway. It was all new as far as body design went, and it was Elwood Engel in full flower. Engel hadn't yet rid himself of his days as a Ford designer, as the 300L patently showed. There were elements of Lincoln Continental and Ford Thunderbird styling present in the 300L and other Chryslers. Even though the L didn't quite have the panache of the 300 Letter Series up to the F, it still had a certain grace, even if it was slightly secondhand. The window area was large and the old windshield design was finally replaced; but Engel persisted in the use of chrome (stainless steel) trim capping the straight-through fender line. Overall length and wheelbase were increased on the 300L to 218.2 and 124 inches respectively. This was up from 215.3 and 122 inches for the 300K. The new dimensions were in common with all Chrysler models, not just the 300L, which, apart from a few little trim differences, was identical to the standard 300 series. There was only the 360 bhp, 413-cubic-inch engine to be had in this, the last of the glorious 300 Letter Series, and that engine was an option on both the stock 300 and New Yorker models. Timing for 0 to 60 was 8.8 seconds, the same as the previous year. There was a four-speed

First year of Valiant Barracuda was 1964, during which 23,443 were built. Car shown is the 1965 model, with high-performance 273 rated at 235 bhp. Unit production for 1965 was 64,596. Compare that with 680,000 Mustangs and the total looks a bit sparse.

manual transmission offered as a no-extra-cost option in place of the familiar TorqueFlite, and a buyer could specify the heavy-duty-suspension and flared-brake-drums package for a mere thirty-five dollars. *Motor Trend*, in its test of the 300L, remarked that the optional suspension and brakes gave the car handling equal to many European sports cars. One wonders which sports cars were compared.

A total of 2,845 300Ls left the factory, of which 440 were convertibles. This was the 300 Letter car's second largest production total in the ten years the Letter Series had been around. The fact that more 300s were sold during 1964 and 1965 might have had something to do with the price, from which Chrysler shaved more than a thousand dollars in 1964. At $4,545 for the convertible and $4,090 for the hardtop, the 300L began to appear more affordable for many who had shied away before.

There had been talk of a 300M, even a clay model made. Its appearance was very similar to the 300L but the big change would have been under the hood. If the car had been built, it would have had the 426 Wedge-head and 365 bhp. But it wasn't to be. On November 27, 1964, word came in the form of a product-planning letter that the 300M had been canceled. As noted earlier, Chrysler felt there was more to be gained by going for large-engined intermediates. This, as it turned out, was a wise move.

Of course the general public knew that Chrysler had a second-generation Hemi engine on its hands, an engine meant only for racers. In 1965 Dodge created a drag-racing Hemi-Charger automobile, a ferocious machine meant only for quarter-mile runs. The car was a Coronet built on the Plymouth Belvedere's 115-inch wheelbase; properly prepared, it would run rings around the opposition. People would shake their heads in awe and whisper how these Hemi-powered Dodge dragsters

would do over 210 and crack the distance in under eight seconds. Dick Landy was a famous dragster who delighted drag-racing crowds with his 110-inch wheelbase Dodge Coronet, doing exhibition runs and wheelies. There was even what was called Hurst's Hemi Under Glass Barracuda, which took off almost vertically . . . hardly surprising considering the Hemi engine was mounted in the rear.

Plymouth had their own version of the same car, and both models cleaned up on the drag-racing circuits. And well they might. They each weighed three thousand pounds, had the Hemi engine, and were midsize. Obviously John DeLorean wasn't the only one who thought midsize cars with big engines were more practical for street and strip.

Besides a leaning toward midsize cars, there were the compacts, too. The Valiant Barracuda had become a separate model and there was the special-edition Formula S, a performance package distinguished by unique insignia and racing stripes. The Barracuda Formula S came with the 273 Commando V-8 rated at 235 bhp. A four-barrel carburetor, 10.5:1 compression ratio, high-lift, high overlap camshaft, solid lifters, dome-shaped pistons, heavy-duty suspension, firm shock absorbers, and front antiroll bar helped to make the popular model a very sporty piece of equipment.

Even while the intermediates were flexing their muscles, full-size powerhouses still dominated the new additions built on what had been farmland two years previously. One such was the Plymouth Sport Fury with quad headlights stacked one atop the other. The 209.4-inch-long Sport Fury could be had with the 426 Wedge-head motor developing 365 bhp. It was a handsome-looking brute capable of 0–60 in 8.2 seconds and a somewhat conservative 120 mph top speed. Still, it could do the quarter in 16.1 seconds at 86 mph, which wasn't at all

In 1962 Chrysler introduced the non-Letter Series 300, much to the chagrin of the 300 purists. Car was similar in many respects to the 300. The pseudo-300 sat on the same 122-inch wheelbase and had the 383 rated at 305 bhp as its only engine. Car shown is the 300 for 1966. Wheelbase had increased to 124 inches, horsepower to 325. Handsome Elwood Engel styling smacks of his 1960 Lincoln Continental with chrome fender strips running the length of the car. Interior was attractive, quite sporty.

bad for a showroom stock automobile weighing forty-two hundred pounds.

Plymouth's smaller, lighter Belvederes did well in NASCAR's Grand National. In one race, the USAC-sponsored Yankee 300, Plymouth Hemi-Chargers came in 1, 2, 3. Pity poor Richard Petty; his Plymouth developed a terminal sickness and dropped out after fifty-three laps. But it was a good day for Chrysler products, with five places in the top nine positions. The winning Plymouth averaged 78.024 mph for the race, which was held at Indianapolis Raceway Park's 2.5-mile road course.

Road courses, though not as popular, are actually superior to the oval tracks for several good reasons. The twists and sudden turns, sharp lefthand or righthand corners, are far better to gauge a car's potential. If there are any weaknesses in suspension geometry or handling response, brakes and transmissions, it is the road course that will show them up. The Europeans have always favored courses and tracks with lots of twists and turns, perhaps because so many roads were like that before autobahn-type roads became the norm. Therefore manufacturers like Mercedes, BMW, Jaguar, and others built cars with vastly superior, and safer, handling

two or three decades before the Americans.

There was little doubt that horsepower, and more horsepower, had returned with a vengeance by 1965. There was nobody out there who didn't have a hot car to offer the baby boomers in their late teens and early twenties. Most youngsters lived for the Rolling Stones, the Beatles, and the other musical greats from across the Atlantic; and Stan Lee was keeping

Astoundingly fast NASCAR & drag-race winner, the 1966 Hemi-powered Plymouth Belvedere Satellite. Standard mill was 273/180 bhp V-8. Good looks helped sell 38,000 Satellites in 1966. With Chrysler Tech Center and 1995 Viper as backdrop, the 1966 Satellite seems at home even if the Center wasn't around when this car was made.

INSET: Imaginative emblem is set below fastback window. It is part of a car that grows on you.

them hip, baby, with imaginative new comic-book heroes like Spider-man, the Incredible Hulk, and the Fantastic Four. There was, though, a dark cloud, a very dark cloud, that hovered over the young. Vietnam.

Somehow, perhaps without thinking, certainly not considering the frightful consequences, America had gotten itself embroiled in a civil war far from home, in a place nobody knew, or particularly cared about. Vietnam had always been a thorn in the side of the West: first it was the French against the tough little insurrectionists who had an almost religious belief in bringing communism to all Indochina. After the French quit trying to defeat Ho-chi Minh and his followers, Vietnam was split in two; the communists had the north and a so-called democracy ruled the south. Peace reigned for a time. Then the north attempted to take the south. In came the Americans, first as "advisers," then with a huge military task force to try to eradicate the revolutionary Viet Cong. Soon, America's young were being served draft papers . . . there would be no Dodge Coronet 426 street machines for a while.

As already noted, everyone had discovered the intermediate. People began to see the sense in the downsized 1962 Dodge and Plymouth models, though a little too late to help them. Since 1963 Plymouth had turned its fortunes around with a decent, well-made product, and had climbed back up the sales charts to reach a respectable fifth place by 1964. And while Plymouth certainly had some hot goodies under its belt, it was Dodge who was marking time as Chrysler's hot car division.

One particularly attractive car was the new intermediate launched by Dodge in 1965. This was the Coronet, built on a 117-inch wheelbase. The new car covered all body styles, from sedan to station wagon, but it was the attractive two-door hardtop that garnered much of the praise. Especially when it was given the 365-hp 426 Street Wedge to storm the Saturday night boulevards with.

In the 365 horsepower tune, the 426 engine certainly nailed one's seat to the floor. According to a *Car Life* road test, the Coronet could do 0–60 in 7.9 seconds, the quarter-mile in 15.4 seconds at 89 mph, and zoom to 100 in 21.4 seconds. Top speed was a little more than 120 mph. Which, given the fact these engines were built with low-end oomph in mind, wasn't bad. *Motor Trend's* testers drove a Coronet with the same engine from 0 to 60 in 7.7 seconds, 0 to 30 in 2.9 seconds. Now that's going some for a showroom stock car.

There was another version of the 426 Wedge that was even wilder. It was the one with 425 hp and with 480 lbs./ft. of torque at 4,400 rpm. It also had a wild compression ratio of 12.5:1, and the engine had solid lifters and factory exhaust headers. Called the Ramcharger V-8, this engine mated to Chrysler's four-speed manual would just about blow off course anything that tried to take it on.

A Coronet 500 two-door hardtop cost a base $2,674, but the 365-horse 426 added a further $513, the even larger engine a little more. Like the Plymouth, Dodge offered the Hemi. Again it only appeared in full racing tune, and was bought purely for drag racing, where Dodge and Plymouth were virtually unbeatable. But on the NASCAR tracks it was Ford all the way.

Nothing appeared to phase the big Fords in their quest for the Grand National Championship. After all, they were part of Ford's Total Performance program even though NASCAR's quirky and changeable rules banned the special overhead-cam 427 and Chrysler's Hemi-head racing engines from competing. Much annoyed, Chrysler withdrew from participating in the championships, leaving Ford to have a virtual clean sweep of the oval tracks. Unable to use the new racing 427, Ford settled for its Wedge

427 to gain top honors in 1965.

Fortunately, the National Hot Rod Association was far more liberal, much to the benefit of Dodge and Plymouth, who were able to do on the drag strips what Ford accomplished in the NASCAR races. NASCAR aces like Richard Petty and Dave Pearson were set up with special exhibition vehicles to run on the drag strips. Petty had a Hemi-powered Barracuda with the engine mounted behind the front seat, and Pearson took a rear-engined Dodge Coronet to show its paces. Both cars stormed the drag strips at a terminal velocity unheard of a decade earlier when the world marveled at the C-300's 130 mph. By 1965, 170 mph-plus was the norm on the NASCAR ovals, even faster on the straights. In one drag-racing event held in Carlsbad, California, a "Hemi-Cuda" sponsored by the Southern California Plymouth Dealers became the fastest stock-bodied, stock-wheelbase dragster ever to run the quarter-mile. This phenomenal car sped down the track to reach 171.85 mph in 8.88 seconds!

America tends to be a country of extremes; there is rarely a middle road. After the far-right rhetoric of the early fifties, the sixties swung to the left-thinking persuasion. The far right was still there, of course, somewhat embedded in the Republican psyche, in the so-called Christian fundamentalist movements, and in vicious organizations like the Ku Klux Klan and militia groups. And then there was Vietnam, a growing sore in America's side that was gradually splitting the country in two. On the cultural front there was Andy Warhol, Phil Spector and his Wall of Sound, the tremendous influence of the British music scene, and the lad from Minnesota, Bob Dylan. Bob Dylan, the messenger from within, awakened our thoughts to the way it really was: it appeared that Youth was now in control. They held the purse strings, they had the power to dictate what they wanted. And commerce listened; the

car companies especially listened. Hence the Mustang, the Barracuda, the 409, 427, and Hemi 426. No more the doddering, sloppy Buicks of old, with the all-too-soft ride to protect all-too-soft backsides; now it was a road-tuned Buick Wildcat or race-experienced Dodge Coronet that captured the blacktop.

And that's how it was in 1965.

There were many tragedies in the early-to-mid-sixties, events that helped shape America's thoughts and deeds. The assassination of President Kennedy, the alleged, and untimely, suicide of Marilyn Monroe in 1962, the murders of civil rights activists in Mississippi; 136 Americans died in Vietnam in 1964 and President Johnson, with a landslide victory in his pocket, committed fifty thousand more troops to this tragic corner of the earth.

These events, the civil-rights marches, and the rising voice of the world's youth—spurred on by the Rolling Stones' "I Can't Get No Satisfaction" and Bob Dylan's "Times They Are A-Changin' "—certainly had a profound affect on the nation's car makers. The designers and engineers were youthful, eternally so, as creative people normally are. The musical movement spoke of excitement, of free expression, which translated into the utterly unique cars being designed and built in America. Driving a six-cylinder-engined car was no fun anymore. Big-block V-8s with hundreds of cubic inches and bags of power was seemingly what the youth of America wanted. Tool down the fast-lane blacktop in a 1965 426-Wedge Coronet and accelerate to Dave Clark Five's "Bits and Pieces" and oh, this was how it was meant to be. Eternal youth was for the asking, and LSD was just around the corner.

NASCAR changed the rules again in 1966, this time in Chrysler's favor. The rule makers hadn't allowed the Hemi in 1965 but did so in 1966. Quite simply, the Hemi had become a production item, Chrysler having decided to

Dodge's new fastback Charger, introduced in 1966. Car rode on 117-inch wheelbase. Standard engine was the 318, but options included 361, 383, and 426 Hemi. Need we say more?

INSET: Part of the 1966 Charger's interior. Notice round instruments on clean dash. Nicely designed seats supported driver and passengers well. White upholstery could get dirty quickly, though.

release a slightly detuned street version to the public. Now it was Ford's turn to throw a fit, which it did in no uncertain manner. Ford complained bitterly about the reinstatement of the Hemi, and finding the complaints fell on deaf ears, boycotted NASCAR for the season. First it was Chrysler in '65, now Ford in '66; all rather squalid, don't you think?

With Ford out of the picture, Plymouth won sixteen Grand National races, Richard Petty eight of them. All the cars were Hemi-powered, and while they would have probably

defeated Ford, had Dearborn raced, Plymouth's victories were a bit hollow without the big factory-sponsored Ford 427s racing with them. To complete Mopar's trips to victory lane, Dodge helped in no small measure by winning eighteen Grand Nationals and, in so doing, greatly enhanced its image as Chrysler's sporty division.

Although Chrysler announced the availability of the Hemi engine, initially it would be only offered in the intermediate B-bodied cars. The C-bodies (they were the full-size Chryslers,

Dodge Polara and Monaco, and Plymouth Fury) were offering a new 440 "TNT" mill. This engine replaced the 413 and was standard on the New Yorker, but an optional version carried a four-barrel carburetor and dual exhausts. That the B-bodied cars received the fabled Hemi tended to underscore the notion that America's youth was the marketing target. Here, as an example, is the advertising copy for a 1966 Plymouth Satellite advertisement: "Power Play. The new 1966 Plymouth Satellite. This year, you need a quick eye. Satellite is the hottest Plymouth for 1966. The body is all new. The hypothesis, simplicity. And, look, it worked. Beautifully." Note the short, snappy sentences that begin the copy. It follows through to the end with much the same punch, punch, don't let up, prose. Here's a couple more sentences culled from the same ad: "Then we let loose with a fistful of optional V-8s" and "Satellite is making tracks in hot-car country. We give you fair warning: With the Plymouth Satellite, something big has come to pass." Those were the final sentences before the catch phrase: "Let yourself go . . . Plymouth." And of course, above the copy, a great picture of the new car.

Chrysler wasn't the only manufacturer after junior; so were the rest. Mercury's compact Comet added the Cyclone GT to its not-quite-so-compact line: eight inches had been added since 1965, bringing the cars up to 203 inches overall. There was no mistaking who Mercury wanted to see in its showrooms: "Cyclone GT. Greatest new entry in the whole blazing GT world." This was followed, thus: "Performance fans! Here's your breakfast, lunch, dinner, and midnight snack. The big, roomy, new Comet Cyclone GT. With a new 390 4-barrel V-8 roaring under its twin scoop hood, this Cyclone GT delivers go that can shove you right back into your bucket seat." And so on and so on. Very youth oriented but nowhere as subtle as the Plymouth's.

There was little that was actually new over in the Mopar camp for 1966. On the styling front, that is, which satisfied itself with minor facelifts or trim changes here and there. The big news was the availability of the Hemi in the intermediates, dealer-installed optional shoulder belts, and finally, optional front disc brakes. As performance was leading the way on the interstates and back roads as well, some sense of responsibility was creeping into the auto makers' psyche.

While Chrysler's existing cars changed little, there was a particularly interesting new one. Offered early in 1966 as a 1966 model, the fastback Dodge Charger was certainly something to behold. Based upon the Coronet's 117-inch wheelbase, at first glance the new Charger was not unlike American Motors' Rambler Marlin that came out in 1965. But that was where any similarities ended. Standard engine was the agreeable 318-cubic-inch V-8. Then came the options: a 361- and a 383-cubic-inch pair of V-8s, and the King Kong of all, the 426 Hemi.

Producing 425 bhp in showroom trim, the Hemi-powered Charger was all muscle. The obligatory 0–60 times showed a shade over six seconds, exemplary considering the car's 4,330-pound weight and abrupt, unaerodynamic front end (little thought was given to aerodynamics in those days). The 383 engine installed in the same car zipped to 60 in 7.2 seconds, a time not to be sneezed at in those days. Dodge helpfully provided a somewhat optimistic 150-mph speedometer, though the Hemi-powered Charger was quite capable of 130 mph before running out of breath.

Besides the headline-making Hemi, perhaps the most outstanding thing about the 1966 Charger was its fabulous interior. This was truly moon-rocket stuff with rich vinyl bucket seats front and rear (the rear ones folded down flat for extra luggage), which were separated by

The 1967 Dodge Charger was almost identical to the 1966 version. A 318-cid engine was standard, developing 230 bhp. Once again the 426 Hemi was available.

an elaborate center console running the interior's length. The instrument-panel face was black with four large, round silver and black pods that told everything the driver needed to know. The steering wheel was attractive and very sporty, with a fake wood rim attached to three stylish chrome spokes.

All things considered, the Charger was an impressive, well-made car that would move along at lightning-fast speeds with the right engine options. Even with the standard 318 the car was no slouch, and was quite popular in its debut year, which was somewhat shortened by its January introduction. A total of 37,344 Chargers were built, of which only 468 had King Kong under the hood. The Hemi added $877.55 to the Charger's base price of $3,128.

A very attractive car with one of the prettiest roof lines around was the Dodge Coronet two-door hardtop. This was the car Dodge

relied upon to compete in the NASCAR and USAC championships. Equally smart was Plymouth's Satellite, which shared the same B-body platform, the same engines, almost the same everything. Except the wheelbase. The Coronet was an inch longer at 117 compared to its sibling's 116. Overall length differed by four inches. Road tests gave 0–60 figures of 5.3 seconds and quarter-mile dashes of 13.8 seconds at 104 mph. Remember, this was with a stock showroom car anybody could buy, and one readily identified with Mopar's NASCAR racers.

Another engine that was available in the Satellite and Coronet was the 440. Developing 375 bhp at 4,600 rpm, the 440-powered Coronet was not a machine to dally with. *Hot Rod* magazine went from nothing to 60 in 6.3 seconds; it was a 1967 model, but mechanically the same as the '66.

It is worth mentioning Chrysler's full-size 300. No, not the Letter Series: that had passed on in 1965. This was the upstart 300, the interloper who scrounged its thoroughbred brother's name to give itself an image . . . and healthy profits. But with the 440 V-8 under the hood, the car behaved in much the same way its legendary brother did. Fast, very fast. Perhaps it was too fast for its colossal 5,060 pounds of weight. And 7.7 seconds was all it took for this 221.9-inch car to reach 60 mph—in a straight line, of course. *Car Life* testers complained the power steering was way overassisted, with absolutely no road feel whatsoever. Therefore tight bends had to be taken gingerly; if the driver tried to take the bend like a Ferrari, well, he wouldn't. The car would squeal and protest and understeer and go every which way but the right one. At least, with the optional front disc brakes fitted, the 300 would stop better than with an all-drum set-up.

Dodge unveiled all-new Charger in 1968. Beautiful styling was regarded as the best by many automotive journalists. Hemi was optional and the car could do 0–60 in 4.9 seconds with this engine. Hidden headlights remained. Grille was inset and didn't help aerodynamics on the track. Charger did very badly in NASCAR championships due to design of inset rear window and grille. This 1968 Charger fits rural scene very well and brings to mind the *Dukes of Hazzard* TV series, in which a 1969 Charger was the star.

Another Mopar that garnered much praise was the Barracuda Formula S. *Sports-Car Graphic* tried one out and liked it. For $340.40, the tester discovered, the standard-production Barracuda could be changed so much that it, as the reporter said, "becomes an amazing vehicle." By which he meant a great handling, cornering machine.

The $340.40 package consisted of reworking the suspension geometry and including power options that would turn the car into something akin to a European sports car. What the buyer of this delightful car got was a 273-cubic-inch Commando V-8 rated at 235 bhp, heavy-duty tuned suspension, firmer shock absorbers, heavy-gauge fourteen-inch wheels with five-inch rims, quick-ratio manual steering, front disc brakes, a tachometer, and

Beautiful Scat Pack 1968 Dodge Charger R/T sat on 117-inch wheelbase. An impressive 96,108 units were built; people really went for the new Charger in a big way. The building behind this English-owned Charger R/T is the famous Charterhouse School. Edifice is centuries old and serves as one of England's most expensive public (private) boarding schools. Dodge sitting in front of Charterhouse doesn't look too out of place. The little round safety lights on front and rear fenders marked the beginning of the U.S. government's crackdown on the auto industry.

INSET: Under the hood of the '68 Charger is the works: 440 Magnum doesn't dawdle when it needs to move!

special Blue Streak tires. If the buyer wanted, he could load his purchase with a ton of luxury options. So what the proud owner got was a sensibly sized luxury car with performance and handling in the best sports-car tradition.

If the Hemi was the spiritual icon of motoring fans, then Jimi Hendrix was a part of that religion. Discovered in Greenwich Village by Chas Chandler, while base guitarist for the British chart-topping group the Animals, Jimi Hendrix was to music what the Hemi was to motoring. A wild, inspired guitarist, Hendrix was taken to England by Chandler, who successfully put him on the road to world prominence. Hendrix dabbled in the fashionable drug of the midsixties, LSD, which was irre-

sponsibly promoted by one Timothy Leary. What resulted was an incredible mix of blues infused by psychedelic inspiration. It was powerful, energetic, mind blowing. Just like the Hemi. And as will be seen, the car companies noticed.

Ralph Nader had become a household word since the publication of his book *Unsafe at Any Speed*, a damning critique of the rear-wheel-drive Chevrolet Corvair. GM was incensed over the publication of the book, which opened a can of worms not only about the Corvair but also about the auto industry as a whole; the company set detectives onto Nader to see if they could unearth any nasty facts about him. They failed, they were found out, and GM's president had to apologize to Nader publicly before a congressional committee. The result of this was a GM cutback because of declining sales due to Nader and calls for greater auto safety.

Car & Driver considered the Dodge Charger the best-looking car for 1968; the magazine also liked the new Corvette. Front end of Charger is made handsome by its simplicity. Inner body panels and chassis components were shared with Coronet.

Street marches demonstrated more opposition to the Vietnam War, the miniskirt bowled over the male gender, and André Breton, the creator of surrealism, died. Following the late President Kennedy's desire to land men on the moon within the decade, a significant step was made toward achieving the goal with the successful landing of *Surveyor I* on the orb's rubble-strewn surface. In China, Communist party leader Mao Tse-tung launched the Cultural Revolution, which was far more sinister than it sounds. And back home, LSD guru Timothy Leary, age forty-five, was arrested for possessing narcotics. These were some of the events that paved the way for the muscle car and the West's cultural revolution in 1966.

By the midsixties, London, the huge, sprawling metropolis that is the capital of England, had become the mecca for the world. Everything that was anything and everybody who was anybody moved to Swinging London, now home of the great nightclubs where one could rub shoulders with the likes of Mick Jagger, Keith Moon, and Marianne Faithful. London had become the city of new ideas and led the way in clothing fashion. Carnaby Street was the "in" place, with boutique after boutique, coffee bars, and easy livin'. With the communications improving daily, anything that happened in London was instantly known in Paris, Moscow, or New York. In Detroit, London's influence found its way into the muscle-car designs, and particularly into automobile advertising copy, which began to sell four hundred cubic inches of power the way Bob Dylan might have sold shoes.

For new-car launches, 1967 proved to be quite a year. Finally Mustang was no longer alone. Chevrolet came out with the Camaro, Pontiac with the Firebird. Ford's Lincoln Mercury division introduced the Cougar, which in essence was a luxury Mustang. The three new pony cars were very similar to the Mustang in

having a huge array of accessories with which to tempt the customer.

Over at Chrysler, Plymouth had an all-new Barracuda, which was a real jewel of a compact if ever there was one. Beautiful styling persuaded *Car & Driver* to call it the best-looking car of the year. It came in hardtop, fastback, or convertible models and had a load of performance goodies for the go-faster boys. Lowest engine in the line-up was the faithful Slant Six rated at 145 bhp, and at the top of the performance tier was the 273-cubic-inch V-8 rated at 235 bhp and the very hot 383 developing 280 horses at 4,200 rpm. A Barracuda equipped with the latter engine could do 0–60 in a very rapid 6.6 seconds, though economy at 10 to 12 mpg was abysmal. Not that a performance buyer cared about economy; if he did, he'd have settled for the six-cylinder version.

Even more muscle was provided by the new intermediate GTX, which was at the top of the Belvedere line. Top engine option was the 440-cid V-8 stolen from Chrysler's full-size cars. Horsepower was 375 at 4,600 rpm, and with this engine the muscular GTX could run to 60 in 6.6 seconds. Riding on the same 116-inch wheelbase, the GTX, if equipped with the 440 or Hemi 426, was something else on road or track.

Dodge called the 440 Magnum when it was used in the intermediate Coronet series and Coronet's offshoot, the Charger. This potent engine was standard in a new Coronet hardtop called the R/T, the initials standing for Road and Track. Besides the engine the R/T had heavy-duty suspension, plus bigger brakes and wider tires than standard Coronets. The same engine was offered as an option on the Charger, which didn't get an R/T version until 1968, and of course the Hemi was offered at almost a thousand dollars extra. Neither model changed much for '67. Not that they needed to; the formula had proved successful the previous season,

so why change a good thing? Although Dodge sales were down in 1967, the performance-eager public shelled out to buy the Coronet R/T; 10,181 were built of a car that was hard to beat in a traffic-light grand prix.

As increasingly the nation's highways took on the semblance of a drag strip, Plymouth's full-size cars threw in their dollar's worth just for fun. One was unable to order a Hemi in the '67 Fury III, but pinned-to-the-seat motoring was readily available with either the 383 or 440 engines. There were two 383 versions, one developing 270 bhp using a single-barrel carburetor, or the fiercer 325-bhp unit with four-barrel carburetion. *Car Life* magazine road-tested a Fury III convertible equipped with the 383/325 bhp engine.

Taking into account the longitudinal members—the sheet-metal ribs welded into the body sill-box section for greater torsional rigidity, plus added reinforcement to the cowl area—to achieve a 0–60 time of 8.7 seconds speaks well of an engine able to haul a 4,280-pound convertible down the road that fast. The standing quarter took a mere 16.6 seconds in a car that by no stretch of the imagination was aerodynamic. With the 440 no doubt these times would have been improved by a second or so.

"Plymouth's Out to Win You Over," claimed the ad campaign slogan. It was quite catchy, brief, and to the point. Trouble was, its catchiness and brevity fell upon deaf ears, as for the second year in a row, the successful Barracuda excepted, Plymouth sales fell. Apart from the ten thousand or so Coronet R/T 440 sales, Dodge didn't do so well, either. Chrysler's 1967 crop of street muscle was the best to be had in a field of fine contemporaries from rival manufacturers, so why didn't more sell?

For one thing, the cars were aimed at the baby boomer generation with revolution in their hearts and Mick Jagger in their souls.

Over America's young was the specter of Vietnam accompanied by unwelcome draft notices, and this alone probably deterred many possible buyers until they knew whether their lives were to be their own or the government's. For the first time that anyone could remember, the young began to openly defy the establishment and create an alternative lifestyle much encouraged by the British pop heroes and their American counterparts. Long hair, colorful, outrageous apparel, William Burroughs and Allen Ginsberg, marijuana and LSD and faster-than-fast cars—this was the new culture pervading the scene. An escape from the inevitable for many was what much of it was all about.

Richard Petty didn't have to worry about such things. All he had to concern himself with was winning the NASCAR Grand National Championship. Hemi-powered Plymouth Belvederes were his steeds, and the combination

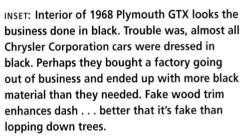

INSET: Interior of 1968 Plymouth GTX looks the business done in black. Trouble was, almost all Chrysler Corporation cars were dressed in black. Perhaps they bought a factory going out of business and ended up with more black material than they needed. Fake wood trim enhances dash . . . better that it's fake than lopping down trees.

The 1968 GTX was one of several supercar variations living under the Plymouth Belvedere banner. GTX, Satellite, Road Runner, and the Belvedere shared almost everything but names. All rode on the Belvedere's 116-inch wheelbase. GTX was a powerful performer, especially with 426 Hemi.

GTX symbol moved around a bit between the years 1968 through 1970. It began down below and eventually moved to the middle.

of the Belvederes and Petty was electrifying. Try as they may, nothing could touch them; Plymouth had obviously got it right, and with the "King"—as Petty was known—doing the driving, nobody else came close. Out of 49 races held in 1967, Plymouth chalked up 31 victories, 27 of which were Petty's, 10 of them in a row. Dodge, on the other hand, managed a mere 5 wins using Hemi-Chargers. Closest rival to Plymouth was Ford, who chalked up 10 wins. Fastest qualifying times were setting new records. At the Trenton Speedway in New Jersey, Petty hit 101.208 mph to set a new fastest-time record for the track. At Daytona International Speedway, Petty qualified at an astounding 179.068 mph in a thirty-four-minute race that averaged 174.583 mph. Naturally Petty won the championship. To this day, nobody has cracked his number of victories in one season, or the 10 wins in a row.

Ever since its Total Performance program came into being in the early sixties, Ford had achieved the impossible by winning everything from NASCAR to Le Mans, the prestigious twenty-four-hour French race. To win Le Mans took some doing, but win it Ford did, the first time in 1966 when the Anglo-American-designed GT-40s crossed the finishing line 1, 2, 3, beating top Europeans like Porsche and Ferrari. Ford continued to dominate Le Mans for several more years, always coming in number one. In NASCAR races, Ford was Plymouth's and Dodge's nemesis, either winning the championship or often being a spirited contender. In 1968 Ford won twenty races compared to Plymouth's fifteen, and once again it was Richard Petty who wracked up Plymouth's wins. Dodge could only manage five wins with the Chargers it fielded, and Mercury won seven races.

The year 1968 was very troubled, not only on the political front, which was dire, but on the motoring scene as well. After Ralph Nader

successfully pointed out the automobile's many safety shortcomings, the federal government stepped in with a basketful of new laws that began to take effect in 1968. Side lights front and rear, strengthened doors, collapsible steering columns—these were some of the items the car makers had to design into each and every car. Another important item was emission controls to help clean up the polluted atmosphere. Unleaded gas would rule supreme within the next decade.

These were minor hiccoughs compared with what was to come in the near future. Thus the 1968 cars continued to blaze a formidable trail of street machines that became wilder and wilder. Once again Chrysler came up trumps with two incredible cars—one a variation, the other arguably the finest design of the entire muscle-car genre. *Car & Driver* called the '67 Barracuda the best-looking car of the year; now the magazine sang the praises of the new Dodge Charger.

Here was an automobile that was beginning to take the principles of aerodynamic design seriously, for the new Charger had a soft wedge

One of the wildest, woolliest cars ever devised: Plymouth's 1968 Road Runner. The Road Runner was a spark of genius, had few frills except where it mattered . . . under the hood. The potent 383-cid V-8 was standard in the Road Runner, but this example has the Hemi. The 1968 Road Runner had Warner Bros. cartoon Road Runner bird on each door, trunk, dashboard, and inside door panels. What was even better was the horn. Painted purple, with a little Road Runner on it, the horn would go "Beep! Beep!"

Wide, semi-flat black stripes adorn 1969 Plymouth Road Runner hood. A 440 V-8 burbles cheerfully within. It's a dark, dark night and the bogeyman's comin'.

shape, a blacked-out grille with hidden headlights, and a body that swelled out around the front- and rear-wheel arches but narrowed in the middle to give the effect of a tightly corseted waist. The styling was not unlike the new breed of wind-tunnel-tested sports racing cars designed for the Can-Am Series, even if the rear roof and back light gave way to fashion rather than form. The exotic shape, which was the inspiration of Dodge design chief Bill Brownlie, did nothing for Dodge in racing competition, the 1968 Charger winning two races; the other three were won by 1967 models. But on the

sales front, the Charger was a major hit—96,108 Chargers were built compared to the 15,788 of the year before.

Dodge made its intentions quite clear in 1968: that it was going all out to become Chrysler's performance king. To help achieve this, Dodge created the Scat Pack. It was made up of a Charger R/T, Dodge Dart GTS, and Coronet R/T. Scat Pack cars were easily identified by their bold bumble-bee stripes wrapped round the rears of the cars. All the models were very attractive, very desirable automobiles, especially when equipped with either the 440 or 425 Hemi. The Dart performed very well with the 340. *Car Life* posted a 0–60 time of 6.3 seconds, and a Hemi-powered Charger whistled to 60 in 4.8 seconds in another test. The Scat Pack cars looked the part, behaved the part, and gave Dodge the performance image it desired— though lowly cousin Plymouth was the one pouring it on in NASCAR competition.

Even though Dodge could pat itself on the back for its beautiful Charger, Plymouth eclipsed everyone (and that included rival manufacturers) with its sensational Road Runner.

Built on the 116-inch Belvedere and GTX wheelbase, and sharing the same identical 202.7-inch body, the Road Runner was stripped for action. Plymouth was beginning to realize that the all-important youth market was starting to fall away as the once-cheap muscle cars were adding dollars by the minute by offering an increasing number of "must have" options. This was not what the nation's youth wanted . . . or could afford. They wanted a plain-jane, taxi-cab-appointed car that had all the requisite performance goodies for a bargain price. This was exactly what Plymouth offered in the Road Runner; a bare-bones car stuffed full of performance that cost a mere $3,034.

What did one get for the price? A specially adapted 383-cubic-inch engine that delivered 335 bhp. It was quite a bit different from Chrysler's three other 383 engines. In the Road Runner, the engine was given the 440-cid Super Commando heads and camshaft, larger intake manifold, the 440's crankcase windage tray, and a Carter AVS 4426S four-barrel carburetor. Then there were twin exhausts and an unsilenced air cleaner, all of which helped to make the Road Runner a rather special vehicle. Even if it did have a taxi-cab interior.

To cope with all this power, the Road Runner had a standard four-speed manual transmission, larger-than-standard torsion bars, high-rate, heavy-duty rear leaf springs, and heavy-duty eleven-inch drum brakes. The latter were disappointing, according to a *Car Life* road test. "During the first panic stop from 80 mph," wrote the magazine, "the cold rear drums locked up tight, the rear end began wagging like a dog's tail, and we had to get off the pedal to regain control." Later in the test, all four drums began to fade, not a good omen if one's inclination was to go fast. Which is what the Road Runner begged you to do. A worthwhile option, an essential one in fact, was to have specified the $72.95 front disc brakes.

"'Beep-Beep!' You know those cartoons? About a rapid bird with a 'Beep-Beep' voice and a penchant for coyote-squelching? Right. Name's Road Runner. Well, Plymouth's built a car with the same name. And personality. Its horn goes 'Beep-Beep!' And the beat goes on." That was part of the advertising copy introducing the Road Runner. A bright red car set against an all-black background. At the top of the advertisement: the Warner Bros. cartoon Road Runner bird in full motion.

It was a brilliant advertising campaign for an undeniably brilliant concept. One with a sense of humor. Whoever thought of getting permission from Warner Bros. to use the Road Runner name and the Road Runner cartoon bird to decorate the car was a genius. And the brilliance didn't stop there. Under the hood there was a purple-painted horn with the Road Runner bird decorating it. "Mee-Meep!" It sounded exactly like the cartoon. "Mee-Meep!"

Plymouth didn't spare the horses on telling the world that this was not any old Belvedere; this was the Road Runner—as could be seen by the little racing bird on the trunk, doors, dashboard, and interior door panels. The Road Runner was love at first sight; everybody adored it,

A man walks up the beach. He's had a tiring day working on his boat. He trudges toward his waiting car. The car has been slightly modified, has fat drag-strip slicks at the rear. A 426-hemispherical combustion-chambered V-8 is the power source. This car goes. Wearily the man gets in, puts the key in the ignition, and starts the engine. It bursts into life, settling down to a staccato, low-key rumble. The man smiles, his weariness gone. He's with the King of the Hill.

wanted it. Eventually 44,599 Road Runners found happy homes; the car became an instant cult, a youth image bar none. Suddenly Plymouth, once upon a time staid old Plymouth, had become part of the youth culture, a rebel. "The Beat Goes On" sang Sonny and Cher, and Plymouth echoed the sentiments using the song's title in its marketing and advertising campaign to great effect.

There were a number of great muscle cars all vying for a piece of the go-faster action, but none came close to the Road Runner for pure imagery. Rival makers all wished they'd thought of it first, this tongue-in-cheek machine with a taxi-cab interior and more power than was healthy to talk about. With the mighty Hemi under foot (1,019 Road Runners were built with King Kong under the hood), a Road Runner was capable of 140 mph and 0–60 in 5.5 seconds. The standing-start quarter-mile run was accomplished in a lightning-quick 13.56 seconds at 105.38 mph. Pretty damn quick for a completely stock car off the showroom floor. Owners of the few Hemi versions built would have had to have very deep

pockets; gas mileage was an uneconomical 7.5 to 10.9 mpg, depending on how heavy your right foot was.

When the Road Runner first appeared, it clicked. Its timing was impeccable. The younger generation had reached a plateau of power that was increasingly worrying the Establishment. But the Establishment had little to offer the young apart from a stone-faced resistance to change. American society was in a turmoil; Timothy Leary encouraged the young to take LSD and "Tune In, Turn On, and Drop Out"—sentiments many followed. Marijuana was being smoked brazenly, openly, and perhaps advocated by the Beatles' ingenious *Sgt. Pepper's Lonely Hearts Club Band* album released the year before. Many said the group's 1968 *White Album* contained "hidden messages." If one was driving a Road Runner at full throttle, perhaps it did.

The Establishment made sure that 1968 wasn't all fun and youthful partying; so much so that French students literally took to the streets and almost brought General De Gaulle's government down. This was the first show of a deeply disillusioned generation collectively taking the law into their own hands. If France was having a bad time of it, so increasingly were America and Britain. Americans were split over Vietnam almost as badly as during the Civil War. On campuses across the country, students demonstrated, marched, rioted against the war. Early in 1968, the Viet Cong launched the Tet offensive. It was a concerted, well-orchestrated effort directed at several cities, including Saigon. Before it was finally crushed, many young lives had been lost. A Gallup Poll found that only 26 percent of Americans favored President Johnson's handling of the war; shortly after, Johnson shocked the nation by announcing he wouldn't run for President in the upcoming elections. Several Democrats, including the late President Kennedy's brother, Robert F. Kennedy, declared themselves as candidates.

Student riots spilled over into Mexico, casting a shadow over the Olympic Games. America won forty-five gold medals compared to its Russian rival's thirty. Guns played their evil part in the assassinations of Martin Luther King, the civil rights leader, and Bobby Kennedy, the second Kennedy to die tragically this way in less than five years. And Andy Warhol, the surrealist artist, was shot and wounded by Valeria Solanis, founder of SCUM (Society for Cutting Up Men). She shot him, she said, because he refused to film a script she wrote! In a very disturbing year, the Russians brutally put down a democratic experiment in Czechoslovakia, sending in tanks and several hundred thousand heavily armed Soviet troops to quell the movement. The events of 1968

provided one of the messiest social backdrops ever to be projected behind some of the most exciting cars ever to leave Detroit.

After a couple of very good years, Plymouth lost the NASCAR Grand National Championship to Ford, although by only four races. Ford scored 20, Plymouth 16, Mercury 7, Dodge 5, and Chevrolet a solitary 1. If the world couldn't live in harmony neither could NASCAR racing teams. Ford and Plymouth continually fought a battle to the death, Ford with its 427, Plymouth with the almighty

America is full of people who are individualists and who want to make a personal statement. Car buffs have their share of folk who like to customize or modify their cars for the same reason. Here we have a 1969 Plymouth Road Runner that is truly a one-off. Body has been pretty much left alone. It's mostly paint and graphics, wheels and interior that have been modified. Entire hood pays homage to the little bird that gave its name to the car. Heart behind refers to Plymouth's 1968 "Beat Goes On" advertising slogan.

INSET, TOP: Thin yellow line curves away below large, colorful Road Runner bird that looks as though he is on the move!

INSET, MIDDLE: Interior shot shows wild but livable seat-back colors, Road Runners stitched into front seats; door panels are done the same way. A yellow line runs all round the interior.

INSET, BOTTOM: Road Runner engine looks like a Hemi but is covered in nonstandard options. This car is undoubtedly quick, quicker than most, and would cut a rug on Hollywood and Vine!

Hemi. Ford's 427 was a terrific engine, make no mistake, and in 1968 it scored better than Plymouth by using the engine in the fastback, slippery Torino. Besides losing the championship, Plymouth suffered another setback when Richard Petty signed on with Ford for the 1969 season. Apparently Lee Petty, one-time NASCAR racer and now head of Petty Enterprises, asked Plymouth for more money to race in the 1969 season. Plymouth refused and off to Ford went the Pettys. Naturally, Ford was only too happy to give the Pettys what they wanted; without Petty, Ford surmised, Plymouth would be in real trouble.

In addition to the amazing Road Runner there were other muscle cars in Chrysler's stable that should not be ignored. The beautiful Barracuda had the 340 V-8, which could zip to 60 in about seven seconds—or the larger, more powerful 383-cubic-inch engine, which knocked half a second off the 0–60 times. Not to be forgotten are the Road Runner's brethren: the GTX, which was just as fast but more expensive and luxurious; and the Belvedere/Satellite combo, which like the GTX and Road Runner could be had with the 383 but not with the larger engines like the 440 or 426 Hemi. For some reason, those engines were the preserve of the GTX and Road Runner; the GTX, incidentally, came standard with the 440. Of Plymouth's full-size cars, the 440 was available in the Fury and Sport Fury.

Dodge had the aforementioned Charger, the Scat Pack Super Bee Coronet, and 340 Dart, the latter being one of the prettiest semicompact cars around, and also one of the quickest with the right engine, suspension, and axle ratio combination. Big, wide, straight blacktops were these cars' domain; Chrysler's Mighty Mopars were the cars to fear in any traffic-light grand prix and were in most cases the fastest on the block. There were exceptions, of course. Ford's Torino was one and, surprisingly, the

Oldsmobile 4-4-2 the other. Both cars were as quick as the Mopars: nothing else came close.

Without Richard Petty driving for them in 1969, Plymouth had the poorest showing since the days when they trundled around with just a flat-head six under the hood. They won only two races out of the fifty-four NASCAR Grand National events run. Dodge made up for the previous years by winning twenty-two races, but once again Ford, with a brand new, slippery Torino Talladega built specially for NASCAR and powered by a colossal 428-cid V-8, beat Mopar by just four races.

Ever since Ford introduced its ambitious Total Performance program in 1962, Dearborn's goal had been to see Fords win every type of automotive sporting event. Falcons won their class in the prestigious Monte Carlo Rally, big Fords won NASCAR, and the fabulous GT-40 road race cars became the first Americans to win the Le Mans 24-Hour Endurance spectacular since a Duesenberg won in 1921. The GT-40s took the first three places in the 1966 race and continued to win for several years after. Ford appeared invincible, and they were for the most part. Except in drag racing and NASCAR, where Dodge and Plymouth fought tooth and nail to beat Ford—and soon did.

Dodge really lost out to Ford in 1968, not because the power trains weren't up to Ford's but purely because of design. Part of the Charger's problem was its attractive tunnelback styling. That is to say, the rear window was set almost upright and deeply recessed between sharply raked c-pillars. It may have been attractive as a styling tour de force but it was about as aerodynamic as a thirty-ton military tank!

"We took the car to Daytona Beach," noted Larry Rathgeb, "and found to our horror that we had terrible, *terrible* front-end lift at takeoff. It was so bad that Buddy Baker [one of Dodge's main drivers] came awfully

Very little was changed for 1969 in the successful Dodge Charger with the exception of a new grille and flashier tail-lights. Engine line-up roared all the way to the 426 Hemi. Inset grille and backlight killed Charger for NASCAR. Engineers installed flush rear window and grille, which improved the Charger's chances when it raced.

INSET: The 1969 Dodge Charger had the name in script with red *R/T* after it.

close to losing the car the first time out at Daytona."

Not wanting Dodge to be embarrassed at one of racing's major events on the motoring calendar, Rathgeb and his colleagues fashioned crude spoilers that were attached to the front and rear of the Charger. The spoilers had the desired effect of keeping the car on the road, but as Larry pointed out, "it wasn't fast enough to be competitive."

Realizing that spoilers were not the answer, Larry and his team looked at the recessed window and raked pillars. Then they knew. Taking a large piece of Plexiglas they shaped it to fit flush over the backlight. They were almost ready to mold the section to the backlight when

George Wallace, Special Vehicles Engineering coordinator, made them stop. "You can't have us run out like a bunch of bozos," he snarled, "and tape this piece of plastic on the back of the car to prove a point in front of God and everybody." As Wallace wasn't a man to argue with, it wasn't until the team returned to the proving grounds that they were able to attach the plastic to prove that point. Which, of course, they did.

By placing the plastic to fit flush with the c-pillars, aerodynamic drag was reduced considerably. At this stage there wasn't time to put the Charger 500 (as it was to be called) into limited production; NASCAR would require a production level of at least five hundred units to homologate the car to qualify it for racing. Dodge would have to sit tight until 1969, when the car would be produced and ready to race.

Besides the flush rear window, the front grille was also fitted flush for better aerodynamics. It was set up to race and race it did. The only trouble was Ford's all-powerful Talladega Torino cars, which were even better aerodynamically. They had rounded front ends and a sloping fastback design that made them slice through the air like a jet plane. After the first two races of the 1969 season, which Richard Petty won driving a 1968 Plymouth—they were Plymouth's only wins—the third race found Petty winning again, only his time he was driving a 1969 Ford!

"Even though we had mounted the grille and back window flush, we still felt we weren't far enough along," said Larry Rathgeb. "So I asked both the Dodge and Plymouth people to come and visit with us as well as the marketing management. I told them we were going to talk with John Pointer, proving-ground engineer, and Bob Marcell, head of Chrysler's Aerodynamic Department, and I requested them to bring along drawings of any current production car and modifications to the same that would lead to improved aerodynamics.

"Well," continued Larry, "Dale Rieker came from Dodge but the Plymouth people wouldn't come. I called to find out why and they said they didn't need engineering when they had Richard Petty." Within days Plymouth would begin to regret its smug, somewhat haughty attitude when the Petty clan walked out and moved to Ford. Suddenly, in the face of the Talladega challenge, Dodge and Plymouth weren't so invincible anymore. Something had to be done and done quickly if Mopar was to have a chance in the Championship. The requisite number of Charger 500s had been built to allow the car to race at

NASCAR, but Rathgeb and his group weren't satisfied. They knew they could do better and sure enough they did. Soon they would be readying what would become the ultimate in supercars.

Chrysler's engine lineup for 1969 remained unchanged from 1967, with the exception that they all met the federal government's clean air standards. New was the optional fresh-air package mounted atop the hoods of the Road Runner, GTX, Charger, and Super Bee. It was identical on all models yet had a different name for each model. For instance, it was an Air Grabber on the GTX, Ramcharger on the Charger, and Coyote Duster (pretty logical, I suppose) for the Road Runner. There were brake improvements, and disc brakes were a worthy option on all Chrysler makes with the exception of the New Yorker and Town and Country, which had the discs as standard.

The standard Charger had new taillights and a deeply recessed split grille and the same backlight that had caused all the trouble at NASCAR the previous year. Engine choices went up to the fabled Hemi even though this was not the Charger racing on the NASCAR circuits. That responsibility was left to the Charger 500 with the flush grille and rear window.

Dodge also fielded the virtually unchanged Coronet in various forms. There was the Coronet 440, the Coronet R/T, the Coronet Super Bee (this was Dodge's answer to the Road Runner) and, introduced midway through 1969, the awesome Super Bee 440 Six Pack.

This was a brute-force car basking in machismo. For instance, it had a flat black fiberglass hood with probably the world's largest hood scoop attached. Unlike many fake scoops, this big one, with large red letters proclaiming *Six Pack* on either side, was all real and gulped dollops of cooling air into the welcoming engine bay. The engine was the 440

Magnum V-8 equipped with an Edelbrock Hi-riser intake manifold plus three Holley two-barrel carburetors just to help the engine sing. What a song that engine could sing, too. It had Hemi-valve springs, low-taper camshaft with flat-face tappets, dual-point distributor, connecting rods that were magnafluxed, and chrome-flashed valve stems to complete the heady mix. To ensure that nobody would mistake the car for anything but a serious street racer, no hubcaps were supplied. Red-line tires added to the image, as did the Hurst manual four-speed transmission. Standard axle was a Dana 9.75-inch Sure Grip with 4.10:1 gears. Wheels were six inches, the tires fifteen.

One magazine breathlessly ripped through the quarter-mile in 13.65 seconds at 105.14 mph and did 0–60 in 6.6 seconds. Another got the 0–60 time down to 5.6 seconds, and another managed 6.3. Of these very special street machines, 1,907 were built out of a total of 27,800 Coronets of all types. One of the most terrifying and exciting cars built in 1969, they were guaranteed to scare the pants off any staid citizen they zoomed past on the street. Oh, and to ensure folks made no mistake about the car (how could they with that whopping hood scoop gulping away up front?), the 440 Six Pack was littered with little Super Bee decals all over the place. The one on the grille was metal, though.

Chrysler-Plymouth Division's full-size cars were huge—the New Yorker was 225 inches

long and 80 inches wide—and had new fuselage styling by Elwood Engel. Plymouth also got the curved glass, rounded-top design for its line of full-size cars, which measured 214.5 inches overall and were 79.6 inches wide. With the four-barrel-carburetor-equipped 383-cid, 330-bhp engine, the big Fury could turn in a 0–60 time of 8.5 seconds; without air conditioning, that time dropped to 7.5. Even in a luxury cruiser like the Fury III, power was the thing.

"Play your cards right, and three bills can put you in a whole lot of car this year." So began the copy for Dodge's newest edition to the Bumblebee-striped Scat Pack, the Dart Swinger 340. Standard equipment included the 340-cid four-barrel V-8, heavy-duty suspension, four-speed manual, full synchromesh with Hurst shifter, dual exhausts, and a hood with die-cast louvers. Plymouth's Barracuda could knock off 0–60 in 6.3 seconds. *Motor Trend* reckoned the Barracuda to be one of the best accelerating cars around and far and away the tops in the sports-personal car stakes. Only the Dart Swinger could come close.

General Motors and Ford had their range of fine muscle cars—the Pontiac GTO, Mustang, Camaro, Olds 4-4-2, and Torino come to mind—but none really matched the stuff Chrysler's young designers and engineers were enthusiastically putting out. Chrysler led the way into the hearts and souls of the young, and many not so young as well, with cars specifically designed for fun, fun, fun. Try as the competitors might, there was nothing quite like a good Chrysler Corporation muscle car; they had everything going for them.

Now unabashedly clothing themselves in pure psychedelia, Dodge/Plymouth advertising copy read and looked like part of the Haight-Ashbury subculture or the Beatles' *Sgt. Pepper* album cover. One real tongue-in-cheek car was the flower-power Barracuda. It could be had in either yellow or orange, had psychedelic flower-

patterned seats, and a flower-decorated vinyl roof! If anything came from *Sgt. Pepper*, this Barracuda did; it was the flower child of the highway, an automobile that belonged to the girl with kaleidoscope eyes.

For Plymouth to produce such a car as the floral Barracuda was strange to say the least. Perhaps it was devised as a tongue-in-cheek, twinkle-in-the-eye recognition of the power the young wielded—a "we-know-you're-out-there-and-here's-a-car-made-especially-for-you" sort of thing. Unfortunately it didn't quite work that way. Very few floral Barracudas were sold, and almost all went to young women whose husbands hated to be seen with or in a car that might make their friends think of them in the same light as Liberace. So the flower-power cars ended up being repainted and having the seats re-covered. So there are extremely few psychedelic Barracudas around today. Which is a shame, because they represent an extraordinary time that will never be seen again.

Motor Trend magazine selected the Plymouth Road Runner for its prestigious Car of the Year award in 1969. The magazine's editors

Dodge Dart began in 1960 as a smaller car on a 118-inch wheelbase. It was smaller compared to the full-size Dodges sitting on 122 inches. There was a colossal range of body styles with names like Seneca, Phoenix, and Pioneer. By 1962, wheelbase was down to 116 inches, and in 1963 to 111 inches, where it remained through 1976. The 1969 Dart 340 GT Sport was very attractive and popular.

INSET: *GTS* on hood of 1969 Dodge Dart means Gran Touring Sport. Nothing like a little class!

gave the Road Runner what is essentially the automotive Oscar for its concept of a distinctive, low-priced automobile without frills or fuss but packed with all the goodies to turn it into a hairy muscle car. It wasn't quite the taxicab sleeper it had been in 1968; there were more options and new standard items such as roll-down rear windows instead of the cheap push-out type the Road Runner had in 1968. Bucket seats were available, as were other options like power windows, TorqueFlite, and natty racing stripes. Standard engine was the 383 mated to Chrysler's four-speed manual, and in this guise the 1969 Road Runner would get to 60 in 7.1 seconds and do the quarter-mile in 14.35 seconds at 101.58 mph. With the available 426/425 Hemi the Road Runner packed an even bigger punch: 0–60 in 5.6 seconds and the quarter in 13.56 at 105.38 mph. In the latter state of tune, the Road Runner was so savage that one man who bought one without appreciating quite what he had soon found out when he floored the pedal; the shock was so immense he had a heart attack! Fortunately he lived to tell the tale.

Such was the Road Runner's success that there was little to touch it. No other car had the use of a world-famous cartoon character with which to identify itself. Pontiac came out with the Judge, Ford already had the Cobra, but both were in-house ideas. The Road Runner became an icon of the supercar species, an entirely American concept that was almost unique in the world of the automobile. America's Big Three built cars in Australia, and there were Aussie muscle cars as well, as will be seen later.

January 1969. After numerous meetings Dodge got the go-ahead to develop and build a supercar to end all supercars, and one that would wipe out Ford's Talladega at the racetrack. Larry Rathgeb, John Pointer, and Bob Marcell had submitted drawings showing how the car should be if it was to win races.

Although both men worked independently of one another, the drawings had an uncanny resemblance to each other.

"It was a sharp-nosed car," remembered Larry Rathgeb. "Much like a Corvette nose with a wing at the rear. An upright wing. I remember saying, 'Do you think that'll do it?' and they both said, 'Yeah, that'll do it.'" Taking the drawings, Rathgeb and Dale Rieker from Dodge went to see Chrysler's racing chief, the legendary Robert M. Rodger, the man behind some of the best engines ever built by a car company, including of course, the Hemis. As seen earlier, he was the person who launched the fabled 300 Letter Series.

Rodger was in complete accord with Rathgeb and Rieker. It was a project after his own heart. As the men turned to leave, Rodger called after them, eyes twinkling: "It's a good thing that somebody in the corporation has an interest in what you're doing. Anyway, you have my blessings. Do what you have to do to get the job done."

Rieker immediately went to see his boss, Dodge general manager Robert J. McCurry, Jr. McCurry was enthusiastic about anything that would help Dodge win races and improve sales. McCurry attended as many races as he could; NASCAR, NHRA Winternationals, IMCA (where Chargers held the crown), and FIA. He would do anything to promote Dodge's image, including exploiting the fashionable youth cult. To this end he created the Dodge Rebellion Girl and Dodge Fever Girl to help promote the cars. The two girls were very successful in promoting themselves as well!

After listening to Rieker and Rathgeb, McCurry thought for a minute, then leaned across his desk and, fixing his gaze squarely on Rieker, asked, "You really think this will get it done?"

"That's what they tell me," replied Rieker. Standing up, a smile crossing his stocky coun-

tenance, McCurry said, "Go ahead then and get it built." It was the last hurdle. Now the program could swing into top gear. The Dodge Daytona seeds had taken and it was about to be born.

The team worked night and day to develop the Daytona. It had to be ready and running in time for NASCAR's inaugural race at its new Talladega track the following September. Much had to be done to make the car a winning machine. It wasn't just a matter of sticking wings and spoilers on an existing car; it meant aerodynamic equations in wind tunnels to get the right shape. This is where Frank Chianese came in.

Chianese was an aerodynamicist at the NASA Space Center in Huntsville, Alabama. The space program was being phased out, which meant Chianese and his colleagues were looking for fresh fields to conquer . . . or new employment. Next thing Chianese knew he and other aerodynamicists had been scooped up by Dodge and sent to Wichita State University with a three-eighths clay model of John Pointer's design. This was to be subjected to aerodynamic tests in the university's 7-by-10-foot wind tunnel. Meanwhile Pointer and Rieker were at Creative Industries, the company that did most of Chrysler's specialist work, and were in the process of building a full-size mock-up.

"We were in constant telephone communication with John and Dale," recalled Chianese. "They would be knocking together sheet metal while we were still doing development work in the tunnel. We would come up with a nose configuration and I would call John and say, 'Hey, John, that nose isn't working out' and later Dale would be on the phone hollering, 'Hey, you guys give me no inspiration. Let's have something 'cause we're pounding sheet metal here!' That's what it was like and it shows how critical the timing was because we were building and testing the car at the same time."

It took almost twelve weeks, working ten to twelve hours a day in the wind tunnel at Wichita State and the considerably larger 16-by-23-foot tunnel owned by Lockheed, which was situated in Georgia. The two tunnels were used for tunnel-to-tunnel correlation studies on the three-eighths-scale models. Occasional tests were conducted on the full-size models, but this was the exception rather than the rule.

Finally a prototype was finished and taken to the proving grounds; it delighted the engineers and designers by lapping in excess of 200 mph the first time out. "And it was the same

Modern, glass-house office block in Farnborough, England, suits racy lines of GTX. England has a lot of Mopar muscle cars. This is one of them. Pillar-box red 1969 Plymouth GTX lets you know it's coming! Wheels are not original but aftermarket accessories popular with many muscle-car fans; Cragar is one well-known brand. The 1969 Plymouth GTX has 375-bhp 440 under the hood; this was the standard engine. A base hardtop retailed for $3,416 in 1969, when 15,602 GTXs were built.

INSET: Standard GTX engine, the awesome 440, slumbers under the hood. If you wake it up, watch out!

day that man landed on the moon," grinned John Pointer.

"It was kinda spooky," chipped in Frank Chianese. "'Cause you would stand in the timing shed, which was alongside the track, and when the 500 went by (tests on the Charger 500 were conducted simultaneously with the Daytona) it damn near took the shed off its foundations. Just a big *wham!* When the Daytona went by, you'd hear this *whop!* . . . and it was gone!"

To be competitive in 1969 meant speeds of up to 200 mph and beyond on NASCAR's high-banked ovals. Large, powerful engines were one thing but speed is no good if the car has no stability or handling—as proven by what happened with the original Charger from which the

Daytona evolved. This is why aerodynamics became so important as the youth-oriented, psychedelic sixties drew to a close. Wind-tunnel experiments had shown that if a car travels at 200 mph, more than 50 percent of its engine power is used to overcome aerodynamic drag. Therefore, better aerodynamics would improve stability while drag would be reduced. In turn this would allow more engine power to be transmitted to the wheels, thereby increasing its maximum speed to the required levels.

What a car the Daytona was. There had never, ever been anything quite like it. This was the ultimate sixties dream, the car Lucy in the Sky would have collected her diamonds in. In essence this was a Charger 500 with an eighteen-inch-long, droopy nose fitted where the grille used to be, and Boeing-type twin stabilizers attached together by a fifty-eight-inch horizontal adjustable aileron positioned at the

---

A 350-horse, 400-cubic-inch V-8 was standard in the 1969 Pontiac GTO, but there were even hotter options. John DeLorean's GTO was the car credited—or blamed—for the intermediate-muscle-car revolution.

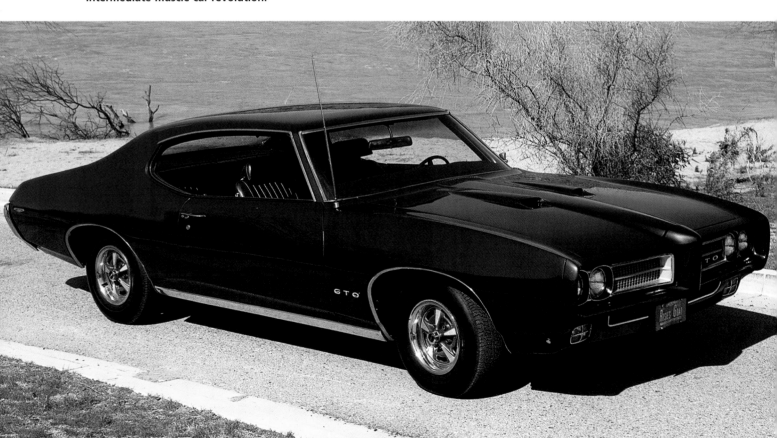

Testers didn't like the 440 'Cuda much. Big block prevented use of disc brakes, power steering, four-speed manual transmission. The 0–60 hits in 5.6 seconds. Best engine in 'Cuda was the 340.

INSET: Interior of Barracuda has fake-wood-rimmed wheel but is quite pleasant. Seats were regarded a little on the hard side.

rear of the car. The stabilizers were twenty-three inches high.

When rival manufacturers first saw the winged Daytona with the rounded, shovel-type nose, they probably snickered up their sleeves. This oddity would never win races . . . and why the wings? Chrysler's engineers proved that the Daytona's tail stabilizers were far more effective for inducing negative lift than the more common rear-deck spoiler.

Under the hood was the Hemi; the choice was unanimous. It had to be the Hemi. John P.

Wehrly was responsible for the design and development of Chrysler's second-generation Hemi engine. It was not the same as the original Hemi that came out in 1951 and none of the parts interchanged. As John Wehrly put it, the engine was only the same philosophically.

"The original 1951 Hemi was a new design Chrysler did, while the 1964 Hemi was based on what we called the B-engine," said Wehrly. "This was the block used for the family of 351, 361, 383, 413, and 440 powerplants. These had a wedged combustion chamber and cylinder head. It was a very strong, beefy engine with a deep skirt block. The original 1951 Hemi wasn't. It was a lighter-duty engine. So we had the opportunity to make the new Hemi a real racing engine. In fact it was made specifically for racing." And it's well known how successful it was.

Dave Cummins, one of Chrysler's senior stylists, now retired, remembers doing a lot of overtime at the time the engines were being tested. "They were so loud," he said, "that they would not run them during the daytime. At nine to ten at night they would run them at 5,000 rpm, then step them up another two grand and run them for another ten minutes until finally they started to stretch and something would miss. Then they shut the things down. They did this day after day after day."

"As a matter of fact," recalled Wehrly, "I remember on my way home the afternoon shift would do a lot of power runs. I could roll down my windows on summer nights and hear those engines a long way off. I could tell when I should turn around and come back by the sound!"

On April 10, 1969, the Daytona made its first public appearance. NASCAR rules required five hundred Daytonas to be sold if Dodge expected to debut on the new Talladega track on September 14. Not that Dodge needed to have worried; hardly had the announcement been made that five hundred Daytonas were to

This is the outrageous Plymouth Barracuda Mod Top. It had a flowery roof and very psychedelic seats covered in floral patterns. Engines ranged from the Slant Six to the 340. Funny how so few people wanted to be seen driving one! Mod Top lasted one season.

be sold to the general public than they were gone. Dodge could have sold five times as many. As it was, order books were overfilled in a matter of days, such was the enthusiasm for the Daytona.

At $3,993 apiece, the Daytona was a bargain. Standard engine was the 440 Wedge developing 375 bhp. It was fast enough to make most would-be racers' hair curl. Optional engines were the 440 Six Pack and, of course, the Hemi, which buyers took at their own risk. Described as a racing engine, the Hemi had no manufacturer's warranty.

Car magazines fell over themselves to get their editorial hands and ink on the Daytona. The October 1969 issue of *Modern Motor* titled its article "the incredible dodge daytona!" (no capitals) and, being who they were, sounded a typical conservative note: "I haven't seen one coming down the highway yet," scorned the writer, "but they're out there somewhere, scaring motorists and pedestrians alike." If only five hundred were made it was a silly observation; after all, we're talking about five hundred sold throughout a continent measuring three thousand miles coast to coast. And scaring people? Well, I suppose at first glance they might have looked like something from H. G. Wells's *War of the Worlds*!

Bill France, NASCAR's tough-as-nails president, had a serious problem. He was standing in the dust at NASCAR's new, much-publicized 2.66-mile asphalt track at Talladega, Alabama, a worried man, indeed. NASCAR's top drivers had boycotted the inaugural race to be held the next day, on September 14, 1969. These drivers, members of the recently formed Professional Drivers Association (PDA), claimed the new track was unsafe to race on. The track's surface was covered with patches and bumps, according to the drivers who had taken their cars out to qualify for pole positions.

Hitting almost 200 mph in the time trials put the wind up many of the drivers who would lose whole sets of racing rubber after four laps on the bumpy surface. "The vibration out there is unbelievable at high speed," top driver and defending Grand National champion Dave Pearson said. "My dash rattled," he continued, "and my gearshift lever jumped around like it wasn't fastened down. The first turn, the worst as far as roughness is concerned, gives you a feeling that your stomach is tearing loose. It's like coming downhill on a roller coaster at 200 mph when you go up and then down across the bumps."

Richard Petty, president of the PDA, led a delegation to Bill France and told him the new track needed better preparation and was unsafe. Couldn't the race be postponed until the track was made roadworthy? The drivers nodded in agreement. The dollar signs in Bill France's eyes clouded a little; he was expecting an enormous turnout for the race; he stood his ground and refused to admit the track wasn't ready or agree that the race be postponed. "We run tomorrow," France said. "If you don't want to run, load your car and go home."

"It's loaded, baby," replied Petty. The drivers had their cars loaded up and home they all went.

Besides being Talladega's inaugural, it was the Dodge Daytona's first time as well. The driver boycott and ensuing troubles almost eclipsed the Daytona's presence. Everybody was looking forward to a real dual between the Daytona and Ford's Torino Talladegas. That was not to be. Ford agreed with its drivers that the track was unsafe, and didn't run. Chrysler went with the drivers as well but left two Daytonas to race. Bobby Isaac, the only non-PDA member, elected to drive as did rookie racer Richard Brickhouse.

Charlie Glotzbach, one of Dodge's drivers who pulled out, set a record qualifying run of 199.466 mph. Ford's Lee Roy Yarborough was a whisker less at 199.350. The hoped-for 200 mph didn't happen, probably because nobody dare try it on the track's lumpy surface.

With factory-supported cars and drivers virtually all gone, the Sunday race was a non-event. Of course, the Daytona won and the winning driver was an excited Richard Brickhouse, who quit the PDA to enable him to run. Jim Vandiver, Ramo Stott, and Bobby Isaac, all driving Dodges, came in 2, 3, 4. Isaac drove the other factory-sponsored Daytona. Average speed for the five-hundred-mile race was 153.778 mph. A hollow victory for Dodge, but at least everyone knew that here was the car that could wipe the grin off Ford's face.

Dodge produced some swinging advertisements in 1969. "Cool it" shouts one for the Coronet Super Bee. "You're sitting watching the Christmas tree, when the thing with scoops on the hood throbs up. There're crazy stripes on the rear and some kind of bee. Goodbye. It's Super Bee. The scoops scoop . . ." And so on in the same—shall we say "groovy"?—manner.

By now, every car company was following Dodge's and Plymouth's lead and talking hip in their advertising copy. Everything was aimed at power-a-plenty. The more horses, the more stripes, cartoon characters, this was it. Not everybody liked or sympathized with all this go-faster rhetoric. Following Ralph Nader's safety suggestions, the federal government had told the car makers that they must build the cars safer, clean up emissions, and look at economy. As the showroom cars got faster and faster, insurance rates spiraled into the blue skies above. People began to get the feeling that perhaps the super cars' days were numbered. They were, but not before a final good-times blitz to come.

On the global front, it wasn't just cars that were getting faster; the skies had their share of speed, too. The year 1969 saw the first flight of the British-French codeveloped Concorde. Soon,

it was hoped, the Concorde would cross the Atlantic at twice the speed of sound, taking just three and a half hours from London to New York. And America achieved President Kennedy's goal; it put men on the moon. "That's one small step for man, one giant leap for mankind," crackled astronaut Neil Armstrong's memorable quote from the moon's surface.

That fateful year, tragic actress Judy Garland died in London, and thousands upon thousands of youngsters attended the fantastic "love-and-peace" pop-music festival at Woodstock, New York. In Northern Ireland, the first seeds of sectarian violence raised its ugly head. Richard Nixon was now President; he ordered a further twenty-five thousand troops to Vietnam. Antiwar activists seized college campuses and 250,000 war protesters marched on Washington. In California Charles Manson and four

Picture yourself driving a rival car at the track and seeing this incredible machine in front of you. It'd be enough to give you the shakes. All said and done, the Daytona is as memorable in car circles as the *Titanic* is to maritime enthusiasts.

INSET: The 1969 Daytona's 440 Six-Pack undressed to reveal three dual carburetors.

hippie followers were charged with the brutal killing of Roman Polanski's pregnant wife, Sharon Tate, and four of her companions; drugs were partly to blame.

And that was how the troubled, exciting, creative, and destructive sixties decade ended. Life would never, ever be the same again. Nor would America's cars. For out-and-out high-performance vehicles, the writing was on the wall. However, Chrysler still had a couple of aces up its sleeve, thus ensuring that the seventies would begin with a real sizzle.

First you don't, then now you see them . . . the headlights, that is. Closed, the headlight doors fit flush with nose.

FUN-LOVING ADS OF THE BEATLES ERA

At the height of the muscle-car boom, Chrysler came out with an astounding series of advertisements. These advertisements were aimed, tongue-in-cheek, at the Beatles-loving, Vietnam-hating youth of America. Copy was couched in language the young would understand. The illustrations were a mixture of cartoons and photographs. Some were openly psychedelic and made no bones about it. Unfortunately we do not have many of the greatest psychedelic cartoon ads here; they are hard to find. Nevertheless, what is pictured on these pages represents some of the best over a three-year period. Enjoy. (Ads © Chrysler Corporation)

A 1967 advertisement for the GTX. It was in 1967 that Mopar and its advertising agency discovered the Beatles generation.

Here's a super 1968 Road Runner ad. Sonny & Cher's song "The Beat Goes On" was Plymouth's slogan for the year.

"Cool it." A wonderful heading for the 1969 Dodge Coronet Super Bee prose. And it's a very psychedelic Super Bee. Where's he been?

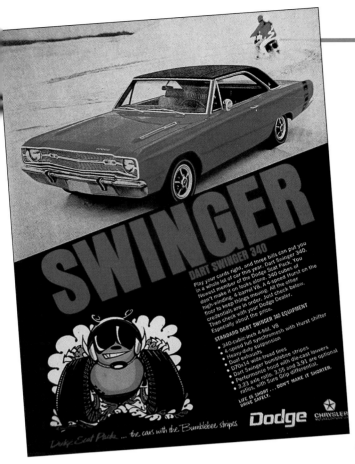

Dodge's Dart 340 was, as the advertisement goes, a "Swinger." The ending is a cryptic "Life is short . . . don't make it shorter. Drive safely." Obviously, Mopar's hot-car stable was getting nervous about the growing clamor from insurance companies and Ralph Nader.

The Duster was new for 1970, as this cartoony advertisement shows. Cute rather than '60s pop.

Here's a lovely advertisement that could have come from the Beatles' *Sgt. Pepper* album. The guy with the psychedelic tie . . . the woman "rushing off in a huff. " Glorious stuff!

A1970 Coronet Super Bee advertisement. Check the offers Dodge was pushing. A racing-style jacket, red with Scat Pack I.D.—only $9.95. And you could choose a collection of Scat Pack decals for free.

Mellow Yellow

Chrysler came out of the sixties in a much better position than when they went in. Lynn Townsend's stint as chairman was obviously proving successful, even though the buying of Britain's beleaguered Rootes Group for $56 million in 1967 proved not to be such a good idea. Rootes made the aging Hillman, Humber, Sunbeam, Singer, and Commer trucks (or lorries, as trucks are called in Britain). An Americanized version of the quite popular Hillman Avenger, christened the Plymouth Cricket, was marketed in America. It was a worse-than-useless car that rusted out faster than one could cry Road Runner.

Why Chrysler bothered to buy troubled European car companies—they also had control of the French Simca Corporation—was beyond most business analysts. Unless it was trying to follow GM and Ford, both of whom had large and very profitable holdings overseas, holdings they'd had ever since the discovery of the wheel! Chrysler couldn't play in the same league as the big boys and shouldn't have tried. They did have better luck with Mitsubishi of Japan, marketing the Mitsubishi-built Dodge Colt small car quite successfully in the U.S. The Mitsubishi connection would grow over the years.

Plymouth's GTX was higher up the Belvedere ladder than its more famous brother, the Road Runner. The latter concentrated on performance; the GTX liked performance, but with a bit of luxury thrown in for good measure. There were 7,748 GTXs built for 1970.

Another area where Chrysler was well established was Australia. Many of the models sold in Australia were American models assembled locally, but with a certain amount of Australian content. In 1962 the Plymouth Valiant was introduced, and while the car used many American mechanical and body parts, the car was built in Australia. Whenever the American parent company changed the design of the Valiant, Australia got the new shape as well, albeit with certain modifications to suit the market.

In 1970 Chrysler Australia introduced the first performance Valiant. This was the Pacer and was initially fitted with a high-performance version of the famous 225 Slant Six. In 1971 a totally new Valiant debuted. This was a wholly Australian car with an Australian design. Its engine was a 265-cubic-inch Hemi straight six. Although smaller by American standards, the car was the Valiant Charger Model VH.

Mid–model year 1970 saw the introduction of Chrysler's first Cordoba. It was nothing like the midsize personal luxury car that was to follow later. The 1970 model was a luxury, performance-oriented, full-size Newport with knobs on, knobs being gold paint, special vinyl roof, and bodyside moldings, and an "Aztec-Eagle" interior. The engine was the 440-cid V-8, which had been designed to deal with the new federal emissions laws. A mere 1,868 were built.

Just 501 units were built of another large Chrysler. This was the 300-H, not to be mistaken for or part of, the original 300 Letter Series. The "H" in the name stood for Hurst, the transmission people. Hurst was used to making special-edition cars; the company had built Oldsmobile and Pontiac specials before turning to Chrysler.

The Hurst was highlighted by its gold-and-white paint job, a customized fiberglass hood

---

Sitting on the knoll in the late afternoon sun. A 1970 Plymouth GTX awaits an unsuspecting Ford Torino Cobra to pass by. Four-on-the-floor mated to the standard 375-horse 440 V-8 versus a 428, 335-bhp machine. Tromp that gas and move into the passing lane for a quarter-miler at the disused airstrip. And we'll have fun, fun, fun . . .

replete with hood scoop, rear deck spoiler, custom interior, pinstriping, and H70 x 15 white-letter tires. A 440 V-8 heavy-duty suspension, and a floor-mounted Hurst shifter took care of the TorqueFlite transmission. The 300-H was a heavy car that had nothing to be ashamed of when it came to performance. While it was no Daytona, the 300-H was more like a big Grand Tourer with enough clout to frighten off most would-be Pettys on the highway.

Speaking about the Pettys, Plymouth wanted to get Richard back. His year with Ford had been pretty spectacular and he was second only to Dave Pearson, who took the driver's championship. But Petty had seen the Daytona in action and was impressed.

"He'd left because of internal politics," explained Larry Rathgeb. "He wanted to drive the Daytona rather than an outclassed car. There was no agreement and no real chance of an agreement with the leadership that we had at that time. So he decided to leave.

"We had a change of leadership in the interim and set about getting Petty back. We went to him, I believe, and told him we could put a Plymouth together, much like Dodge's Daytona, if

Plymouth's AAR 'Cuda 340 was the ultimate Barracuda of all. AAR stands for All-American Racers, the name of Dan Gurney's racing-car group. Gurney was contracted by Plymouth to prepare and race the 'Cuda, built specifically to compete in the Sports Car Club of America's Trans Am series 1970 season. About 2,800 AAR 'Cudas were built to homologate the car according to SCCA's rules to qualify for competing in Trans Am. Barracudas had a new body for 1970, and the 'Cuda, with its blacked-out grille, flat black hood paint, and functional hood scoop was the standout. Unique to the 'Cuda was its strobe-type tape stripes down either side of the car.

INSET: If you want to announce who you are, let's do it big-time. Letters spelling out AAR are a little on the large size, but hey—this is 1970!

he would return to the fold. He agreed and everybody was happy."

"I remember when I first met Richard Petty," laughed Larry. "It was at the 1964 Atlanta race, and when I first saw him he was under his car, under there beating on the vehicle trying to clear his tire. So I walked over and said my name was Rathgeb, I work for the Chrysler team.

"'Good to meet you,' he said. 'Gee. I've got some problems with this car. It doesn't want to do this, that, and the other thing.' I said, 'Well, why don't you put the wheels back on and I'll show you something.' So he put the wheels back on. Then we looked at the wheels and I said, 'Now see where those wheels are pointing?' He kind of looked and said, 'Yeah. They point straight ahead.' I said, 'Now jack the car up right center in the front.' Then the wheels fell down and they pointed in. 'Geez, that's strange,' I said. Next I told him to drop the jack very quickly and watch the wheels.

And when the car went down the wheels actually steered. That happens to cars depending where the tie rods are in or out, relative to each other.

"Petty looked at me and said, 'What can I do to correct that?' So I said I didn't know because I didn't know what his suspension was. I knew that the inner or outer tie rods would have to be moved vertically in order to correct the problem. Then Lee Petty, Richard's father, came up and said 'Geez, Richard, tell them what it is.'

Larry sat back, drew a breath, and continued. "Richard took the upper arm and we moved it back this far and up this far, and so on. I was writing all this down. Then Lee

This car is one of apparently four Dodge Charger R/T SE models built with the 426 Hemi. SE stood for Special Edition, which meant luxuries such as sun roof and leather seats. Racing-style hood pins were unusual for this model, but in those days a person could build his/her car any way he/she wanted.

INSET: Here's the SE Special Edition emblem. It was on the rear roof pillar. Note the Scat Pack bumble bee in the window.

A sight one rarely, if ever, sees. A 1969 Dodge Charger Daytona (green, foreground) being pursued by the equally charismatic 1970 Plymouth Road Runner Superbird (to give it its full title).

said, 'Tell us what we have to do.' To which I replied, 'Lee, I have to put this through the computer.' 'Well, go! Call it in and tell them to put it through the computer for you,' Lee demanded. So I retorted, 'Lee, it doesn't happen that quickly.' 'No, no. Call!' he cried. So he grabbed me by the shoulder and reached into his pocket to grab some change, and he dragged me over to this pay phone at the racetrack—the phone was in the garage area—and he took his handful of change and threw it down and said, 'Now here. Call that man and tell him what we've got for suspension! We've got to get this thing fixed!'

"So I did. I called my designer and I told him what they, the Pettys, had done to their suspension. To which my designer replied that

it was Friday and he couldn't do anything because the computer was solidly booked. 'I probably won't be able to use the computer to put the suspension in until next Wednesday.' I said I'd see him on Monday; and we found out what had to be done to his inner tie rod and went back to fix it. We did so and I was pleased that he had a decent car at last."

That all happened in 1964 and now it was 1969. The "win-a-race-on-Sunday,-sell-cars-on-Monday" corporate philosophy was looking decidedly anemic around Plymouth's door.

Plymouth was desperate: it wasn't winning races. Recalling turning down the offer to participate in the Daytona program, Plymouth swallowed its pride and went, cap in hand, to the engineers and aerodynamicists and said they wanted a car too. The go-ahead was given and work began on what was to become known as the Superbird. Five months was all the team had to build another winged car. This time a different model, the Road Runner, would be the "donor" vehicle and with it would come other problems.

John Herlitz was manager of Plymouth's intermediate car design studio at the time (today he is director of styling). Although a great believer in aerodynamics, he was horrified when he first saw the Daytona. Gary Romberg, one of the aerodynamicists responsi-

ble for the Daytona, remembers Herlitz's reaction well: "Because the Daytona was selling pretty well," said Romberg, "there was talk of making a real production run out of the car rather than just the required number needed for homologation. So we asked John to come over and look at the car and see if there was anything he could do with it.

"Anyway, I remember being over at Creative with him, looking at this car with all those added parts . . . well, his expression was enough. He looked incredulous as he said the Daytona was world-class ugly."

John's first reaction was to ask if he could change the uprights a little. "We had wanted to do that, anyway," said Gary. "If you look at the uprights, the vertical stabilizers on the Daytona versus the Superbird, you will find they are a little bigger on the 'Bird. Track work the engineers had done indicated larger uprights worked pretty well. So that's how the larger stabilizers came about."

There was no question that any changes could be made to the Daytona. There would be no more built after the allotted five hundred were completed. Now it was Plymouth's

---

When Dodge announced it was building the winged Daytona to race on the ovals, NASCAR ruled 500 were needed to be built to qualify. Dodge did that with ease. When Plymouth said they were building the 'Bird, NASCAR upped the number of cars to be built to 1,500. Plymouth smiled . . . and built 1,920 units with ease. Learning from their experiences with the successful Daytona, they improved the 1970 Superbird by giving it taller stabilizers at the rear. They also improved air cooling at the front.

turn to field a winged car for the 1970 racing season. And it was this car on which John Herlitz and the styling studio were able to exert a little influence.

John Herlitz observed that Gary Romberg's efforts on the Daytona only went to prove that "unbridled aerodynamics can really be ugly!" Dale Rieker, who acted as program overseer, suggested taking the Charger front fenders and Daytona nose cone and attaching them to the Road Runner. This wouldn't work because the Charger's fenders had lines that wouldn't match up.

John Herlitz again: "I said I have to work with the Plymouth front fender! There was no question about that. Then we needed to get the little 'guppy' mouth out of the center grille area and put the air intake underneath. Then with the use of graphics I wanted to raise the visual emphasis back on the front of the car so that it didn't look like it melted!"

Suddenly styling became critical when NASCAR's 1970 rules became known. The often-vacillating NASCAR decreed any new model had to produce as many as there were dealers of the make. Plymouth had 1,920 dealers. So to qualify, that was the number of cars that had to be built.

"All of a sudden we had to sell almost two thousand of these things," said John Herlitz. "We had to get the cars to dealerships so it became more important to make the car look more integrated."

As with the Daytona, B bodies were sent to Creative, which carried out the necessary modifications—stabilizers, nose cone, that sort of thing. Interestingly, the nose cone and stabilizers were made from aircraft aluminum alloy but the retractable headlight doors were fiberglass. Neat little touches by Herlitz to enhance the car's looks included blacking out the headlight doors and adding the Road Runner motif on the left headlight door. A black vinyl roof was added to hopefully make the Superbird more palatable to customers.

The word *Plymouth* in either black or white large letters is emblazoned along the rear quarter panels. And Herlitz got his way with the stabilizers; the Superbird's are wider, swept back further, and taller than the Daytona's.

"In the rush to get everything finished over at Creative," said Herlitz, "we were working on the car trying to figure out how to size the circumference for a big Road Runner bird decal to stick on the stabilizers. Would you believe that here we were in Engineering and we couldn't find a compass to draw this circle. So we ended up using the bottom of a wastebasket!"

Pressing the bottom of the wastebasket against the stabilizer, John traced the outline of the circle that became the guide for 3M to go to work to produce the decal featuring the Road Runner cartoon character encircled by the words *Road Runner Superbird.* Strange how a simple wastebasket saved the day in this technological age of ours.

Wind-tunnel work on the Superbird was kept to a minimum. What testing was done produced almost identical results to the Daytona. Both cars were based upon Chrysler's intermediate B-body, even if the outer sheet metal was different. Next time you see a Superbird or a Daytona, take a close look at the front

fenders, especially those on the 'Bird. Let John Pointer tell the story:

"The Daytona was the Charger 500. We used the '69 body but the '70 Charger had a bowtie type of bumper that backed onto the front fenders, which had a raw, flush-fitting edge. So we used the '70 fenders, matching the nose cone up to them.

"The Coronet had a fairly similar front bumper so we used this model's front fenders and hood on the Plymouth Road Runner body. Now the Dodge had a center peak or crease that finished before the nose cone, while the Superbird carried the motif into the cone. As for the Coronet, this was modified and extended with the use of a piece of metal that was welded along the front. Why? To lengthen the hood to fit flush with the nose cone. Just a metal patch pop-riveted onto the production hood."

Finally the Superbird was finished. It was better looking than the Daytona due to the styling touches exacted by Herlitz. It was also

Road Runners to become Superbirds were designated such. Somehow this 'Bird was sprayed a Road Runner hue; probably there was a hitch on the line. When it reached Creative Industries, the company that did specialized work for Chrysler, it was noted with consternation that the body was the wrong color. What to do? Hurried meetings were held at the assembly line and at Creative, then between the two. In the end it was adjudged to be cheaper to let this one out as it was, rather than send it down the line again for a repaint. And that's the story of this special Superbird. Although the runt in the litter, this 'Bird proved it was just as good as any other under the paint. Chrysler historian Galen Govier of Wisconsin has verified this car is genuine, and therefore unique.

INSET: Hefty Hemi powered all NASCAR Superbirds and a few street versions as well. The engine added almost $1,000 to the price of the car. In 1970, Superbirds and Daytonas won 38 out of 48 NASCAR races.

incredibly fast. Hemi-powered racing versions ran at over 220 mph while the more docile 440, which was the standard engine in the street cars, was still capable of 150.

At the 1970 Daytona contest, Superbirds and Daytonas left everybody standing. Richard Petty was back and driving as well as ever. Pete Hamilton drove his 'Bird at a nearly 150 mph average for the big race. By the season's end, Superbirds beat all comers, particularly Ford, to win twenty-one Grand Nationals out of the thirty-eight first-place finishes taken by Chrysler products. Ford won only six, Chevrolet none. NASCAR didn't like it at all. For 1971, NASCAR would only run cars carrying engines no bigger than 305 cubic inches.

For 1970 Plymouth fielded one of its biggest model lineups ever to hit the streets.

Many of them could be had as plain janes or out and out supercars; besides the already mentioned Superbird, Plymouth pitched a new compact called the Duster. This one was a big surprise; nobody expected it. There were two versions—the ordinary, economical Duster with a new 198-cubic- inch six that replaced the old 170 mill. The 198 engine shares most of its components with the 225-cubic-inch six. Based on the Valiant, which it replaced, the Duster was designed to be all things to all people. But in its performance suit of clothes, the Duster comes alive. Powered by the 340-cubic-inch V-8 with high-flow cylinder heads and high-performance camshaft, manifold, and carburetor, the Duster had a standard three-speed, floor-mounted manual, though most performance buyers would have probably

opted for the four-speed manual with Hurst linkage as the way to go. TorqueFlite automatic was also an option.

Though not as quick as some of the cars in Plymouth's stable, it more than holds its own. According to *Hot Rod* magazine, the quarter could be reached in 15.38 seconds at 91.55 mph. It was a pretty car, with looks that would please the local pastor as well as the car-dreaming kid down the avenue.

An especially nice vehicle was the new 'Cuda. If zipped into its AAR 'Cuda suit, it was wild. *AAR* stood for racing driver Dan Gurney's All American Racers, based in Santa Ana, California. Built to take part in the SCCA's Trans Am series, the AAR came with the 340, which used a six-pack carburetor for the first time. The AAR is also distinguished by its flat black fiberglass hood held down by racing pins. A huge, functional hood scoop delivered ram-air into the engine when needed.

Nobody should have missed an AAR 'Cuda. It had a tell-tale dash-to-ditto racing stripe, which ended in big *Cuda* letters and an *AAR* shield. Colors were wild: Hot Pink, Purple, Lemon Twist, and Lime Green to name a few. As far as performance went, the 340 could fly by to 60 in 5.8 seconds and the quarter-mile was achieved in 14.3 seconds at 99.5 mph. Top speed was estimated at 130 mph, and the car had front disc brakes as another desirable option.

As pony cars go, the Barracuda and its 'Cuda derivatives were among the best looking around. They had psychedelic colors, which really turned 'em on down Haight-Ashbury way. The AAR was better than most. Prepared by the experienced Dan Gurney and his team, and built by Creative Industries in Michigan, the AAR was expected to do better than it did in the Trans Am races. While it was a great street car, the AAR was new, a virgin on the track compared to the very experienced Pontiac Trans Am, Mus-

tang Boss 302, Z-28 Camaros, and all. Some say the 'Cudas were rushed, not given enough preparation to take on competition as tough as the Trans Am. An excellent showing by Mark Donahue's Roger Penske–prepared Javelin and Mustang's obviously unbeatable formula (Mustang won the 1970 championship, by the way) put to flight the Chrysler challenge.

Mention should be made of Dan Gurney's contribution to Chrysler. He had been involved with various aspects of car racing for a long time. Formula 1 racing had always had a big place in his heart, and he designed his own engine and car in which he won the Formula 1 Spa-Francorchamps race. Then he worked for Ford, but left after a disagreement over policy. After that he signed up to help Plymouth prepare for Trans Am.

Another terrific car, this one from performance-minded Dodge, was the very slick Challenger. It shared its new, unitized E-body with the Barracuda but had a 110-inch wheelbase, which was a little longer and heavier than the

Here's an interesting Superbird. Note big wheels, moon-style hubcaps, tell-tale parachute bag at rear. This particular 'Bird dragraced. Engine was a Hemi so the car, with its plentiful aerodynamic qualities, would have won more than lost.

INSET: Unforgettable Superbird motif was the Road Runner bird. Size of roundel was determined by using the bottom of a wastebasket—the designers didn't have a compass and team was under starter's orders to get the car ready in time. Stabilizer tails and the nose cone were made from aluminum alloy; yet retractable headlight doors were fiberglass.

Barracuda's. Quad headlights were a Challenger feature instead of the Barracuda's duals. Although both cars had the same shape, there were enough styling differences to tell the two apart. A bodyside creaseline followed the Challenger's handsome contours (the Barracuda had no such line), and the rear was not so busy as the Challenger's.

Engines in both cars were the same. Life started in the six-cylinder mold with the venerable Slant Six. This was fine for Grandma to visit her chiropodist in, but the young preferred some extra zap. And buyers of either the street Challenger or Barracuda got real power no matter what hot V-8 combination they ordered. There was the 340 'Cuda, 440 Six Pack 'Cuda, and the Hemi 'Cuda. Each car ran wild and free . . . or could be made to run that way provided there was nothing around to get in the way. Of all the 'Cudas, the 340 was the best. It was far better balanced than the other two, weighing 95 pounds less than the 440, and was 255 pounds lighter than the

Hemi version. The strong, lightweight 340 engine was a fraction more than a half second slower to 60 than the Hemi—6.4 seconds versus 5.8 seconds. The 440-6 on the other hand, was in-between the two; and 0–60 happened in 5.9 seconds. The 340's quarter-mile run was 6 mph slower than the Hemi: 14.5 seconds at 96 mph, 14.4 at 100 mph (440-6), and 14.0 at 102 mph.

Much the same results were obtained from the Barracuda sister ship, Dodge's new Challenger pony car. The Challenger T/A 340 Six Pak (Dodge's spelling) was the high-profile street version of the Trans American Sedan Championship racing car. The racing car's design was conducted in-house by Dodge designer Pete Hutchinson. He created the car needed to race, and Dodge farmed out the building of the vehicles to Autodynamics. The racing cars had a highly tuned 305-cubic-inch V-8 pumping out 440 horsepower, while the street machine had the excellent 340, which developed 290 horses.

The Challenger's name and concept was conceived by Dodge Division executive stylist Bob Brownlie. He also brought about the Charger. "The Challenger is not a scaled-down Charger," he said at the time. "The long hood, short deck give the Challenger a definite, traditional Grand Touring look. We call it road appearance."

To keep all that engine power in its place, Dodge gave the T/A the special Rallye Sport suspension. This consisted of an extra-large front sway bar, one at the rear, increased rear spring camber, heavy-duty shocks all around, and Sure-Grip differential. This worked pretty well, but there was a tendency for the rear wheels to hop in sudden or panic braking.

Like the 'Cudas, Dusters, and Darts, the Challenger employed wild paint schemes and outrageous graphics. A flat black fiberglass hood—few, if any, ever fitted properly—contrasted with the rainbow-bright hues adorning the cars. One of the colors, a sort of lime green, was called Sublime by Dodge. A very pleasing black side stripe sandwiched in between a much narrower black line began at the tip of the front fenders and moved gracefully to the C-pillars, where it ended. *T/A* in big block letters was displayed prominently within the stripe, just ahead of the front windshield frame.

SCCA required 2,500 Challenger T/As and

2,500 AAR 'Cudas to be built to homologate the cars for racing. Dodge made 2,539 for the model year, Plymouth 2,724 AAR 'Cudas. And that was that. The Trans Am Sedan Championship began in 1966 and called it a day after the 1970 season. A wind of change was beginning to blow through the corridors of Detroit and Dearborn. The Feds were breathing down

Here are some of the men who create the cars we love. These men were responsible for the "winged warriors," the 1969 Daytona, and 1970 Superbird. They are, from left to right: John Pointer, Gary Romberg, Larry Rathgeb, John P. Wehrly (he designed the second Hemi engine), Frank Chianese Jr., and R. L. Lajoie. All were either specialized-vehicle engineers, aerodynamicists, or engine designers.

A 1969 Dodge Daytona with a 440 Six-Pack and a 1970 Plymouth Superbird with the 426 Hemi get ready for a brief but exotic sprint. To see the two together was rare indeed, especially on a public highway.

the auto makers' necks with more and more safety requirements to be met by such and such a date; for example, 5 mph safety bumpers had to be on all cars by 1973. So Ford pulled factory support from the race, and so did Chrysler and the others. This heralded the beginning of the end of an extraordinary era in American automobile manufacture, an era that has already gone down in history as the most exciting in three-quarters of a century of car making.

A wind of change may have been blowing, but there were still some good cars to come. It turned out that 1970 was the last really wilder-than-wild year. Plymouth promoted all its muscle under the Rapid Transit System banner, and what muscle it was. The Road Runner, GTX, and Satellite could be had with a new Air Grabber flip-up hood scoop that was operated by an under-the-dash switch. When the driver wanted air—presto! He got it in spades by flipping said switch. Once again the free-

thinking Plymouth stylists designed the sides of the Air Grabber with much the same cartoony eyes and teeth that distinguished the legendary P-40 fighters belonging to the Flying Tigers squadron in World War II.

Dodge called its latest campaign Scat City. "Scat City is anywhere competition is hot, keen, and sanctioned," began the copy for an eight-page advertisement. The first photograph is of a Daytona winging its way to victory, which more or less tells the reader what to expect. Well, Dodge hired some of the top dragster and racing drivers to try out the new 1970 cars. Which seemed a logical thing to do, all things considered. After all, Dodge cars were winning the drag-racing championships and beginning to show the way on the oval circuits as well.

Almost as if it were destined to happen simultaneously, the world's most influential and successful pop group disbanded. John, Paul, George, and Ringo decided to call it quits while still so far ahead. It was Paul McCartney who was the main motivator behind the split, and with their end a great void opened up that has yet to be filled. Jimi Hendrix died, so did Janis Joplin, both from drugs. A dreadful tragedy overtook student protesters at Kent State University, Ohio, when National Guardsmen fired indiscriminately into a crowd of youngsters. Two young men and two girls were killed, eight others injured.

The way things were going, one might be forgiven for thinking pop stars had a wish to be in the obituary columns. It started with Otis Redding's death in a plane crash in 1967, then Frankie Lymon dying from a heroin overdose in 1968. Rolling Stone Brian Jones drowned in his swimming pool in 1969, Hendrix and Joplin were gone in 1970. In 1971 a troubled Jim Morrison of the Doors died in Paris; 1950s rock 'n' roller Gene Vincent passed away from a bleeding ulcer; and Duane Allman was killed in a motorcycle accident. There was an uneasy feeling abroad that the youth movement was fast fading away, and the muscle-car revolution was about to die like its rock 'n' roll mentors.

Chrysler hung on in 1971 with all-new models. The real King of the Hill, the Superbird, was gone, never to return. But the restyled Road Runner was an attractive package, all said and done. The very curvaceous, rounded fuselage-shaped body was shared by the GTX and both were models of the Satellite series. Wheelbase was 115 inches and the cars had a three-inch wider rear track, which helped handling considerably.

A new chrome oval bumper circled the front plastic grille, but the buyer had a choice of color-keyed bumpers if he/she so wished. As in previous years, the 383-cubic-inch engine was standard, though horsepower had dropped by 35 in the Road Runner, 30 in the GTX. Pressure was being exerted on Detroit to cut back on performance across the board. Mopar wasn't quite

---

Apart from the fabled 300 Letter Series, Chrysler didn't bother too much about performance, preferring to leave such things to its lesser siblings to play with. Chrysler did have the assembly-line 300 series, which used to be the Windsor until 1962. Engine was the big 440 putting out 350 bhp. Almost 225 inches long on a 124-inch wheelbase, the Chrysler 300 truthfully belonged to another age. Its rounded "fuselage" styling was introduced in 1969. The 300 weighed 4,175 pounds and cost $4,580 in 1970.

An impressive 24,817 Duster coupes were built. This was the 340 version of 1970. It came with tuned suspension, wide tires, front disc brakes, and an economical price. With the 340, Duster was on a par with other compact Mopars.

so ready to comply as was Ford, GM, and AMC, but it lowered horsepower on the 440 by 5, to 385 horses. The Hemi was still offered with no change in specifications.

Road tests of the two cars produced 0–60 times of 6.7 seconds and 14.84 at 94.5 seconds. Top speed was probably in the region of 130 mph. Overall handling was good in the American idiom, though understeer and wheel hop were still disconcertingly present. Straight-line performance had been the American Way since the fifties, and nothing could touch a muscle car on its own turf. Give it a few sharp left and right handers and life took on a new meaning: if you survived the experience, that is! To be fair, these cars were quite good if an adept driver was piloting them, but a Hemi-powered Road Runner in inexperienced hands could be dangerous.

Speaking of Hemi engines, 1971 would be the last year Chrysler offered them. They were only available in the Road Runner and GTX, the latter of which was in its final year. Its ride was as hard as nails, much harder than any other Chrysler intermediate. So hard that it was like riding an unforgiving plank on an equally unforgiving washboard road. Road testers hated the ride, saying it wasn't justified because it only made the car's handling "adequate." As people say about roving tomcats, the GTX had a short life but a merry one. Born in 1967, it was gone by the end of 1971, the victim of circumstance . . . and insurance companies. That the public was distancing themselves from muscle cars in droves by 1971 is evidenced by the sharply declining sales across the board; only 2,942 GTXs were produced, and the Road Runner dropped to 14,218 units.

Plymouth's compact Duster had been a hit when it was introduced in 1970. It shared the Valiant sedan's 108-inch wheelbase and much else besides. There was a range of engines on tap, from the Slant Six, a 318 2-bbl V-8, and the raunchy 340 2-bbl V-8, the latter developing 275 horsepower. All the suspension and performance goodies were available for what was Plymouth's least expensive muscle car. In all, 218,000 Dusters left the factory in 1970, 24,817 of them being 340 versions.

Graphics were all the rage on the 1971 Duster 340. A flat black hood could be ordered with the numerals *340* emblazoned in white across the driver's side. Within the *4* of the *340*, the word *Wedge* was stenciled in orange. A black stripe curved its way along the sides of this fancy and still potent Duster, ending in the graphics *340*. Highback buckets filled the interior; they, or headrests, were one of the safety features all cars had to have from 1969 on.

Sister division Dodge was beginning to feel the performance pinch, although it wasn't knuckling under as fast as other makes. After all, Dodge had built an enviable performance image for itself and wasn't too keen to lose it overnight. The 1971 Challenger was a case in point. Apart from a recessed split grille and new graphics, the Challenger was the same as the previous year. There were some casualties in the Challenger lineup; the RT/SE and R/T convertible were dropped, and so was the 440 Magnum V-8 (the 385-hp 440 Six-Pack remained); but the 426 Hemi stayed. Sales in 1971 crashed 60 percent over 1970, with only 4,630 Challenger R/Ts made. Of these, a desultory 71 were Hemi equipped. There was a new model cloned from Plymouth's Duster compact. Called the Dodge Demon 340, it replaced the Dart Swinger as the division's performance compact.

Only eighty-five Hemi-powered Dodge Chargers were built in 1971, the last year the Hemi would be offered, though it would continue to be available to racing teams. Chargers for 1971 came with an all-new, svelte "coke bottle"–shaped, semi-fastback design that was extremely handsome to look at. Standard engine was the 318 rated at 230 bhp, followed by the optional 383 in 275- or 300-horsepower guise. Standard engine on the Charger R/T was the 440-cubic-inch developing 370 hp or an optional 385. These slippery, long-hood, short-rear-deck Chargers gave a good account of themselves at NASCAR in 1971 and would continue to do so for a little longer. Motown was hurriedly winding down its performance image in the face of ballooning insurance premiums underscored by new surcharges if the car happened to fit into the muscle category. Really, it was just an excuse for the insurance companies to take more money off the backs of the embattled motorist who enjoyed a little

Measuring 209.7 inches overall, the Super Bee sat on a 117-inch wheelbase. Like most Dodges for 1970, the Super Bee was identified by its large, chrome-wrapped split grille. No other Dodge had split grilles; they had one-piece loops in heavy chrome.

Standard engine for a car known for its muscle was the famous 225-cid, 145-horse Slant Six. This 1970 Challenger didn't have that engine; it had the sprightly 230-horse 318. As can be seen, this model is the convertible, of which 3,173 were built in the lowest price range. A step up was the R/T.

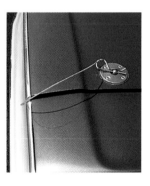

INSET: Gas cap on side of fender emulates racing type. Challengers did race in the Trans Am competition.

Another Challenger R/T racing touch is the hood pins. Many ultra-sporty cars had these.

excitement in his driving. In Australia, the opposite was happening when it came to performance.

Australia had favored American or American-type cars ever since the thirties. A haughty Britain still considered its overseas dominions as "captive" markets for its wares. With no regard to vastly different climatic conditions in Australia as compared to Britain, car manufacturers exported homespun products with no modifications to cope with the different environment. "If it works in blighty, it'll work anywhere, old boy" was the credo.

Many British-built cars still contained quite a bit of wood in their manufacture, at least up until the mid-to-late thirties. American mass-production cars had tossed out wood by 1934 and were of all-steel construction. And with the various climates America possesses, Detroit built cars to cope with heat and cold. So Australia was a good bet to sell cars.

Down Under has a lot of desert regions mostly peopled by termites. Large, hungry termites. One sniff of a British-built car with all that mouthwatering wood in the body was enough to send the little creatures into a state of frenzied excitement. Any farmer who owned a Humber or Morris, and had a termite city close by, would shortly find the termites had invaded his car and had either eaten or carted off the wood within. Result: one collapsed and useless vehicle.

But not so with the Americans. There was nothing more galling to a self-respecting termite than an all-steel car. It was either move on or starve. Naturally Australians took to the big, comfortable Yankee cars in a big way. Therefore, it wasn't long before GM, Ford, and Chrysler had most of Australia's car market to themselves. Ford had been in Australia since 1914, when it began shipping Model Ts in, CKD (completely knocked down) for local assembly. GM arrived in 1931, when it took over Australia's most famous make, the Holden. Chrysler came along much later.

Shipping American, or Canadian-built American cars, for assembly in Australia went on for years. Chrysler started building the Valiant from 1962. Then, in 1971, Chrysler introduced the Valiant Charger.

The Charger was wholly designed and built in Australia along with an all-new Valiant VH Series, which was also completely Australian. It was a fastback design and showed its American lineage with its recessed rear window and flowback C-pillars.

It was an amazingly fast car, powered by a Hemi OHV in-line six-cylinder 265-cid engine that developed 270 bhp at 5,000 rpm. The engine was fitted with 3-2 barrel Weber carburetors, had a compression ratio of 10, and could easily make 120 mph with its three-speed manual transmission. Suspension was like U.S. Dodges: torsion bars and leaf springs. Brakes were eleven-inch disc/drum.

Road testers for Australia's *Modern Motor* magazine were high in their praise for what was considered the best supercar around (the others

The 1970 Dodge Diamante Challenger is a one-off show car with a fancy body and down-home Challenger underpinnings. It had the Hemi, of course. This is a two-seater pony sports car, and quite a good looking machine at that. Joe Bortz, famed show-car collector of Chicago, owns this one.

were Ford's Falcon and the Holden Monaro). Its 0–60 was 6.3 seconds, and its quarter in 14.8 seconds at 91 mph.

One of the reasons Chrysler built the Charger was quite evident: for stock-car racing. For the Australians, racing on road and track wasn't as dramatic or as successful as for their American cousins; there were certainly no clean sweeps. Part of the problem was Ford's highly developed Falcon GT-HO Series, which won virtually everything in sight. By 1974, the tables turned. Australian racing champion John McCormack was approached to race in the increasingly popular Sports Sedan class. He agreed and decided to go with the Charger. They debuted at Adelaide International Raceway in February 1974.

Competition was fierce in the free and easy Sports Sedan class, where rules allowed almost as much improvisation as needed. McCormack won the Adelaide race against some pretty tough contenders. For the next couple of seasons, the Super Charger won almost everything in sight. There was one major disadvantage, though, and something that would never be allowed in American racing: the Charger was powered by a Repco-Holden 5-liter V-8! In other words, a rival make's engine.

It wasn't long before those not in agreement with fast cars started to make their opinions

Movie companies tended to use Mopar cars for the rough stuff. The villains used a Dodge Charger in *Bullitt,* a Challenger in *Vanishing Point,* and of course the *Dukes of Hazzard* wouldn't have got anywhere without their Dodge Charger. A bunch of them were used in the TV series. The 1970 Dodge Challenger R/T convertible was a sleek, attractive pony. After 1971, there would be no more convertibles from Chrysler for some time.

felt. Just as in America, the Australians suffered politicians trying to make a name for themselves by attacking or wanting to ban some aspect of the automobile. "Bullets on wheels," accused one politician in the middle of a media blitz on supercars. At the time, Chrysler was making a limited two-hundred-unit run of a special Charger dubbed the E49. With all the flack bursting about them, Chrysler stopped thinking about building more E49 models. So too did Ford and Holden, both of whom were likewise putting together limited runs of super specials.

During its short life, the Australian Charger offered several engine options. There were three Hemi sixes (215-, 245-, and 265-cubic-inch displacement engines) and two V-8s (a 318 and 340), which were American designed. In 1972 the Charger finally got a four-speed manual transmission as a $155 (Australian) option in place of the less desirable three-speed unit. It was designed, developed, and built in Australia

THE BEAT GOES ON . . . IN AUSTRALIA

Here's something similar but very different. An Australian-built 1968 Chrysler Valiant four-door sedan (above). Although the Valiant had been assembled in Australia since 1962, it was mostly from U.S. parts. As time went on Valiants became increasingly Australian sourced. When this Valiant was assembled, a lot of original Australian design was going into the cars. Although still being assembled with a lot of imported U.S. parts, the Valiant was becoming more Australian by the day. Six-cylinder power was the standard engine in the early days. Rear shows similarity to U.S. Valiant, though Australian Valiant features more chrome trim than its U.S. counterpart. Australian-designed grille is quite different from American Valiant's of the same year.

INSET, TOP: Valiant's interior is very American in concept, even feel. Seats, door panels are blue . . . refreshing after all the black ones seen in America. Dashboard design is finished off in fake wood and blue plastic. Overall, the car has a very neat, attractive interior.

INSET, BOTTOM: Attractive taillights and lots of chrome distinguish sturdy Valiant. Car was a favorite in Australia due to its robust construction and indestructible mechanical parts.

This is a 1973 Valiant Charger 770 in an English setting. The first Australian Charger came out in 1971 and was an immediate hit. Although a few hundred Aussie Chargers were exported to England, almost all were 770s, which was considered the luxury model of this otherwise high-performance automobile.

Australia shares much in common with the U.S. Both are large
countries originally colonized by the British, have similar weather
patterns, and have a strong independent spirit. And like latter-day
Americans, Australians thought muscle cars were the way to go.
Hence the all-Australian Chrysler Valiant Charger shown here.
Australian 1972 Charger is just that . . . Australian. Totally, completely. The car was designed and assembled in Australia and featured a hemispherical six-cylinder engine that, like the kangaroo,
was not found anywhere else. With a length of 173.5 inches, the car
was three feet shorter than the U.S. Charger's 208 inches. Here the
Charger sits atop a hill overlooking the famous City of Portsmouth,
the major British naval base. Far away in the distance, you can see
the sea.

INSET: Interior of Charger 770 is very American in design. I could
have sworn that steering wheel was lifted from the 1970 AAR '
Cuda. There were several distinct Charger models. The base Charger,
Charger XL, Charger 770, and high-performance Charger R/T. The
Australian magazine *Modern Motor* road-tested an R/T equipped
with the 265-cid, 270-bhp Hemi straight-six Six Pack, and achieved
0–60 in 6.3 seconds. There were three versions of the Hemi, all
designed and built solely in Australia.

RIGHT, MIDDLE: Kick-up rear spoiler is an integral part of Australian
Charger. Note Charger script on side.

RIGHT, BOTTOM: Chargers exported to Britain all had V-8 power. The
most powerful was the 340 developing 275 bhp. This engine is
the 318 V-8 rated at 230 horses.

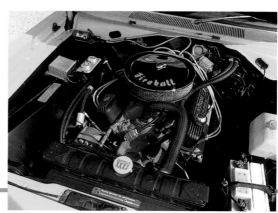

by Borg Warner, in the hope that it might give the attractive car a better chance on the racing circuits.

By 1976 Charger sales had dropped from 50 percent to a mere 8 percent of Valiant sales. Performance cars across the board felt the pinch from the vocal minority that had now become the majority. After four years' production the Charger passed on to that great motorpool in the sky. A few years later, 1981 to be exact, Chrysler's new chairman, Lee Iacocca, sold what was left of Chrysler Australia to Mitsubishi due to the American parent company's deteriorating financial health.

Aussie Chargers were not exported to the United States, though several hundred of the 31,857 total production were sent to England. It is believed there is one residing in Georgia, and it may well be the only one in the country. The Valiant and Valiant Charger shown on these pages were photographed in England.

It had become painfully obvious that the seventies were going to be devoid of the excitement and creativity of the sixties. The anti-Vietnam protest continued to disrupt America's social conscience even though half the troops had been withdrawn. Louis Armstrong, the world's greatest jazz trumpeter, died, as did the Soviet Union's flamboyant ex-premier, Nikita Krushchev. Talk of high car insurance, gas economy, and smaller engines prompted America's car makers to think along new lines. Only Chrysler, overloaded with huge, fuselage-shaped behemoths, paid little attention to what was coming . . . and almost lost the shirt off its back as a result.

In 1972 America's motor industry switched to SAE net horsepower ratings to describe engine power. On paper this looked as though horsepower had been drastically reduced, which was not the case at all. The old gross horsepower system measured what an engine put out from just the block and heads. SAE meant the

true horsepower once the engine had everything attached. If an engine had been rated at 385 bhp gross, under the SAE system that had been used in Europe since time began, that horsepower was "down" to 280. Which is where it always was, anyway.

None of Chrysler's intermediates or compacts changed much for 1972. Only the large cars got a moderate facelift with new grilles and trim. To comply with the new low-lead gasoline requirements and stiffer emissions standards, Chrysler reduced compression ratios across the board. Torque outputs were reduced and Six-Pack carburetors were becoming a thing of the past. Still, a late supercar buyer could take comfort in the fact that the 340 was available in the 'Cuda and Challenger Rallye (this replaced the R/T model). Standard engine in the Challenger was the docile 318 with the 340 as an option. The 'Cuda fared better; the 340 was its standard mill.

The year 1971 found an all-new Dodge Charger. *Car & Driver* magazine said that "far and away it's 1971's best styled new car." It was Highland Park's last real gasp on the muscle-car set. The movement was winding down dramatically.

INSET: With the block-busting 440 Magnum, the Charger could still hurtle up to 60 in a reasonable 6.5 seconds. In 1968, though, a Charger could roar to 60 in 4.8 seconds.

As for the once-glorious Road Runner and Dodge Charger, engine sizes and power were reduced. The Road Runner was demoted from the 383 (this excellent engine had been consigned to the scrapheap) to the 340. The Charger's biggest engine was the new corporate 400-cid V-8 rated at either 190 or 255 SAE net. The Demon/Duster pair had the 340 as standard and remained quite potent.

There were still a couple of innovative rock bands and singers around in 1972, mostly from England. David Bowie released his excellent, cult-defined *Ziggy Stardust* album and almost became the part. Debut albums also came from the outrageous Alice Cooper and Roxy Music, the latter whose sexy album sleeve was probably more memorable than the record within. In world political events, Vietnam dragged on; President Nixon visited China as a prerequisite to better relations; three months later came the Watergate break-in, which eventually led to the breaking of a President. Britain suspended Northern Ireland's provisional government and imposed direct rule on the troubled province. At the Olympic Games, tragedy struck when Arabs massacred eleven Israeli competitors.

It was 1973 and, in the automotive world, 1955 all over again. Sales reached record levels with over 11 million new cars sold. Chrysler was happy to have had a hand in the numbers sold: Plymouth broke its own production record with almost 900,000 cars built. Dodge was next with 665,000 units produced, and Chrysler manufactured 234,000, including its millionth car on June 26.

All cars had to have five-mile-per-hour-mandated bumpers, front and rear. These were bigger and uglier than ever before and were attached to springs that telescoped in and out if the front or rear if the car was hit.

And in 1973 President Nixon was suffering mightily over the embarrassment of Watergate.

According to the *Washington Post*, whose reporters, Bob Woodward and Carl Bernstein, uncovered the sordid affair, the White House was more than implicated. Several White House aides resigned and a Senate committee began hearings on the case.

For those who hadn't gone to Vietnam or died of drugs, the days of psychedelic music and muscle cars were noticeably on the wane. They had reached adulthood, gotten married, were having children, and thinking of house payments and sensible family cars. Not cars to hold a dance in, but small, economical cars. Like the ones from Japan. Chrysler imported Mitsubishis that were called Dodge Colts. They sold extremely well because they were cheap to buy, had the sort of quality control Detroit appeared to have forgotten about, and were

economical. Plymouth, on the other hand, was saddled with its awful English import, the Cricket. The car was terrible; it was everything the Japanese cars were not. It failed dismally. In 1975 Plymouth gave up on a bad job.

The events of October 1973 would have a profound effect on the world, an effect that has been reverberating ever since. The Arabs shut off their oil for what comes naturally . . . essentially, more money. The winter of 1973–74 was long and bitter for American motorists standing in long gas lines.

Car production fell by 24 percent during the year in which President Nixon, faced with the threat of impeachment, resigned. He became the first U.S. President ever to do so. That year, 1974, was not a good one for America; somehow the nation lost its way. Chrysler also lost its way, with total company car sales down by 26 percent. Stuck with Big Berthas designed in happier days, Chrysler found its compact

The 1971 Challenger poses in an idyllic landscape. Challenger also had the idyllic engine in the form of the 340 developing 275 horses.

Completely new fuselage-type styling complemented the 1971 Plymouth Road Runner and its midsize siblings. Road Runner came with 383-cid V-8 developing 300 bhp.

cars were the ones selling. Hot cars across the board were not. The best-selling Charger was the luxury-oriented SE, which like the standard hardtop coupe, could be had with the 400- or 440-cubic-inch engines.

Really quite attractive was that year's Road Runner, with its over-the-roof stripe that started behind the headlights. Standard engine on what was once one of the hottest muscle cars ever to see blacktop was the 318 with nothing else to offer. Not that anybody wanted anything else; the public would have been happy with any engine so long as it was economical. However, the Road Runner's sibling, the Satellite, did offer a 275-horse (SAE net) 440 for a little more go.

Things got worse in 1975. The big talking point was the huge price increases meted out by the car companies. They blamed Washington and its politicians for forcing them to raise prices to recover the costs of all the safety and emissions controls the government ordered. Of course the politicians countered with the premise that the auto industry created its own mess.

Chrysler chairman Lynn Townsend, who had guided the company to many years of profitability, hiked prices for the third time in a year. He had no love for politicians. With a deepening recession touched off by the oil embargo, Townsend responded to the government's criticism by saying it hadn't done anything to help sales of new cars. With the chairman of America's third largest auto company blaming the government, Michigan's senators and congressmen quavered a bit when Chrysler laid off eighteen thousand workers. An election year was fast approaching so it is not improbable to suppose these politicians were kneeling at the foot of their beds praying frantically for salvation.

The company's sales tumbled alarmingly (by 34 percent) in 1975. One Chrysler that did surprisingly well was the new Cordoba two-door personal car. Exactly 150,105 were built of this quite handsome machine that looked as though it had borrowed a few ideas from Chevrolet's Monte Carlo (at least it didn't have front swivel seats). Standard engine in this car with vertical opera windows and a half vinyl roof was the 360; options included the 318- and 400-cid units.

It might be worth mentioning what kind of acceleration figures the Cordoba was getting with the 400-cid option: 0–60 took 12.5 seconds. In light of the car's two-ton weight, emissions controls, and a compression ratio of 8.2:1, this really wasn't too bad. However, fuel economy was pretty terrible: 13 mpg was the combined average with the 400-cid developing 175 net horsepower. Not exactly what the Feds were looking for, methinks!

Lynn Townsend retired as chairman of Chrysler Corporation on October 1 at the age of fifty-six. Whatever one might think of Townsend, he gave Chrysler some pretty good years. It was going to be interesting to see how the new chairman, John Riccardo, would make out.

With two seasons to go before the end, the Dodge Challenger. Standard engine was a 318. Then came the 340 followed by the 440. This model is the 1973 Challenger Rallye and only 8,123 units were built; more than 32,000 standard Challengers were made in '73. As pleasant to behold as it was, seeing the Challenger in profile makes you realize that the bumpers were there for decoration only. A slight thump, front or rear, would mean real damage. Small wonder the feds insisted upon 5 mph impact bumpers.

All in all, 1975 was an American nightmare, the year the well ran dry. Everything that could go wrong did go wrong. A humiliating, ignominious pullout from Vietnam signaled the nasty business was finally over, but at what cost? Almost sixty thousand young Americans who returned home in pine boxes—that was the cost. There was spiraling inflation and prices everywhere were higher. Most of the new cars had an inflationary spiral of their own, and one that would cheerfully continue unabated until they were well into five figures.

The nice but somewhat dull-looking, sporty Duster continued in 1976, the year a little known peanut farmer, Jimmy Carter, from the equally little known town of Plains, Georgia, won the presidency. A famous Chrysler bit the dust, the luxurious Imperial. Well, it did and it didn't. It returned as the Chrysler New Yorker Brougham . . . the same car, different moniker. Energetic Dodge supremo Robert McCurry was now VP for the Chrysler Division and was more than pleased when the Brougham sold almost forty thousand units.

Dodge and Plymouth fielded a new car each this spartan year. Both were compacts built on a new F-body platform. They were announced

midyear and were intended to replace the Valiant and Dart, the parents to the once-upon-a-time excitement of the 'Cuda and Challenger. The new cars were the Plymouth Volare (the late Dean Martin had a hit single with a song called "Volare" once) and the Dodge Aspen, which was probably named after the famed Colorado ski resort. Both had Chrysler's venerable 225-cubic-inch Slant Six as standard, and the 318 V-8 was an option if the buyer wanted a little more pep.

Though entirely conventional in every way, the Aspen and Volare were volume-car hits. Production was 220,000 for the Aspen, 300,000 for the Volare. There were several models for each car, varying from low to luxury. But no muscle. In fact nobody bothered much with performance cars; small cars, economical cars were wanted.

People who traded in their indestructible Valiants and Darts for the new compacts were in for a big disappointment. The Volare and Aspen weren't a patch on the cars they replaced. According to Lee Iacocca, in his 1984 book, *Iacocca: An Autobiography*, Chrysler hadn't given enough time to developing the cars. They

It turned out that 1974 was the final year for the unique American muscle car. In light of the Arab oil embargo, expensive gas, emissions, safety, and insurance companies charging more for less, cars like the 440-powered 1974 Plymouth Road Runner, once the hero of the young, were alone and unwanted. Even with the 440, the '74 Road Runner had lost much of its power due to lower compression ratios, reduced horsepower—that sort of thing. But it went out in a smart suit of clothes knowing that it would never be forgotten by a world that loved the days when ultimate road power was king. Exactly 11,555 Road Runners were built before production ended in March 1974.

were full of problems: poor workmanship/quality harkened back to 1957, hoods would fly open, they would stall when one stepped on the gas. I remember renting a Volare in 1976 only to have the embarrassment of the car stalling when trying to accelerate from a traffic light. And like the '57s, Volares and Aspens rusted out prematurely, particularly the fenders.

To give Chrysler its due, the company honored the mistakes. Three and a half million Volares came back to the dealerships and were repaired at Chrysler's cost at a time when it could ill afford to cough up a lot of money. A further $109 million was spent on replacing rusted-out fenders, fenders that should never have rusted out if somebody had thought about rustproofing them. Having come back from the brink of destruction after the 1957 workmanship fiasco, Chrysler really didn't need a repeat of that disaster.

Another nonperformance car was the very successful Cordoba. There was little problem with quality or workmanship here. In sales it was second only to the Monte Carlo, from which it got its reason for being. Mind you, the Cordoba's 120,000 production total was three times less than the Monte Carlo but still surprisingly good.

Two new compacts, the luxurious Chrysler LeBaron and Dodge Diplomat, entered the fray in 1977. Both were on the new corporate M-body, which was based upon the F-body platform. Both cars sold quite well, the LeBaron nearly 55,000 units, and the Diplomat 38,000. Optional T-bar roofs came with the hot-selling Cordoba and its kissin' cousin, the Dodge

Charger SE. The latter had lost all its muscle to become another soft-riding luxury automobile.

If the late seventies were lacking in imaginative automobiles, they certainly didn't lack for tragedy. On August 16, 1977, Elvis Presley was found dead in his Graceland home from heart failure that had been compounded by weight, drugs, and other complications. The world wept at his demise. Later in the year British singer Marc Bolan of T Rex died in a car accident. He had hits with "Telegram Sam," "Get It On," and "Hot Love."

Not counting the Mitsubishi-built Plymouth Arrow coupes, the GT, GS, and 160, there was nothing remotely muscular in Chrysler's camp for the rest of the seventies, not even boy-racer, go-faster stripes. The Arrow coupes had go-faster badging and stripes purely for affect. There were no guts in the standard 1.6-liter engine, a little more in the 2.6 Silent Shaft motor. The corporation made news in 1978 by producing the Dodge Omni and Plymouth Horizon. Both were subcompacts on the new L-platform. Both Omni and Horizon were the very first American front-drive small cars. The engine was an overhead-cam 1.7-liter four supplied by Volkswagen. Both cars sold like

---

Personal luxury had replaced the great performance cars of the past; the Charger was gone and in its place came the 1979 Dodge Magnum, replete with all the goodies plus T-tops. Standard mill was the famous 318, and optional was the 360 rated at either 150 or 195 horsepower (NET), depending on which engine was picked.

hotcakes: almost 82,000 Omnis and close to 107,000 Horizons.

Even with healthy compact and subcompact sales, Chrysler was sinking into what could be described as a quicksand. Already sunk like the dinosaurs of old were Chrysler's traditional big cars. They had sung their last hurrah and would be consigned to limbo forever more. The Dodge Royal Monaco and Chrysler Newport/ New Yorker were gone after 1978. Appearing for one year only was the svelte Cordoba 300. More of a luxury option package rather than an updated version of the legendary 300 Letter Series, the Cordoba 300 contained none of the rip-roaring power delivered by its namesakes in the fifties and sixties. Never mind that it had a 360-cid V-8 delivering 195 bhp NET, the engine was sanitized and gutless to the point that four-cylinder Japanese go-faster cars would whistle by with the minimum of effort. However, as a luxury personal car, the 300 was one of the nicest around, and a great starlet hauler on L.A.'s Mulholland Drive.

Things were looking particularly bad at

The Chrysler Cordoba personal luxury car had been a huge hit for Chrysler; between 1975 and 1978, over half a million Cordobas had been built. In 1979, a special, all-white edition of the Cordoba was announced: the Cordoba 300. Once again the great name had been revived; Cordoba's 300 had the traditional blacked-out grille, was well made, and came with an all-red interior upholstered in Corinthian leather. Luxury abounded, but alas, no performance. While it had the 360 V-8 rated at 195 bhp as standard, the engine was lame compared to the "good old days." Nevertheless, the Cordoba 300 was a standout car in dull 1979.

Chrysler, so bad in fact that John Riccardo approached the government for temporary financial assistance. Washington's response was initially unsympathetic; they said they would look into what could be done. Possibly guarantees for private loans to Chrysler. President Carter said the troubles were Chrysler's own fault; they should build more fuel-efficient cars. Then help came. A possible savior. Lee Iacocca, the motoring whiz kid behind so many of Ford's successes, joined Chrysler on the day the company announced a third-quarter loss of almost $160 million.

A fine and proud company was at death's door.

There's a Viper in My Soup

As it turned out, Lee Iacocca was the right man for the daunting task at hand: to save Chrysler from following the road to oblivion like so many car companies had done before. He was to be Chrysler's guardian angel, a man with faith in his commitment to put the company back on track. The year 1980 was a depressingly dark time at Highland Park; one could almost sense the Angel of Death hovering at the end of each corridor.

Iacocca was born of Italian parentage, a first-generation American whose parents arrived in the New World in 1902. His father, Nicola Iacocca, was only twelve when he came to America, and lived with older brothers who had already settled here. Working hard as an apprentice shoemaker in Allentown, Pennsylvania, young Nicola saved enough money to return to Italy in 1921, ostensibly to bring his widowed mother back to America with him. While in the country of his birth, Nicola met,

Once Lee Iacocca successfully brought Chrysler back to the land of the living, thought of sporty cars returned when Bob Lutz joined the company. There were a number of go-faster boy racers, such as 1984's Laser Turbo, with its 2.2-liter Mitsubishi engine. However, there was a bit of oomph in the very-limited-production, one-year-only Dodge Spirit R/T four-door sedan. It had a DOHC intercooled multivalved four-cylinder engine that really could move. Rear of Spirit has a typical early-nineties Chrysler look. Rather boxy and square with a touch of deja-vu about it. Think of the Chryslers that you could wear your hat in. European-type turn signals were a sensible feature. Bright red color, solid finish marked the 1993 Dodge Spirit as quite a quality car. Trouble is so few knew about the car that it virtually sank without a trace. Grille, bumpers, even wheels are color-keyed to the Spirit.

fell in love, and married a seventeen-year-old girl named Antoinette. Shortly afterward, he returned to Allentown with his bride and mother and set up house. Three years later, on October 15, 1924, Lee Iacocca entered the world.

By the time Lee was born, his father had opened a successful hot dog restaurant called the Orpheum Weiner House. Soon it became a family business with Lee's uncles as partners. To this day, Lee's cousins still make hot dogs; and there was a time Lee thought he might go into the hot dog business himself. Fortunately for Ford and Chrysler, he didn't. Fate took a hand in ensuring the young Iacocca stayed away from restaurants and food when his father, now running several enterprises, decided to go into the car-rental business. So he bought into a national chain called

U-Drive-It. Soon Nicola Iacocca had a fleet of rental cars numbering thirty in all . . . and most were Fords.

Because of his father, Lee was around cars a great deal of the time and soon developed a fascination for them. A friend who was an auto retailer encouraged young Lee's interest and from that moment on, Lee knew that cars were the only way for him to go.

A serious bout of rheumatic fever sidelined Lee for six months. When he tried to enlist at the beginning of World War II, Lee was turned down as a 4F. He tried to convince the air force he was perfectly healthy, but his pleas fell on deaf ears. Fate, it appears, had taken a hand once again, because Lee enrolled at

Chrysler's latest LeBaron model first arrived on the scene in 1987 and became an instant hit, reasons for which are obvious. It was the best looking car ever to appear on the J-car platform. It was curvy instead of being square, it looked youthful, feminine, the convertible version appealing to young women buyers. Changes were so minor over the years, it was difficult to tell whether a LeBaron (1992 model shown) was the first or last of the breed (in 1993 the headlights became more aerodynamic and there was a smaller grille). Powered by an overhead-cam, four-cylinder 2.5-liter engine rated at 100 bhp, the 184.9-inch LeBaron's base price was almost $13,000. Add the optional turbo-charged version or the Mitsubishi-built 3.0-liter (181-cid) SOHC V-6 and the price started to go up. During its existence, the LeBaron convertible was the darling of the young, footloose, and fancy-free. It became the most popular convertible in the world.

Like its name implies, a Viper coiled and ready to strike. It really depends how you liked to imagine the new car from Dodge that became the talking point in every bar, country club, and yachting marina across the country in 1992. Some considered the Viper so voluptuous that, according to the *Car & Driver* description, it was Jayne Mansfield reincarnated as a sports car. If it was, it's hard to say which is preferable. Profile of the Viper is like nothing you've seen before. Because there is nothing like it, anywhere. Whole front lifts up for easy access to V-10 engine, hence the deep crease that extends into the doors. If nothing else, there's plenty of room to get lost trying to find the spark plugs! Based on the Dodge truck motor, Lamborghini refined the Viper, turned it into an all-aluminum engine developing a whopping 400 bhp NET. Design was a collective effort between Italy and Chrysler in Detroit. Look at the design. Doesn't it echo the 1968 Dodge Charger R/T in a more exaggerated way?

INSET: Interior of Viper is very smart, well thought-out. Note the heavy roll-bar roof support at rear. Only a convertible was offered in 1992. Besides the Charger, there's also much of Carroll Shelby's Cobra in the Viper. Shelby was part of the team that created the Viper when Chrysler president Bob Lutz suggested they make a sports car with the same appeal as the Cobra.

ABOVE, MIDDLE: Wheels are cast aluminum and are a large 17" x 10" in the front, and a colossal 17" x 13" at the rear. Note the word *Viper* on the disc brakes and the snake's head in the center of the wheel.

ABOVE, RIGHT: There's the Viper image again, this time adorning the rear of the car. There are seven snake's-head emblems on the car, if you count the wheels.

Lehigh University to try for a scholarship in engineering.

Studying for eight semesters, Lee was rewarded with a bachelor's degree. The war was still raging across the globe and young men with Lee's talents were in short supply. Although he had a wide choice of jobs, Lee wanted to work for Ford; a company that could build a stunner like the 1940 Lincoln Continental, he figured, had to be worth working for. Then he got a flyer from Lehigh's placement director outlining an offer to go to Princeton. He had already been to Ford, where they were very impressed with him, but they told him to take up the Princeton offer and promised him to hold a position once he graduated. It reads like one of those early James Stewart movie scripts, doesn't it?

The rest is history. Lee got himself a master's degree in engineering, was taken on by Ford, quit engineering and became a highly successful Ford dealer with ideas that made the company sit up and take notice. By the late fifties he was back working for Ford, and in the time it takes for Bruce Wayne to change into Batman, Lee found himself vice-president and general manager of the Ford division. Soon he was made head of the division; he cleared the way for Ford's Total Performance program and fathered one of the world's best-loved cars, the Mustang. Fourteen years after the Mustang's birth, Henry Ford inexplicably fired Lee Iacocca. Ford was on top of the world, having completed its two best years in the company's history. To get the full story, you have to read Iacocca's book. What happened left a bitter taste in Lee's mouth and a deep pain in his heart. The truth is that Henry was a class snob; Lee didn't fit in, so he had to go.

So fast was Chrysler going down that it was breaking the ladder's rungs in a freefall pattern. That Lee Iacocca was no longer with Ford was, from the beleaguered company's viewpoint, the best thing that had happened since sliced bread.

Yellow was a new color added in 1994 and suited the Viper quite well. There are faster cars but none quite as charismatic or exciting as the Viper, whose 400 bhp propels the car at a high rate of knots. Top speed is around 180–185 mph.

On November 2, 1978, Lee joined Chrysler. His mission: to save the company.

As far as Lee Iacocca was concerned, everything that could be wrong in a company was wrong at Chrysler. There was no organization; no planning; the left hand didn't know what the right one was doing. In his autobiography Lee tells a sad tale: "Chrysler didn't really function like a company at all. Chrysler in 1978 was like Italy in the 1860s. . . . The company consisted of a cluster of little duchies, each one run by a prima donna. It was a bunch of miniempires, with nobody giving a damn about what anyone else was doing.

What I found at Chrysler were thirty-five vice-presidents, each with his own turf. There was no real committee setup, no cement in the organizational chart, no system of meetings to get people talking to each other. I couldn't believe, for example, that the guy running the engineering department wasn't in constant touch with his counterpart in manufacturing. But that's how it was. Everybody worked independently. I took one look at that system and I almost threw up."

Investigating further, Lee discovered that

A black 1995 Viper R/T 10 Roadster. See how the light picks out the bumps and bulges of this curvaceous design? Coming almost intact from the 1989 Viper concept car, one can see the enthusiasm of the design team etched into the state-of-the-art plastic-composite-materials body.

INSET: The Viper's ten-cylinder engine is beautifully turned out the way 1930s European exotic car engines were finished. A nice job indeed.

each department didn't know what the others were doing. "The manufacturing guys would build cars without ever checking with the sales guys," Lee wrote. "They just built them, stuck them in a yard, and then hoped that somebody would take them out of there." Everything, Lee discovered, was done for the short term, without consideration for the future.

Over the next three years, Lee fired thirty-three of the thirty-five vice-presidents and let many others go. He hated doing it, he says, but to make Chrysler an efficient entity again the sackings had to be done. The situation at the country's tenth-largest company was akin to a Broadway farce, but without the laughter. At one point, in the summer of 1979, there were a hundred thousand—yes, believe it, a hundred

thousand—unsold cars on Chrysler's back lot slowly rotting away.

Lee set to work to get rid of $600 million worth of cars. He went to the dealers and told them there would be no more fire sales; Chrysler had become used to regular fire sales, which meant the dealership would get the vehicles at a special price. Under Iacocca, this practice ceased. It took time, he said, to get rid of the huge inventory, but they did. The dealers bought the vehicles and they were told Chrysler in the future would only build to order.

Painful decisions were made to streamline Chrysler, but streamline Highland Park operations Lee did. Many people had to be let go, subsidiaries sold off, factories closed. Then Chrysler tackled the federal government for a

The 1995 Chrysler Atlantic Show Car is so good that it really needed to be considered as a production vehicle. According to Tom Gale, vice-president of product design and international operations, the charismatic era of elegant, classic two-door coupes, such as a late-thirties Delahaye, is no more. He said that today's sedans portray what the coupe used to do. Which is why the Atlantic would not be produced. While what Tom Gale says is probably true, this surely doesn't mean a two-door car as beautiful as the Atlantic wouldn't sell if it was produced. This doesn't gel with public reaction; people would like to own a truly artistic statement like the Atlantic. Look at the design, those outstanding chrome "moon" wheels, the only chrome on the car.

INSET: Any way you look at the Atlantic, it looks right. From above or below, front to back, side to side, there is nothing in its proportions that jar the nerves. The Atlantic has perfect symmetry and is a clear indication of the true artistic talent working in Chrysler's design studios. Under the elegant hood is a DOHC, 32-valve, 4.0-liter straight-eight engine, which develops an estimated 325 horsepower. Independent suspension is all round, the brakes are four-wheel disc with ABS, and the drive train is an Auto Stick Transaxle. Interior is Neutral and Dark Rosewood leather. Wheelbase is 126 inches, overall length 199.5 inches. The Atlantic brings the best of yesterday into the world of tomorrow. Why not take a chance, Chrysler, like you did with the Prowler, and put it into limited production?

loan to help save Chrysler and give it time to build new, sensible cars.

It took Lee Iacocca and John Riccardo (he was still Chrysler's CEO; Iacocca was president) time to finally convince a suspicious Congress and Senate to grant a loan guarantee worth $1.2 billion. The loan was granted by a two-to-one vote in the Democratic-controlled House but was closer in the Senate. Nevertheless Chrysler could breathe a little easier again.

And to set an example, Lee reduced his salary to a dollar per year.

What really saved Chrysler was the K-car. The front-wheel-drive, four-cylinder-engined small car was the creation of Hal Sperlich, a friend of Lee who came to Chrysler from Ford in 1977. Almost immediately Sperlich began to develop the K-car idea. The little compacts got 41 mpg on the highway, 25 in the city. The first pair, the Dodge Aries and Plymouth Reliant, were launched in October 1980. Initially there were problems, but sales picked up early in 1981, and by year's end, Chrysler's new K-cars had captured 20 percent of the market.

At this critical time in Chrysler's fortunes, the company did not give muscle cars much thought; throughout the eighties, nobody did. Uppermost in Motor City's mind was how to stave off the Japanese, whose cars were claiming 25 percent and more of the American car market. It was a time for retrenchment, for products that could take the Japanese head on. Ford set the ball rolling with first its British/German-built Sierra. The car was rounded, aerodynamic, had front-wheel-drive, independent suspension all around, and four-wheel disc brakes. Shortly after, Ford launched the amazing Taurus, in 1985. It was a kissin' cousin of the European Sierra, but longer and wider. Suddenly square-mobiles were out, aerodynamics were in. Everybody went jelly-mold, became fuel-efficient, and unless you were in Cadillac or Lincoln country, it was bye-bye V-8.

Chrysler didn't follow the aerodynamic formula for some years. Lee Iacocca's reorganization had paid dividends, the government loans were paid off early, seven years early, in fact, and the K-cars sold and continued to sell. By the end of 1983 Chrysler had bounced back into the land of milk and honey with a profit of $925 million, the largest in the company's history.

K-cars were everywhere—with the exception of the beautifully made bustle-back Imper-ial (this splendid luxury car only lasted three seasons), the terminally ill Cordoba and Dodge Mirada passing away at the end of the 1983 model season. There were still some M-bodied rear-drive cars like the uninspired Plymouth Gran Fury and Dodge Diplomat. The Gran Fury, incidentally, sold quite well to police forces across the country. But Chrysler's emphasis would be on the K-car platform, which now had the smart LeBaron convertible and coupe, the New Yorker, Dodge 600, and two sportier cars, the Dodge Daytona and Chrysler Laser.

On the L-body platform were the subcompacts like the Omni and Horizon. They did quite well, and by 1982 the Dodge 024 Charger and Plymouth TC3 Turismo coupes were added. Powered by Chrysler's little 2.2-liter four-cylinder engine, the cars tried to reflect some of Europe's and Japan's sportier hatchbacks with special paint, stripes, and trim, though not really much else. Compared to the golden years of performance, these cars were nonstarters in the sporty-car field.

Being a car enthusiast at heart, Lee Iacocca talked his old friend Carroll Shelby into building a go-faster car that would actually go faster! Iacocca and Shelby went back to the halcyon days when they both had something to do with the Mustang: Lee for dreaming the idea up in the first place, Carroll for creating a legend out of the car with the GT-350/500 Shelby Mustangs. Set up at Chrysler's expense, in a state-of-the-art facility near Los Angeles, Shelby put together the Dodge Shelby Charger.

There was no doubt about it, the Shelby Charger looked as though it might get up and go. It had front and rear spoilers, rocker panel extensions, blue and silver paint with contrasting blue and silver side stripes, fifteen-inch Goodyear radials on aluminum wheels, a special interior with color-keyed bucket seats, and much else besides. Under the hood was a reworked 2.2-liter four-cylinder engine sporting a 9.6:1 compression ratio and developing 107 horsepower (versus the standard 94).

Bearing in mind the engine's size, the 0–60 time of 8.5 seconds wasn't bad, especially when compared to the old performance V-8s of the fifties/early sixties. Even the fabled 300 was hard put to better those times thirty years earlier.

On the world front, by the mideighties quite a lot had happened, little of which was reassuring. B-movie star Ronald Reagan was elected President in 1980, the same year a gun-crazy cretin shot and killed ex-Beatle John Lennon. World terrorism was a constant headache, and Natalie Wood drowned falling off a boat. All this was in 1981. In 1982, Argentina invaded the hotly contested Falkland Islands, two hunks of bleak and inhospitable rock belonging to Britain, inhabited by a minority of people and a majority of sheep; British Prime Minister Margaret Thatcher mounted an invasion of the islands that was quick, fierce, and bloody and resulted in the Argentineans being routed. Thus the Falklands were returned to the sheep.

Alfred Hitchcock died; so did Princess Grace of Monaco, in an automobile wreck. Princess Grace came to fame as Grace Kelly the movie actress, and had starred in three of Hitchcock's films, including *To Catch a Thief*. After America lost its way in the seventies, President Reagan encouraged the nation to pull itself out of its gloom in the eighties, a time when the rich got richer and greed was the name of the game. Youth, as the world knew it in the sixties, was nowhere to be seen.

In 1984 the new-look Chrysler debuted the Plymouth Voyager and Dodge Caravan minivans. These were practical people movers that could carry seven on a trip. Built on a 112-inch wheelbase, the Voyager and Caravan were the same length as the K-cars, at 175.9 inches. The vans were powered by the 2.2-liter four or Mitsubishi's Silent Shaft 2.6-liter unit. A five-speed OD manual transmission or the three-speed TorqueFlite were available.

Both minivans were the first of their type to be designed and built in the U.S. and were a tremendous success. Rivals GM and Ford fretted that they hadn't thought of the idea first. They didn't, thus leaving Chrysler to lead the way, consolidate its position, and stay on top of the minivan market with 50 percent of the sales to this day. In 1987 there was a healthy increase in power with the arrival of the Mitsubishi-built, 3.0-liter, 136-horsepower OHC V-6. A larger version, the Grand Caravan, was introduced. It sat on a 119.1-inch wheelbase and had an overall length of 190.5 inches.

On the mini/sporty front came a turbocharged option on most of Chrysler's captive import vehicles. That's Mitsubishi in Japan, Dodge/Plymouth Colt, Vista, Conquest, etc., etc., and etc. in America. Turbo-charging was the name of the game in the mideighties and a lot of fun if one happened to have the right car. Carburetors' days were numbered as fuel injection, in a load of permutations such as PFI, TBI, MFI or PBI, swept the board. Before one knew it, the American car was no more; they had become international cars with fuel injection, front-wheel drive, independent suspension and four-cylinder engines. The days when one could tell a country by the cars built there have gone. Last night I went to bed wrapped in Old Glory; this morning I dressed up in my United Nations suit!

On June 3, 1986, an event not considered terribly important at the time occurred at Highland Park. Robert A. Lutz became executive vice-president of Chrysler Motors. If people but knew it, Lutz's appointment would have earth-shaking consequences for the company. Why? Because Lutz was an automobile man, somebody who loved fine cars, tinkering with

Two legends take stock of each other. One is fresh, exciting, and new, the other millions of years old: the Hennessey Viper and the famed White Cliffs of Dover. On a cold, gray day on the English Channel, the Viper's yellow hue stands out against the dull landscape.

INSET: Rear-view shot of Hennessey Viper coupe. Note the British license plate . . . grammar's a bit off: *A 8 LTR*. But you can't have an extra letter to make *A* into *AN*.

cars, and most of all, driving cars. Just the right qualifications for a man whose personality, charisma, and influence would help make Chrysler the most forward-thinking car company in America.

A new 2.5-liter Chrysler-designed-and-built engine became available in 1986. It was derived from the reliable 2.2-liter and was offered in the go-faster Dodge Daytona, Chrysler Laser front-wheel-drive sport coupes. The twins, which is what they were, looked snazzy and could handle quite well even if they weren't in a hurry to go anywhere. Not that Chrysler really cared at this point. The K-cars and all their

derivatives had hit a nerve in the by now quite conservative American psyche. Under Lee Iacocca's direction, the new-look Chrysler was making money and profits and consolidating its gains. But there were those within the company who wanted to see Chrysler return to the good old days, to produce excitement like the 300s, the Road Runners, again.

And one of those was Bob Lutz.

As noted, Lutz was a car enthusiast in the truest sense. Garaged at his beautiful home in Ann Arbor is an array of fast, distinctive cars and motorcycles. He has a 1955 Chrysler C-300, a Cunningham C-3 (both cars are in

CHRYSLER IN THE FAST TRACK, 1990s STYLE

After a long absence, Chrysler has gone back into motorsports with a vengeance. Whatever the competition, Chrysler is there. Not yet in Formula One, but don't count your chickens that Mopar won't in the next few years. Chrysler returned to racing in 1996 with the Viper GTS-R (below and inset), Dodge Stratus Super Touring Car, and the Dodge Ram NASCAR Craftsman Truck. Then there's the PPG Neon Challenge Series and SCCA Neon Club Racing. After only two years in the field, the Chrysler factory development team, the French Viper Team ORECA, won the FIA GT2 Driver's Championship with British driver Justin Bell. FIA, which is the world sanctioning body for motorsports, awarded its Manufacturers' Championship to ORECA after a clinching one-two win in Sebring, Florida. In turn, ORECA, run by Hugues de Chaunac, presented the award to Chrysler CEO Robert Eaton at a ceremony at the Chrysler Technical Center, Auburn Hills. More than thirty years ago, Ford won the world's most prestigious endurance race, Le Mans. This

tough twenty-four-hour race is the one everybody wants to win. Up to 1997, the Viper GTS-R hadn't. The Viper Team was going for it in 1998, and that year indeed won their class, 1, 2. Truck racing is a popular and growing sport. Chrysler has entered the NASCAR Craftsman Truck competition with a series of Dodge trucks run by Mopar and supported independent teams. New to the sport, the Dodge trucks have yet to win, but win they will provided this practical way of improving the product sold to the consumer is allowed to survive. (Photos courtesy Chrysler Corporation)

ABOVE AND INSETS: **1996 Neon Racers.** (Photos by Mark Weber)

1997 Pennzoil Dodge.
(Courtesy Chrysler
Corporation)

1997 Mopar Dodge. (Courtesy Chrysler Corporation)

1997 Dana Dodge.

1997 Cummins Dodge.

1996/97 World Champion Viper GTS-R. Viper body is constructed from carbon fiber, has steel space-frame and polycarbonate windows. Tires are a massive 11 x 18 inches front and rear, with Michelin Pilot SX radial slicks. Striking blue and white American racing colors add to the illusion

INSET, LEFT: Viper Champ's interior is nothing remotely like a stock pro-duction car. Look at the aircraftlike panel to the right of the driver.

INSET, RIGHT: Low-angle shot of 1996/97 World Champion's stabilizer wing. Small stabilizers attached to horizontal wing remind one of Superbird and Daytona. Few realize those cars were capable of 220 mph and would more than hold their own against today's racers.

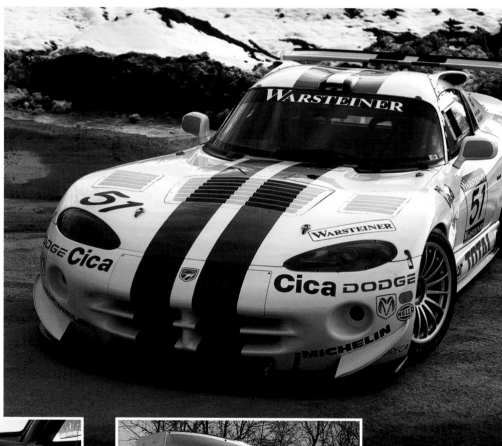

All photos courtesy
Chrysler Corporation

December 17, 1997. Here Team ORECA and the Chrysler Development Team stand together around the FIA Manufacturer's Championship Viper. Silver-haired man by driver's door is Viper Team ORECA boss, Hugues de Chaunac.

Here's the Viper GTS-R heading for victory at Le Mans in 1998. The car proved itself a true thoroughbred and, thanks to Chrysler's engineers and Team ORECA, can take its place alongside the best in the world.

INSET: The 1998 Viper GTS-R Le Mans winning team. From left to right we have David Donohue (U.S.A.), Luca Drudi (Italy), and Justin Bell (Great Britain).

this book), a midthirties Riley sports car, a thirties Citroen Traction-Avant (front-wheel drive in English), and of course the new American sports car his ideas helped create. Lutz also has a couple of BMW motorcycles. An accomplished driver, Lutz served in the Marines as a jet pilot from 1954 to 1959, and a few years later received his MBA from the University of California—Berkeley.

Lutz's first automotive position was with Opel, part of General Motors' European operations. He held several senior positions before moving on to BMW, where he stayed three years as executive vice-president of sales. He went to Ford of Europe after BMW, and served as chairman and executive vice-president of Ford's International Operations. He spent a further twelve years with FoMoCo as executive vice-president of Truck Operations. The next step was joining Chrysler.

One car Lutz always liked was the AC Shelby-Cobra. Ex–race driver and car builder Carroll Shelby took the British-built AC and shoveled Ford's small-block V-8 under the hood, thus creating the 260/289 Shelby Cobra. Sports-car lovers everywhere were fascinated by

the brute power and force behind the Shelby, especially when it was given Ford's whopping 427; it became a legend overnight. This was the car Lutz wanted to see recreated, but using all the benefits of modern technology.

February 1988 and Tom Gale, Chrysler's talented chief of design, was wandering down the corridor past Lutz's office—Lutz was then president of operations—when he was called in. "I can remember it like it was yesterday," recalled Gale. "Bob called me into his office—it was only a few minutes' discussion—and he said, 'I've been thinking more and more. We really ought to kick off a project like a reborn Cobra.' That was our intent right from the beginning."

Like Bob Lutz, Tom Gale is a committed car nut. He likes to mess around with hot rods and loves to drive his Plymouth AAR 'Cuda. The thought of a sports car of a type Lutz described excited him. It was outrageous, not the sort of thing a responsible car company should be doing. Anyway, there was already an American sports car, the legendary Chevrolet Corvette. Would there be room for another?

The answer came at the Detroit International Auto Show. A team of gifted engineers and designers was formed to work on what was to become the Dodge Viper. Within eleven months, the team had a running prototype painted red. It held center stage at the 1989 Detroit show, where visitors crowded around

Here the 1997 Viper burns rubber in controlled slide. Car never gets out of hand, always remains steady. It is very difficult to get into trouble with this car . . . unless you drive it off the Golden Gate Bridge, that is. (Courtesy Chrysler Corporation)

Cary Grant has become the Viper and there's no cornfield, but the scene is *North by Northwest* in modern terms. Front of car has definite reptilian look about it. So did the Shelby Cobra, for that matter.

INSET: There are Viper emblems everywhere on the car. Here we find one on the underside of the hood. There are more on the engine, as well. Reminds one of the old MG, which had a thing about its octagonal badge . . . they were everywhere. (Courtesy Chrysler Corporation)

the stand to look at what became an overnight sensation. Everybody wanted to see the Viper RT/10. Letters poured into Chrysler by the hundreds, from enthusiasts pleading for the car to be put into production. Some even sent deposit checks, which were returned.

Reaction to the show car was so positive that Chrysler chairman Lee Iacocca said that a decision whether to build the Viper or not would be forthcoming in the second quarter of 1990. On May 18, 1990, it was announced that the Viper would be built in limited numbers for sale to the general public. A new motoring leg-

end was born that day, and car people everywhere rejoiced.

Overseeing the complete technical and engineering program for the Viper was Frenchman Francois J. Castaing, vice-president of vehicle engineering. Castaing worked for American Motors, joining the company in 1980 after ten years with AMC's new partner, the French state-owned Renault car company. He came on board Chrysler's ship when it bought AMC in 1987.

Castaing relished the Viper program. He said in an interview that the Viper had been an experiment in many ways. "If you think about it," he said, "it's unique for a major car manufacturer to build a one-of-a-kind car, show it to the public, and then say, 'If you like it, then we'll make it for you.' " This was unheard of in large motoring corporations and terribly refreshing. Since Iacocca's reorganization of Chrysler, there has been a happy, free-thinking feeling in the air at the impressive Chrysler Technical Center in Auburn Hills, near Detroit. "Neither Ford nor GM encourage the easygoing way we do things here," said John Herlich. "We have car enthusiasts heading Chrysler, people who are willing to try something unique and different."

Carroll Shelby had been building limited-edition, high-performance K-car Dodge Shadows in the eighties and was working on an idea to build a sports car of his own and trying to interest Chrysler in his idea. That was when Bob Lutz and Francois Castaing approached him. "Why don't we build a sports car, something like the old 427 Cobra—only let's build a 1990s version of it?" said Lutz. The three men sat down and conceived how the car should be. However, Shelby would not be directly involved with the Viper; he was awaiting a heart transplant. It was a remarkably successful transplant, performed in 1990 when Shelby was sixty-seven years old. Less than a year later he was driving the Viper that paced the 1991 Indianapolis 500.

Not that it mattered whether Shelby was involved or not. Mere mention of his name was enough to inspire confidence in those physically or mentally attuned to the Viper program. His 1960s Cobra was the inspiration; Lutz wanted an updated Cobra using modern technology without resorting to the glitzy paraphernalia inherent in most sports cars today. In other words, pure simplicity. Just like the sports cars of old when a lightweight body, a pair of seats, a powerful engine, precise steering, close-ratio manual transmission, and good brakes were all that was needed.

Which is exactly how the Viper came to be.

Especially important was the engine. Some suggested the old 426 Hemi, but Castaing nixed the idea. He didn't care for the idea of trying to reproduce a legend. When the concept car was put together, Dodge was working on a big, cast-iron V-10 truck engine. Everybody agreed this was the type of powerplant that would be unique for the car. But not in its present form. As Carroll Shelby kept saying, weight had to be lost, not gained.

There was not a V-10 available at the time of the concept Viper's creation. Tom Gale said this was the engine of choice, so the Viper team cobbled together a V-10 by taking the 360-cid V-8 and adding two extra cylinders. It was after a jetlike blast down a suburban street that Iacocca gave his okay for the Viper to be put into limited production.

By the middle of 1989 Chrysler still hadn't built the V-10 truck engine. "We knew the Viper Team was working at least eighteen months ahead of the truck engine," said Castaing, who telephoned Lamborghini Engineering, the Formula 1 research and development wing of the famous Italian sports car then owned by Chrysler. He discussed the engine problem with Mauro Forghieri, Lamborghini Engineering's head. A bunch of Team Viper engineers flew to Italy with a sackful of V-10 engine drawings, and as Castaing said, by this time it had been decided that the engine would be all aluminum, unlike the cast-iron beef of the truck version.

An agreement was put together whereby Lamborghini Engineering would help to redesign the block and head from the drawings to enable the parts to be converted into aluminum. Then the Italians would cast the parts for fifteen engines. Two complete engines were put together to check for tolerances; then everything was shipped back to Chrysler. From that point, everything else was done in Detroit.

Team Viper was created by Roy H. Sjoberg, who had come to Chrysler from GM in early 1985. He announced he was going to build a team that would have nothing else to do but research and develop the Viper. Two hundred eager employees applied, out of which Sjoberg selected twenty addicted car enthusiasts. This was the first time a team like this had been assembled at Chrysler, or anywhere else for that matter, though Ford jumped on the bandwagon with its similar Mustang skunkworks group. One of Team Viper's first tasks was to see how quickly the car could be put into production and, most importantly, how much it would cost.

About the time the Viper skunkworks team was assembled, the Viper Technical Policy Committee was formed. It consisted of the four Viper founding fathers: Bob Lutz, Francois Castaing, Tom Gale, and Carroll Shelby. Team Viper would meet TPC every three months to discuss progress. And three months after being formed, Team Viper reported to TPC that they could deliver a finished car in three years for only $50 million—figures unheard of in modern-day Detroit, where new car development can run into hundreds of millions.

How did the Viper get its by-now-legendary name? Bob Lutz was how. He said he thought it up on an airplane trip. "We couldn't use the Cobra name," Lutz recalled, "but we wanted a snake." He thought of Asp but that wasn't too good; then Sidewinder, which was out because people might think the car goes sideways or it had military connections. Lutz considered Python but as he said, "Pythons—they're big and fat and swallow pigs and then lie around in the sun for a week." So the Python was a no-no. Then Lutz hit upon Viper. It sounded right. The name, he said, rolled off the tongue. So Viper it became.

Design and construction of the Viper was aided by computer. Always mindful of weight concerns, the designers and their computers developed a steel-tube space frame monocoque. The frame is extremely rigid and costs less to build than current platform chassis.

Once the frame had been developed, it was decided the body panels would not be crafted in steel like the show car but in a new resin-transfer molding process, or RTM for short. Roy Sjoberg was selected by Castaing to handle development of the body panels due to his experience with plastics at GM.

Dead on time and strictly to budget, the first full-production Viper rolled out of the New Mack Avenue Assembly Plant in Detroit. The plant used to be Chrysler's Mack Avenue facility but was renamed for the Viper. About 130 workers, under a five-year agreement with the United Auto workers, were employed. They were to be called "craftspersons"; this was the only classification at the plant. All the craftspersons were delegated responsibility for quality, obtaining materials, and for working together as a team. Hence they became Team Viper members. This was groundbreaking stuff for Detroit and an exciting concept that has worked. The craftspersons are loyal, dedicated, and share total enthusiasm for this, the coolest of cool cars.

Since the Viper was developed, Chrysler has been on a roll, always doing something exciting, never sitting still, never resting on its laurels and always going forward. While the Viper is the obvious flagship of this born-again, rejuvenated company, there has been no letup in the 1990s to always be in the news. Design chiefs Tom Gale and John Herlich have feeling and enthusiasm, plus great talent and love for designing automobiles. This can be witnessed by the first LH Cab-Forward series of cars, which literally knocked the industry off its feet much in the same way Chrysler's previously inspired designs of 1957 managed to do. The Concorde, LHS, Intrepid, Stratus,

Here's a car Chrysler took a chance on and it worked. The 1997 Plymouth Prowler. Here is the world's first production hot-rod, smacking of all the things Gene Barris and Mad Daddy Roth lived for. It does 0–60 in seven seconds; has short length of 165 inches; has a drag-limited top speed of 117 mph (which means it'll be faster if the drag limiter was off). OK, so it doesn't have a V-8. The Prowler's engine is a belt-driven, single overhead cam V-6 developing 214 bhp (SAE net). The motor goes, and it could be made to go even more. Prowler production sells phenomenally well every year, no doubt to all those who remember the Beach Boys.

INSET: Interior of Prowler is impressive with full instrumentation, comfortable ergonomic seating. Gears are automatic, which is not quite the hot-rod way. Prowler literally stops on a dime (from 70 mph in 168 ft.), making it one of the best braking cars in the world.

Sebring, Avenger, the outrageous Dodge Ram pickup and the little Neon—these are memorable, beautiful, and practical designs that have left the opposition in disarray. And the latest Concord, Intrepid, and LHS shout, "Suddenly it's 2010!"

It is highly probable that designer Tom Gale had something to say about the cheekiest production car on the block. Being a lover of hot rods, the idea for a production hot rod must have come from him. That hot rod is the Plymouth Prowler, introduced in 1997.

There is no mistaking the Prowler for anything else but a rod. It has a sort of '32 Ford grille (or should we say 1938 Plymouth?), cycle front fenders that turn with the wheels, odd-looking bumperettes that stick out securely in front of the grille and happily passed the 5 mph crash test, and projecting lamps each side of the grille that give the front a look like something out of *The X-Files*. And in true hot rod fashion, the rear wheels are quite a bit larger than the front ones.

Although the steering wheel is impossibly fat and modern and hides an air bag in its center, the delightful dashboard and instruments harken back to the days when Gene Barris was a little fella in short pants. A large, round black-on-white speedometer sits in the middle of the dash, flanked by four smaller pods that tell one everything one needs to know. Under the hood there's no old Hemi sitting there—just a neat SOHC 3.5-liter V-6 pumping out 214 bhp at 5,850 rpm (the same engine powers your local pastor's Concorde), and it will growl and snarl up to 60 in 7.0 seconds. Top speed is around 120 mph.

Where the Prowler loses sight of its Holly-wood-and-Vine-on-a-Saturday-night heroes is in brakes and comfort. Few rods had eleven-inch front and thirteen-inch rear disc brakes, which pull the Prowler to a very rapid and safe stop from 70 mph. According to road-test reports, these brakes are even better than the Viper GTS units. And that's saying something.

Comfort levels are excellent. The ride is sporting in nature and doesn't jounce around like a cockroach that's just been sprayed with Raid. The suspension is independent all round, which certainly helps the Prowler's exceptional handling. Another area where the Prowler contradicts its hot rod heritage is in its level of standard features such as air conditioning, power steering, window and door locks, cruise control, tilt steering, rear defroster, and AM/FM radio with seven speakers, CD, and cassette player. And we must not forget this is a convertible, the top folding down into the rather shallow trunk.

The price of thirty-five thousand dollars may sound like a lot for a car, but not this one. Only three thousand are built in a year, and the buyer is assured of having a most talked-about vehicle. Not that anybody will get one of these terrific cars in a hurry: the entire yearly production is sold out before it begins.

Under the auspices of Tom Gale and John Herlich, Chrysler has perhaps one of the best automobile design teams in the world. For sheer artistic beauty, the 1995 Chrysler Atlantic show car is hard to beat. It is a successful marriage of the sort of styling favored by Zagato and the best to come out of modern-day Detroit, Chrysler in this case. Long, swoopy hood, pontoon-style fenders, and fashionably laid-back, modern windshield design. A beautiful design that could easily and successfully be put into production, but probably never will.

During the seventies and eighties, Chrysler turned its back on motorsports. They kept Richard Petty on until 1979, but it was a half-hearted effort compared to the halcyon, golden days of the sixties. At one period in the seventies, Chrysler sold would-be racers a complete car kit. This consisted of a chassis, engine, and other mechanical parts that the buyer would have to put together himself. He could also purchase body parts or a complete body to tack on once engine, transmission, and chassis had been assembled, or he/she could put their own custom-made shell on the chassis. These hybrids were quite successful and a couple of hundred were sold to racers.

As we march across the bridge into the twenty-first century, Chrysler has returned to motorsports with a bang. Lee Iacocca was for sports; his successor as chairman of Chrysler, Robert Eaton, and of course Bob Lutz have been enthusiastic about motorsports. In the midnineties, Chrysler launched itself unashamedly back into the sporting arena. Not with a couple of intermediates with big-block V-8s, no, that's for the birds. With an enthusiasm not seen since the discovery of the wheel, Chrysler has gone in for almost every type of motor racing competition.

We all know the Neon, don't we? That diminutive car that one GM designer exclaimed was a winning design, practical, and with no afterthought add-ons. In 1995, the first PPG Neon Super Cup race was held at Road America and the response from SCCA Neon Club racers was remarkable. Fifty-seven Neons raced in a thirty-minute event that was televised. This led to the Neon Challenge Series.

There were five races in 1996, four in 1997. Forty Neon racers scored points in 1996 and points were awarded to the twelve Club racing competitors in each class. At the Road America finale the top ten in each class were able to compete in the 1997 series.

Neon racing is fun racing. Watching identical cars that differ only by their rainbow-bright racing colors is quite something. Having identical cars pushes the drivers to the fore because it is ultimately a race in which the most skilled driver wins.

Another form of motorsport is pickup-truck racing. Several teams compete for honors in the NASCAR Craftsman Truck Series. Of course Mopar is well represented, backing the teams driving Dodge Ram 1500 pickups powered by 5.9-liter Magnum cast-iron-block carbureted V-8s. You can't buy engines like this from your local friendly Dodge dealer: horsepower is 650-plus and the top speed is 160 mph. The NASCAR Craftsman Series is growing in popularity all over the country, but especially in the South and Midwest. Dodge trucks also enter drag racing events, with good results.

Mopar officially returned to racing in a big way in 1996. Chrysler's Motorsports activities have been channeled into a single operation, directed by Louis Patane, executive director, Chrysler Motorsports Operations. "Chrysler's involvement in racing," said Patane, "is more than just for publicity or image. There must be tangible benefits to the company that extend beyond the racetrack. Our motorsports programs are truly an integral part of our product development processes."

Like the Team Viper effort, Chrysler's

Motorsports Operations consist of engineers, designers, technicians, teams, and sponsors who work together as one union, interacting with each other daily to ensure maximum cooperation across the racing board. This solid team approach pioneered by Chrysler with Team Viper support has produced results such as the Viper Team ORECA's FIA GT2 Drivers' Championship and Manufacturers' Championship.

In 1996 Chrysler entered into sponsorship of the French racing team ORECA owned and run by Hugues de Chaunac. According to Richard Myers, racing manager for the Viper team, Chrysler had an interest to go into European endurance competition to promote its name. Chrysler now has a large presence in Europe and Great Britain, with Jeeps and Neons being sold all over the continent. Neons are built in Austria with European specs, and Jeeps, though still assembled in Detroit, arrive in England in right-hand-drive form. Vipers are also sold in England by Chrysler Jeep Imports UK, in Dover. So far, about a few dozen Vipers have found homes in Britain.

"The Viper racing program was conceived by Bob Lutz and Francois Castaing," said Myers over lunch, on a dark and rainy day near the Chrysler Tech Center. "We prepared Vipers for their first race at Daytona," continued Myers, "and two cars were entered.

"We really didn't do so well that time; one crashed and the other had transmission failure. It was a Baptism of Fire . . . maybe a Baptism of Labor would be a better term," Myers chuckled.

A lot of preparation went into making the Vipers fit for racing on the tough endurance courses of Europe. Le Mans, for instance. The twenty-four-hour race at Le Mans is the endurance event to end all endurance events—and the one to win. Bentley, Jaguar, Mercedes, Porsche, Ford, Ferrari have all raced at

New features on the 1998 Viper are the center and side hood scoops. Shown is the styling prototype.

INSET, LEFT: Shades of the old Dodge Charger. A racing-style gas cap, fitted not to the fender but to the roof pillar.

INSET, RIGHT: Closeup of left-hand, rearward-facing scoops. Unlike many cars of old, these scoops actually work.

Viper emblem does not change and has been the same from day one.

Le Mans with varying degrees of success. Ford won the race several years in a row from 1966 and succeeded in taking the wind out of Ferrari's sails.

Dick Myers explained that the racing Viper's success was due to an incredible team effort. Many parts—such as the Borg-Warner transmission, which was uprated—came from outside suppliers. The differential was supplied by Dana. Suppliers were approached to help with the project; Dick said that while some weren't too keen at first, they "all pitched in and came to the party."

Much of the Viper was designed by computer. "We were able to design the front exhaust headers in-house," explained Myers, "the roll-cage and all that sort of thing. It was all done on a computer. Even though we use

the computer we are typically team oriented. We have some very talented artists. It comes from the efforts of everybody. It's not just the tool we use but the people using the tool [the computer]. Computers are just speed."

Warming to his subject, which he obviously has a lot of feeling for, Myers said: "The car tells you what it needs and if you want to listen to the car, then you can make it faster. If you walk in there with some preconceived notion that this car should be just like that car over there . . . well, it won't work. Not the way you want it to. Sometimes what the car wants is completely the opposite . . . you've got to ask the car what it wants. Maybe what it wants is completely the opposite of conventional wisdom. We've found that out a couple of times here. We learned so much. Not only have we learned so much racing the Viper, but we learned so much by watching the competitors. It is all a learning process, a process that makes a better car."

An interesting point Myers mentioned was about the engine. Prior to 1996, the Viper V-10 engine had been worked on by Lamborghini. After 1996 the in-house Viper team redesigned the whole engine and removed eighty pounds of weight and changed every dimension. The water-distribution system in the cylinder head was redesigned . . . in fact everything in the engine was changed. This is what comes of racing experience.

Ford took four years before it won Le Mans with its GT-40 endurance cars. There was a lot of money involved. Compared with Ford's expenditure, Chrysler might appear very frugal. Yet, in less than two racing seasons, Viper Team ORECA of France won the FIA (Federation Internationale de l'Automobile) GT2 Championship, and one of Viper Team ORECA's drivers, British-born Justin Bell, walked off with the FIA GT2 Drivers' Championship.

Viper Team ORECA is owned and run by Hugues de Chaunac, a successful force in European motorsports with twenty championship titles to his and ORECA's credit. Chrysler couldn't have chosen a better partner than de Chaunac and Team ORECA to run its Vipers in competition. Lou Patane of Chrysler Motorsports said of the partnership: "ORECA is an accomplished race team with proven expertise in turning out champions and a championship product. We are proud to partner with such a world-class and well-known organization."

ORECA's success continued into 1998 when the specially built Viper GTS-Rs returned to compete in the legendary Le Mans 24-Hour Endurance race. Porsches dominated the field, yet the Vipers came in 1, 2 in the GT2 category, thus establishing the first victory by an Ameri-

can manufacturer in twenty-three years . . . yes, that's how long it has been since Ford led the way. The leading Viper was driven by American David Donahue, Justin Bell from Britain, and Italian Luca Drudi. The winning car completed 317 laps, a distance of 2,681.8 miles, at an average speed of 111.7 mph—though the car approached 200 mph four times on each lap. And each lap found the drivers changing gear 43 times . . . or 13,500 times during the day-long marathon, which says much for the durability of the transmission. It also says a great deal for the effort that has gone into making the Viper such a tremendous car, especially since the racing machines are developed from the production Viper R/T 10 and are not pure racers built merely for competition.

The genuine enthusiasm and love for the Viper is catching; one feels it as soon as one walks into Chrysler's fabulous Technical Center or the motorsports buildings less than a couple of miles away. This enthusiasm is better than any amount of money that could be spent on the Viper racing program. Very few cars can claim to have a personality; Ferrari is one, Viper the other. Both are built with immense pride and feeling for the job in hand, and it shows.

Having clinched the historic class win at Le Mans, Viper Team ORECA went on to capture the 1998 FIA GT2 Championship for the second time in two years. The final race was at Laguna Seca Raceway in California, and the winning drivers were Olivier Beretta from France and Pedro Lamy. Beretta also took the Driver's title. As in 1997, the Viper GTS-Rs won or placed in the top three in most of the 1998 races. So great has been the Viper's performance that Chrysler and ORECA have agreed to continue their successful partnership into 1999 and beyond.

In 1997 Chrysler, in partnership with ORECA, first made the racing world sit up and

The GT2 class-winning Viper GTS-R that took the title at Le Mans in 1998. Nice graphics highlight the car, which would hit 200 mph four times each lap during the 24-hour marathon. Swoopy looks are made for speed as well as being distinctive and handsome. This car averaged 111 mph during the entire Le Mans race. Changeable weather from rain to dry necessitated several tire changes.

take notice. Seven first-place finishes, six second-places, and five thirds clinched the FIA championships for ORECA and Chrysler. A creditable tenth place was scored in 1996 at Le Mans, the Viper's first year out. They failed in 1997, but were determined to go all out in 1998 to improve their performance in the fabled endurance race. As we have already seen, not only did the ORECA team do better, they drove their Vipers to a 1, 2 finish in the prototype class. The strain on drivers and crew was immense: Dick Myers was still exhausted but happy several days after the event!

It had been twenty-three years since Ford's GT-40s last won Le Mans, thirty-two since that historic day in 1966 when 7-liter Ford GT-40s crossed the line 1, 2, and 3. Multimillions had been spent to build the perfect race-winning car, for Henry Ford II was determined to beat Ferrari, especially after Enzio Ferrari snubbed Henry's offer to buy him out. Ford kept on winning for a number of years

If you have $325,000 to spend on a race winner, you can plunk your money down on a Viper GTS-R. ORECA, in an agreement with Chrysler, is building and selling Viper GTS-R racing cars to select private racing teams

around the world. In addition to the cars, ORECA has put together a customer-service department to supply spare parts and technical support to GTS-R owners. As Lou Patane remarked, the GTS-R program continues to "yield great success for Chrysler, and we've set out not only to build a strong racing heritage for the Viper but to establish a means of offering private race teams the design, engineering, and race-readiness of a Viper GTS-R so they are capable of winning on any level at a reasonable cost." And speaking of money, Dick Myers said the whole Viper racing program costs ten times less than the money spent by Porsche. To give an instance of economic management, Viper engineers installed 1957 Imperial control arms because they were as durable and capable of taking maximum punishment as any especially built for the car.

Followers of motorsports will know how

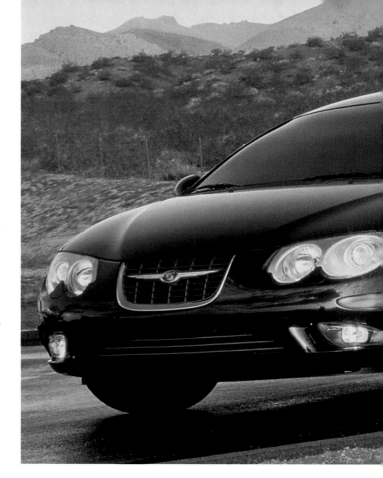

finicky racing organizations are when it comes to race guidelines. Often they will change the rules in detriment to the racing drivers and their cars. However, the FIA World Council announced, in October 1998, new guidelines that are beneficial to ORECA. The new ruling allows production-based GT cars to go for overall victories instead of just GT2 class wins. "I'm looking forward to competing in the new championship for overall wins," chuckled Hugues de Chaunac, when the new rules were announced.

What of the standard, road-going Viper R/T 10 that can be bought by the lucky few? Either in original roadster or coupe form, the Viper is inspired. Unique styling sets either car apart from the crowd . . . there's nothing around that looks remotely like it. The Viper is a class act. As ORECA race-driver Justin Bell put it, the Viper is pleasantly agreeable to drive, surprisingly versatile, and very responsive under all sorts of conditions.

Underneath the huge resin-transfer-molded plastic hood lies the business. The business of course being the red, all-aluminum V-10 pushrod, 8-liter engine that develops 450 bhp (SAE net); its 0–60 is between 3.8 and 4.0 seconds, and the top speed is drag limited to around 177 mph. Without this encumbrance, there's probably an extra 10 mph to add to the speed. But oh! Does this reptile move!

A six-speed manual transmission moves the car with alacrity. Shift into first, stomp on the gas pedal, and go. Change swiftly, smoothly into second . . . the gears are close together, so close in fact that you could miss third entirely until you find the right gate. Start again. Brooks Field airport at Marshall, Michigan, has a nice quarter-mile runway. Airport manager Scott Southwell wants to try the car; he was brought up on Mopar muscle in the good old days.

You're at the start of the runway and there are no planes to impede your progress. You put the transmission into first and rev, holding

your left foot on the brake. You let go, the car weaves just a little, and you are away. Slam into second, then third. The world whizzes by, the runway a blur. Now you're in fourth, the quarter-mile is coming up dreadfully fast. You look at the speedometer: 135 mph and you have to brake. You try several more runs, and manage fifth gear on one occasion. This is one helluva car.

Scott takes the wheel. He smiles and he tingles all over. An airplane pilot, ex-dragster, terrific driver, he goes through the gears, but can only manage five in one run, four in a couple of others. He hits 140 but the governor spoils it. Scott throws the car into a broadside, stands on the brakes, and whirls the Viper every which way. Smoke billows from the enormous 17-inch wheels sporting 13-inch rims at the rear, 11 inches up front. The car handles all the abuse without even straining. "Never once," said Scott, "do you lose control. It's as steady as a rock, and can be thrown around without any fear."

Hopefully Dodge engineers will do some-

Dodge. This is the Viper ACR—the letters stand for American Club Racer—and the car is designed to compete in grassroots racing in the U.S. Which means anybody who chucks off his business suit at weekends can go racing in a competition-ready Viper and dream that he/she is driving hell for leather down the Mulsanne Straight at Le Mans. What a way to spend the weekend: pure Valhalla!

In 1990, Chrysler was in a parlous state once more. Now it is a profitable, high-flying company, thanks to the extraordinary zeal and enthusiasm Chrysler workers have. The year 1999 marks the company's seventy-fifth anniversary, and there is a lot to celebrate.

Look at the Viper and you see the new, aggressive Chrysler reflected in its clear coat. This new Chrysler is an updated, modern company that has a sense of humor, is willing to take chances, and loves what it is doing. There is little doubt that the creation of the Viper, and then the cab-forward series of cars, did much to boost morale.

What of Chrysler's future? In a surprise move in 1998, Chrysler tied the knot with German luxury-car and sports-car builder Mercedes-Benz. Of course the world's oldest car company made sure it had controlling interest in a venture that should be extremely advantageous to Chrysler. Certainly the people that are running a very successful show don't want a return to the bad old days.

There is plenty going on, plenty planned. In 1998 there was the launch of the new 300

thing about the hard, bumpy ride in the R/T 10 convertible before too many people entranced by the car notice it. On rotten, pot-holed roads like Michigan's atrocious I-94, the Viper quivers like someone who's had too much caffeine; the normally sensitive, responsive steering isn't sure of itself, wanting to get lost on the snow-cracked road filled with miniature Grand Canyons.

One thing, though. The Viper exudes charisma. It has a strong personality that makes one think the car is a live person. Even at $72,000-plus, the Viper is worth every penny.

The spirits of four men have left indelible shadows upon the Viper. Just-retired Bob Lutz, Francois Castaing, Tom Gale, and Carroll Shelby are the shadows; they're in every Viper made. For 1999, there's a new Viper from series. Based on the LH series, the 300M has a more powerful engine and sportier suspension—and has the genius of Tom Gale in its radical and attractive design. And Plymouth has designed and built a state-of-the-art sports car in its West Coast design offices. Called the Pronto Spyder, the little car was thought up by John Herlitz, Tom Gale, and Bob Lutz. It has a diminutive wheelbase of only 95.0 inches, is 156 inches in length, and can do 0–60 in 5.3 seconds. The Pronto is a two-seater, has a nice size, and would sell like crazy. Folk would be lining up to get into Chrysler showrooms to buy the Pronto. There is absolutely no doubt that Plymouth should build this car. And with Mercedes's input, there' s every reason to suppose that there are going to be some phenome-

nal cars coming our way as we cross the bridge into the twenty-first century.

Today Chrysler's quality control is much, much better than it was a few years back. But there is still a ways to go. Interior materials still need to be upgraded. Chrysler continues to build some of the greatest cars ever to see the road, and it would be shame not to see some of the greatest workmanship as well.

But when it comes to performance—well, Chrysler need never worry. The 300 Letter Series, Fury, Charger, Road Runner, Super Bee, Daytona and Superbird, Prowler and Viper—these are the very best.

Chrysler, we salute you. In performance and style, you did it better than anyone else. Walter P. would have been proud.

APPENDIX: *Specifications*

1951 Chrysler New Yorker. Wb. 131.5 in., overall length 214 in. Engine: hemispherical V-8, 331 cid, 180 bhp (SAE gross). 34,286 built of 6 different models. Base price: $3,378.

1954 Chrysler New Yorker DeLuxe 4-door sedan. Wb. 125.5 in., overall length 215.5 in. Engine: hemispherical V-8, 331.1 cid, 195 bhp (SAE gross). 34,322 built of 5 different models. Base price: $3,443.

1955 Chrysler C-300 2-door hardtop coupe. Wb. 126 in., overall length 218.8 in. Engine: hemispherical V-8, 331 cid, 300 bhp (SAE gross). 1,725 built. Base price: $4,110.

1956 DeSoto Adventurer 2-door hardtop coupe. Wb. 126 in., overall length 220.9 in. Engine: hemispherical V-8, 341 cid, 315 bhp (SAE gross). 996 built. Base price: $3,728.

1956 Chrysler 300B 2-door hardtop coupe. Wb. 126 in., overall length 222.7 in. Engine: hemispherical V-8, 354 cid, 340 bhp (SAE gross). 1,102 built. Base price: $4,419.

1956 Plymouth Fury 2-door hardtop coupe. Wb. 115 in., overall length 204.8 in. Engine: V-8, 303 cid, 240 bhp (SAE gross). 4,485 built. Base price: $2,807.

1957 Chrysler 300C 2-door hardtop coupe. Also convertible. Wb. 126 in., overall length 219.2 in. Engine: hemispherical V-8, 392 cid, 375 bhp (SAE gross) or 390 bhp. Optional high-lift cam version. 1,918 hardtops, 484 convertibles built. Base prices: $4,929 (hardtop), $5,359 (convertible).

1957 DeSoto Adventurer 2-door hardtop coupe and convertible. Wb. 122 in., overall length 221 in. Engine: hemispherical V-8, 345 cid, 345 bhp (SAE gross). 1,650 hardtops, 300 convertibles built. Base prices: $3,997 (hardtop), $4,272 (convertible).

1957 Dodge D-500 2-door club sedan. Also convertible. Wb. 122 in., overall length 212.2 in. Engine: hemispherical heads, V-8, 325 cid, 285 bhp (SAE gross). There was the Super D-500 engine rated at 310 or 340 bhp (SAE gross). Note: D-500 was optional performance package for Custom Royal and Coronet series. 82,220 2-door hardtops and 6,960 convertibles built. Base prices: $3,314 (club sedan), $3,670 (convertible).

1957 Plymouth Fury 2-door hardtop coupe. Wb. 118 in.,

overall length 206.1 in. Engine: V-8, 317.6 in., 290 bhp (SAE gross). 7,438 hardtops built. Base price: $2,900.

1958 Chrysler 300D 2-door hardtop and convertible. Wb. 126 in., overall length 220.2 in. Engine: hemispherical V-8, 392 cid, 380 bhp (SAE gross). Optional fuel-injected engine developed 390 bhp (SAE gross). Only 16 300Ds were so equipped and most converted to carburetors. 618 hardtops and 191 convertibles built. Base prices: $5,173 (hardtop), $5,603 (convertible). Fuel injection was a $400 option.

1958 DeSoto Adventurer 2-door hardtop and convertible. Wb. 126 in., overall length 218.6 in. Engine: V-8, 361 cid, 345 bhp (SAE gross). 350 hardtops and 82 convertibles built. Base prices: $4,071 (hardtop), $4,369 (convertible).

1958 Dodge D-500 2-door hardtop and convertible. Wb. 122 in., overall length 212.2 in. Engine: V-8, 361 cid, 305 bhp (SAE gross). Super D-500, V-8, 361 cid, 320 bhp (SAE gross); dual 4-bbl version, 333 bhp (SAE gross). Note: D-500 was special performance package for Coronet and Custom Royal series. They were a very small percentage of the 133,953 units produced by Dodge for model year 1958. Base price between $3,500 and $3,800; there are no records for cars with the D-500 option.

1958 Plymouth Fury 2-door hardtop. Wb. 118 in., overall length 206 in. Engine: V-8, 317.6 cid, 290 bhp (SAE gross). Optional Golden Commando V-8, 350 cid, 305 bhp (SAE gross). 5,303 units built. Base price: $3,032.

1959 Chrysler 300E 2-door hardtop and convertible coupe. Wb. 126 in., overall length 220.9 in. Engine: wedge V-8, 413 cid, 380 bhp (SAE gross). 550 hardtops, 140 convertibles built. Base prices: $5,319 (hardtop), $5,749 (convertible).

1959 DeSoto Adventurer 2-door hardtop and convertible coupe. Wb. 126 in., overall length 221.1 in. Engine: 383 cid, 350 bhp (SAE gross). 590 hardtops, 97 convertibles built. Base prices: $4,427 (hardtop), $4,749 (convertible).

1959 Dodge D-500 2-door hardtop. Wb. 122 in., overall length 217.4 in. Engine: D-500 V-8, 383 cid, 320 bhp (SAE gross) or 345 bhp (SAE gross) with dual 4-barrel carburetors. D-500 was option package only; there are no separate production figures. Base price between $3,500 and $3,800.

1959 Plymouth Sport Fury 2-door hardtop and convertible. Wb. 118 in., overall length 210 in. Engine: 317.6 cid, 260 bhp (SAE gross). Optional Golden Commando V-8, 360.8 cid, 305 bhp (SAE gross). 17,867 hardtops, 5,990 convertibles built. (Sport Fury was regular series, not limited-edition Belvedere model like previous Fury.) Base prices: $2,927 (hardtop), $3,125 (convertible).

1960 Chrysler 300F 2-door hardtop and convertible. Wb. 126 in., overall length 219.6 in. Engine: 413 cid, 375 bhp (SAE gross). Optional engine, 413 cid, 400 bhp (SAE gross). 964 hardtops, 248 convertibles built. Base prices: $5,411 (hardtop), $5,841 (convertible).

1960 DeSoto Adventurer 2-door hardtop (now a complete series). Wb. 122 in., overall length 217 in. Engine: V-8, 383 cid, 305 bhp. (SAE gross). 3,092 2-door hardtops, 5,746 4-door sedans, and 2,759 4-door hardtop sedans built. Base prices: $3,663, $3,579, and $3,727 respectively.

1960 Dodge D-500 (engine option package available on Polara, Matador, and Phoenix models). Wb. 122 in., overall length 212.6 in. Engines: V-8s, 361 cid, 295 bhp; 383 cid, 325 bhp and 330 bhp (all SAE gross). 73,175 Phoenix, 27,908 Matador, and 16,728 Polara models built. Base prices, hardtop coupes only: $2,737, $2,996, and $3,196 for Phoenix, Matador, and Polara respectively.

1960 Plymouth Fury 2-door hardtop coupe (Sport Fury discontinued). Wb. 118 in., overall length 209.4 in. Engine: V-8, 361 cid, 305 bhp. This was largest engine option offered in all full-size Plymouths (SAE gross). 18,079 hardtop coupes and 7,080 convertibles built. Base prices: $2,599 (hardtop), $2,967 (convertible).

1961 Chrysler 300G 2-door hardtop coupe and convertible. Wb. 126 in., overall length 219.8 in. Engine: 413 cid, 375 bhp (SAE gross). 1,280 hardtops and 337 convertibles built. Base prices: $5,413 (hardtop), $5,843 (convertible).

1961 Dodge (D-500, Super D-500, Ram-induction D-500 V-8 engine option packages available in Dart, Polara). Dart: Wb. 118 in., overall length 209.4 in. Polara: Wb. 122 in., overall length 212.5 in. Engines: D-500 361 cid, 305 bhp (Dart); D-500 383 cid, 325 bhp (Polara); Ram-induction D-500, 383 cid, 330 bhp (Polara); Super D-500 V-8, 413 cid, 375 bhp. All engines SAE gross. 100,547 Dart V-8 models built; 14,032 Polara models built. Base prices: $3,470 to $4,005 (Dart models); $2,966 to $3,409 (Polara models).

1961 Plymouth Fury 2-door hardtop and convertible. Wb. 118 in., overall length 209.5 in. Engines: 6 high-performance V-8s offered to combat Ford, Chevrolet hi-po models. 317.6 (318) cid, Super Fury V-8 260 bhp standard engine; 360.8-(361-) cid, Golden Commando V-8, 305 bhp; 383-cid V-8, 325 bhp; 383-cid V-8, 330 bhp; 383 cid, 340 bhp; 413.2-cid V-8, 350 bhp and 413.2-cid

V-8, 375 bhp. All figures SAE gross. 54,215 Furys (all models) built. Base prices: 2-door hardtop and convertible, $2,718 and $2,967 respectively.

1962 Chrysler 300H 2-door hardtop and convertible. Wb. 122 in., overall length 215.3 in. Engine: V-8, 413 cid, 380 bhp (SAE gross). 435 hardtops, 123 convertibles built. Base prices: $5,090 (hardtop), $5,461 (convertible).

1962 Dodge Dart, Polara 500, Custom 880. Bodystyles: various. Dart and Polara: Wb. 116 in., overall length 202 in. Custom 880: Wb. 122 in., overall length 213.5 in. Engines, high performance only: 361 cid 305 bhp, 413 cid 410 bhp, and 413 cid 420 bhp (SAE gross). Note: 413s were the famous Ramcharger engines so successful in motorsports. Dodge model year production: 165,861 units. Base prices: $3,185 (Dart 2-door hardtop), $3,019 (Polara 500), and $3,030 (Custom 880).

1962 Plymouth Fury, Sport Fury. Wb. 116 in., overall length 202 in. Engines: 361 cid 305 bhp, 413 cid 410 bhp and 420 bhp (SAE gross). Calendar-year production of all Plymouths: 331,079 units; model year production: 172,134 (full-size cars). Base prices: Sport Fury, $2,851 (hardtop), $3,082 (convertible); ordinary Fury: 2-door hardtop $2,693, convertible $2,924. Note: 413 engine used mainly for drag racing and produced for that purpose.

1963 Chrysler 300J 2-door hardtop. Wb. 122 in., overall length 215.5 in. Engine: Firepower 390, 413 cid, 390 bhp (SAE gross). 400 built. Base price: $5,184.

1963 Dodge 330, 440, Polara. Wb. 119 in., overall length 208.1 in. Engines: V-8s; 383 cid, 330 bhp. The following engines were built primarily for drag racing and NASCAR, and were unbeatable: 426 cid, 4-bbl, 385 bhp; Ramcharger V-8, 426 cid, 415 bhp (dual 4-bbls); Ramcharger V-8, 426 cid, 425 bhp (all SAE gross). Model year production: 64,100 Dodge 330 models; 44,300 440 models; 39,800 Polara models (figures do not include Dart compact models or full-size 880 models). Base prices (2-door hardtops only): 330 2-door sedan (no hardtop), $2,352; 440 hardtop coupe, $2,477; Polara 2-door hardtop, $2,732.

1963 Plymouth Fury/Sport Fury 2-door hardtops. Wb. 116 in., overall length 205 in. Engines: V-8s. With the exception of the Golden Commando 383-cid, 330-bhp engine, others were built primarily for motorsports, where they were invincible: Super Stock 426-cid Wedge, 385 bhp; 426-cid Super Stock II, 415 bhp; 426-cid Wedge, 425 bhp, dual four bbl (SAE gross). Model year production (Fury/Sport Fury 2-door hardtops): Fury, 13,832; Sport Fury, 11,483. Base prices: $2,693 and $2,851, respectively.

1964 Chrysler 300K 2-door hardtop and convertible. Wb. 122 in., overall length 215.5 in. Engines: 413 cid, 360 bhp (standard 300K engine); optional: 413 cid, 390 bhp (SAE gross). 3,022 hardtops and 625 convertibles were built (a new 300 production record). Base prices: $4,056 (hardtop), $4,522 (convertible).

1964 Dodge Polara 330, 440, 880, Custom 880. All

bodystyles. Wb. 119 in. (880, Custom 880: 122 in.), overall length 209.8 in. (880, Custom 880: 214.8 in.). Engines: 383-cid V-8, 305 bhp; 383-cid V-8, 330 bhp; Ramcharger V-8, 426 cid, 415 bhp; Ramcharger Eight-Barrel 426 cid, 425 bhp; Hemi-Charger V-8 (NASCAR only). Hemispherical combustion chambers, 426 cid, 400 bhp; Hemi-Charger V-8, 426 cid, 415 bhp; Hemi-Charger V-8, 426 cid, 425 bhp (all SAE gross). Production totals: Polara V-8, 66,988; Polara 500, 17,787; 330 V-8, 46,438; 440 V-8, 68,861; 880, 10,526; Custom 880, 21,234 (production totals do not include 6-cylinder models). Base prices, V-8 models only: 330, $2,372–$2,863; 440, $2,508–$2,962; Polara, $2,745–$2,994; Polara 500, $2,978–$3,227; 880, $2,826–$3,270; Custom 880, $2,977–$3,420.

1964 Plymouth Savoy, Belvedere, Fury, Sport Fury. Wb. 116 in., overall length 206.05 in. Engines: 383 cid, 426-cid Wedge, 426-cid Hemi. Engines identical to Dodge; please check 1964 Dodge for horsepower ratings. 426 Wedge and 426 Hemi built expressly for drag racing and NASCAR. Hemi engine cost around $1,800 "in the crate" for professional racing teams and was unavailable to the public. Only 6,359 426-cid-powered cars were built in 1964. Production totals: Savoy (2-door sedans only), 21,326; Belvedere (2-door hardtop coupe only), 16,334; Fury, 36,303 (hardtop coupe), 5,173 (convertible); Sport Fury, 23,695 (hardtop coupe), 3,858 (convertible coupe). Base prices: Savoy, $2,224 and $2,332; Belvedere, $2,444 and $2,551; Fury, $2,706 (V-8 only) and $2,937 (convertible); Sport Fury, $2,864 and $3,095.

1965 Chrysler 300L (the last Letter Series 300). Wb. 124 in., overall length 218.2 in. Engine: 413 cid, 360 bhp (SAE gross). 2,405 hardtops, 440 convertibles built. Base price: $4,090 (hardtop), $4,545 (convertible).

1965 Dodge Coronet Hemi-Charger, Coronet, Polara, Monaco, Custom 880. Wb. (three different) 115 in., 117 in., 121 in. Overall lengths 201 in. (an approximation on a special Coronet race car built solely for competition. A few were sold to the public for $3,165 per unit), 204.2 in., 212.3 in. Engines: 383 cid, 330 bhp; 413 cid, 340 bhp; 426-cid Wedge, 365 bhp; 426-cid Hemi, 415 bhp; 426-cid Hemi, 425 bhp. Production totals: 209,393 Coronets (including Hemi-Charger), 134,771 Polara/Custom/Monaco models. Base prices (not including 6-cylinder models): Coronet, $2,353–$2,688; Coronet 440, $2,499–$2,868; Coronet 500, $2,674–$2,894; Polara, $2,837–$3,259; Custom 880, $3,085–$3,527; Monaco, $3,355.

1965 Plymouth Barracuda Formula S. Wb. 106 in., overall length 188.2 in. Engine: Commando 273-cid V-8, bhp 235 (SAE gross). 64,596 Barracudas built; this included Formula S package. Base price: $2,535.

1965 Plymouth Belvedere, Fury, Satellite. Wb. 115 (Belvedere I SS), 116 in. (Belvedere, Satellite), 119 in. (Fury I, II, III). Overall length 203.4 in., 209.4 in. Engines: All V-8s, 383 cid, 330 bhp; 426-cid Hemi, 425

bhp dual 4 bbl ($1,800 for this engine); 426-S, 426 cid, 365 bhp; 426-R Hemi, 426 cid, 415 bhp (SAE gross). Belvedere Super Stock, n/a. Production totals: Belvedere II, 24,924 (2-door hardtop), 1,921 (convertible coupe); Satellite, 23,341 (hardtop coupe), 1,860 (convertible coupe); Fury III, 43,231 (hardtop coupe), 5,524 (convertible coupe); Sport Fury, 38,348 (hardtop coupe), 6,272 (convertible coupe). Base prices: Belvedere I SS, $4,671; Satellite, $2,649 and $2,869; Fury III, $2,691 and $3,048; Sport Fury, $2,960 and $3,209.

1966 Dodge Dart GT hardtop coupe and convertible. Wb. 111 in., overall length 195.9 in. Engine: 273-cid V-8, 235 bhp (SAE gross). 30,041 GT models built, though few had the hi-po engine. Base prices: $2,545 (hardtop coupe), $2,828 (convertible coupe).

1966 Dodge Charger, Coronet, Polara, Monaco. Wb. 117 in. and 121 in., overall length 203 in. and 213.3 in. Engines: V-8s. 383 cid, 4-barrel, 325 bhp; 426 Hemi, 426 cid, 425 bhp; 440-cid Wedge V-8, 365 bhp (all SAE gross). 37,344 Chargers built. As production figures for Coronet, Polara, and Monaco run into hundreds of thousands and do not single out high-performance cars, the figures are not included. Base prices: Coronet 440, $2,551 (hardtop coupe), $2,766 (convertible coupe); Coronet 500, $2,705 (hardtop coupe), $2,921 (convertible coupe); Charger, $3,122; Polara, $2,874 (hardtop coupe), $3,161 (convertible coupe); Monaco, $3,107 (hardtop coupe); Monaco 500, $3,604 (hardtop coupe).

1966 Plymouth Barracuda. Wb. 106 in., overall length 188.3 in. Engine (high-performance only): 273 cid, 235 bhp (SAE gross). 38,029 built, the majority with smaller engine configurations. Base price: $2,556/$2,637.

1966 Plymouth Belvedere, Fury. Wb. 116 in. and 119 in., overall length 200.5 in. and 209.8 in. (Belvedere includes Satellite; Fury includes VIP). Engines: Commando V-8, 383 cid, 325 bhp; Street Hemi, 426 cid, 425 bhp; Race Hemi (competition only), 426 cid, 425 bhp and 440 cid, 365 bhp (all SAE gross). Production totals: Belvedere II, 36,644 (hardtop coupe), 2,502 (convertible coupe); Satellite, 35,399 (hardtop coupe), 2,759 (convertible coupe); Fury III, 41,869 (hardtop coupe), 4,326 (convertible coupe); Sport Fury, 32,523 (hardtop coupe), 3,418(convertible coupe). Base prices: Belvedere II, $2,430 (hardtop coupe), $2,644 (convertible coupe); Satellite, $2,695 (hardtop coupe), $2,910 (convertible coupe); Fury III, $2,724 (hardtop coupe), $3,074 (convertible coupe); Sport Fury, $3,006 (hardtop coupe), $3,251 (convertible coupe); VIP, $3069 (hardtop coupe), $3,133 (convertible coupe).

1967 Dodge Dart GT 2-door hardtop and convertible. Wb. 111 in., overall length 195.4 in. Engine: 273-cid V-8, 235 bhp (SAE gross). 38,225 built. Base prices: $2,627 (hardtop coupe), $2,860 (convertible coupe).

1967 Dodge Charger 2-door sport hardtop coupe. Based on Coronet chassis and running gear. Wb. 117 in., overall length 203 in. Engines: 318-cid, 230-bhp V-8 (standard); 383 cid, 325 bhp; 426 Hemi, 425 bhp; 440 cid,

375 bhp (all optional). 15,788 built. Base price: $3,128 (hardtop coupe).

1967 Dodge Coronet, Polara, Monaco. Wb. 117 in., 122 in.; overall lengths 203 in., 219.6 in. Engines: 383 cid, 325 bhp; 426 Hemi, 425 bhp, 440 cid, 350 bhp, 440 cid, 375 bhp. Production totals: Coronet 500 Series (includes performance R/T): 39,260. Polara 500: 5,606 hardtops and convertibles built; Monaco 500: 5,237 hardtop coupes built. Production figures of other Coronet, Monaco, and Polara series and bodystyles not included. Base prices: Coronet 500 $2,773 (hardtop coupe), $3,013 (convertible); Polara 500 $3,155 (hardtop coupe), $3,443 (convertible); Monaco 500, $3,712 (hardtop coupe).

1967 Plymouth Barracuda. Wb. 108 in., overall length 192.8 in. Engines (Barracuda had five different engine options; the following were the highest performers): 383 cid, 280 bhp.; 383 cid, 325 bhp. Production totals: 19,997 (hardtop coupe); 2,840 (convertible coupe); 22,575 (fastback coupe). Base prices: $2,605 (hardtop), $2,907 (convertible), $2,762 (fastback).

1967 Plymouth Belvedere, Satellite, GTX, Fury, VIP. Wb. 116 in., 119 in.; overall length 208.1 in., 200.5 in., 213.1 in. Engines: Commando V-8, 383 cid, 325 bhp.; Street Hemi V-8, 426 cid, 425 bhp.; Super Commando V-8, 440 cid, 375 bhp. Production totals: Belvedere II, 34,550 (hardtop coupe); 1,552 (convertible coupe); Satellite, 30,328 (hardtop coupe), 2,050 (convertible coupe); GTX, n/a; Fury III, 37,448 (hardtop coupe), 4,523 (convertible coupe); Sport Fury, 28,448 (hardtop coupe/fastback hardtop coupe), 3,133 (convertible coupe); VIP, 7,912 (hardtop coupe). Base prices: Belvedere II, $2,457 (hardtop coupe), $2,695 (convertible coupe); Satellite, $2,747 (hardtop coupe), $2,986 (convertible coupe); GTX, $3,178 (hardtop coupe), $3,418 (convertible coupe); Fury III, $2,872 (hardtop coupe), $3,118 (convertible coupe); Sport Fury, $3,033 (hardtop coupe), $3,062 (fastback hardtop coupe), $3,279 (convertible coupe); VIP, $3,182 (hardtop coupe).

1968 Dodge Dart GTS. Wb. 111 in., overall length 196 in. Engines: 340-cid, 275-bhp V-8; 383 cid, 300 bhp. Production total: 8,745 (hardtop coupe and convertible coupe). Base prices: $3,189 (hardtop coupe), $3,383 (convertible coupe).

1968 Dodge Charger R/T. Wb. 117 in., overall length 208 in., Engines: 440 cid, 350/375 bhp; 426-cid. Hemi, 425 bhp. Production totals: n/a. Base price: $3,506 (hardtop coupe).

1968 Dodge Coronet, Polara, Monaco. Wb. 117 in., 122 in.; overall length 207 in., 219 in. Engines: 383 cid, 290 bhp; 383 cid, 330 bhp. 383 cid, 335 bhp; 426-cid Hemi, 425 bhp; 440 cid, 375 bhp. Production totals / base prices: Coronet 440, 116,348 (includes new Super Bee option), $2,733 (hardtop coupe), $3,027 (Super Bee); Coronet 500, 40,139, $2,879 (hardtop coupe), $3,036 (convertible coupe); Coronet R/T, 10,849,

$3,379 (hardtop coupe), $3,613 (convertible coupe); Polara, 99,055, $3,027 (hardtop coupe), $3,288 (convertible coupe); Polara 500: 4,983, $3,226 (hardtop coupe), $3,487 (convertible coupe); Monaco, 37,412, $3,369 (hardtop coupe); Monaco 500, 4,568, $3,869 (hardtop coupe).

1968 Plymouth Barracuda. Wb. 108 in., overall length 192.8 in. Engines: "Formula S" 340 cid, 275 bhp; "Formula S" 383 cid, 300 bhp; 426-cid Hemi, 425 bhp. (A few Barracudas were fitted with Hemi engines for drag racing and could do a mile in under a 11 seconds, at top speeds of over 130 mph.) Production totals / base prices: 19,997, $2,579 (hardtop coupe), $3,383 (convertible coupe); 22,575, $2,736 (fastback coupe); 2,840, $2,907 (convertible coupe).

1968 Plymouth Road Runner. Cheap and sporty variation of the Belvedere model. Wb. 116 in., overall length 202.7 in. Engines: 383 cid, 335 bhp; optional 426-cid Hemi, 425 bhp. Production totals / base prices: 29,240, $2,896 (coupe); 15,358, $3,034 (hardtop coupe).

1968 Plymouth Satellite / Sport Satellite, GTX, Fury / Sport Fury. Wb. 116 in., 119 in.; overall length 202.7 in., 213 in. Engines: Satellite, GTX: 383 cid, 290 bhp; 383 cid, 330 bhp; 426-cid Hemi, 425 bhp; Fury: 440 cid, 375 bhp. Production totals / base prices: Satellite, 46,539, $2,594 (hardtop coupe), 1,771, $2,824 (convertible coupe); Sport Satellite, 21,014, $ 2,822 (hardtop coupe), 1,523, $3,036 (convertible coupe); GTX, 17,914, $3,355 (hardtop coupe), 1,026, $3,590 (convertible coupe); Fury III, 60,472, $2,912/$2,932 (hardtop coupe/fastback hardtop coupe), 4,883, $3,236 (convertible coupe); Sport Fury, 6,642, $3,206 (hardtop coupe), 17,073, $3,225 (fastback hardtop coupe); 2,489, $3,425 (convertible coupe).

1969 Dodge Dart GTS. Wb. 110 in., overall length 195.4 in. Engine: 340 cid, 275 bhp. Production totals / base prices: 6,702, $3,226 (hardtop coupe), $3,419 (convertible coupe).

1969 Dodge Charger/RT/500. Wb. 117 in., overall length 207.9 in. Engines: 383 cid, 290 bhp; 383 cid, 330 bhp; 426-cid Hemi, 425 bhp (R/T and 500); 440 cid, 375 bhp (500). Production totals / base pricse: Charger, 38,931, $3,001 (hardtop coupe); R/T 9,732, $3,711 (hardtop coupe); 500 (built specifically for racing), $3,139 (hardtop coupe).

1969 Dodge Charger Daytona. Wb. 117 in., overall length 208.5 in. Engines: 440 cid, 375 bhp; 426-cid Hemi, 425 bhp. Production total / base price: 503, $4,000.

1969 Dodge Coronet, Polara, Monaco. Wb. 117 in., 122 in.; overall length 206.6 in., 220.4 in. Engines: 383 cid, 290 bhp; 383 cid, 330 bhp (option), Super Bee, 383 cid, 335 bhp; 426-cid Hemi, 425 bhp (Coronet); 440 cid, 375 bhp (Polara and Monaco). Production totals / base prices: Coronet 440, 105,882, $2,692 (hardtop coupe); Super Bee, 27,846, $3,076 (coupe), $3,138 (hardtop coupe); Coronet 500, 32,050, $2,929 (hardtop coupe), $3,069 (convertible coupe); Coronet R/T, 7,238, $3,442 (hardtop coupe), $3,660 (convertible coupe); Polara, 83,122, $3,117 (hardtop coupe), $3,377 (convertible coupe); Polara 500, 5,564, $3,314 (hardtop coupe), $3,576 (convertible coupe); Monaco, 38,566, $3,528 (hardtop coupe).

1969 Plymouth Barracuda, 'Cuda 340. Wb. 108 in., overall length 192.8 in. Engines: 340 cid, 275 bhp (both); 383 cid, 330 bhp; 440 cid, 375 bhp ('Cuda). Production totals / base prices: Barracuda, 12,757, $2,780 (hardtop coupe); 1,442, $3,082 (convertible coupe); 17,788, $2,813 (fastback hardtop coupe).

1969 Plymouth Satellite, Sport Satellite, GTX, Fury, Sport Fury, VIP. Wb. 116 in., 120 in. (Fury and VIP); overall length 202.7 in., 214.5 in. (Fury and VIP). Engines: 383 cid, 330 bhp; 426-cid Hemi, 425 bhp; 440 cid, 375 bhp. Production totals / base prices: Satellite, 38,323, $2,659 (hardtop coupe); 1,137, $2,875 (convertible coupe); Sport Satellite, 15,807, $2,883 (hardtop coupe), 818, $3,081 (convertible coupe); GTX, 14,902, $3,416 (hardtop coupe), 700, $3,635 (convertible coupe); Fury III, 44,168, $3,000 (hardtop coupe), 4,129, $3,324 (convertible coupe); Sport Fury, 14,120, $3,282 (hardtop coupe), 1,579, $3,502 (convertible coupe).

1970 Chrysler 300-H (Hurst). Wb. 124 in., overall length, 224.7 in. Engine: 440 cid, 375 bhp. Production total / base price: 485, $5,939 (hardtop coupe). Note: Chrysler 300 Hurst was prepared by Hurst Performance Research Corporation and sold through Chrysler/Plymouth dealers—essentially a promotional package advertising Hurst.

1970 Dodge Dart Swinger 340. Wb. 111 in., overall length 197 in. Engine: 340 cid, 275 bhp. Production total / base price: 13,785, $2,631.

1970 Dodge Challenger R/T (T/A). Wb. 110 in., overall length 191.3 in. Engines: 383 cid, 290 bhp; 383 cid, 330 bhp; 383 cid, 335 bhp; 426-cid Hemi, 425 bhp; 440 cid, 375 bhp; 440 cid, 390 bhp. Production totals / base prices: Challenger, 53,337, $2,851 (hardtop coupe), 3,173, $3,120 (convertible coupe); SE, 6,584, $3,083 (hardtop coupe); R/T (includes T/A), 14,889, $3,226 (hardtop coupe); 1,070, $3,535 (convertible coupe); SE, 3,979, $3,498 (hardtop coupe).

1970 Dodge Charger, 500, R/T. Wb. 117 in., overall length 208 in. Engines: 383 cid, 290 bhp; 383 cid, 335 bhp; 426-cid Hemi, 425 bhp; 440 cid, 375 bhp; 440 cid, 390 bhp. Production totals / base prices: Charger and 500, 39,431 (hardtop coupe); Charger, $3,001 (hardtop coupe); 500, $3,139 (hardtop coupe); R/T, 10,337, $3,711 (hardtop coupe).

1970 Dodge Coronet, Monaco, Polara. Wb. 117 in., 122 in.; overall length, 210 in., 220 in. Engines: 383 cid, 290 bhp; 383 cid, 330 bhp; 426-cid Hemi, 425 bhp; 440 cid, 375 bhp. Production totals / base prices: Coronet Super Bee, 3,966, $3,012 (coupe), 11,540, $3,074 (hardtop coupe); Coronet 500, 8,247, $3,048 (hardtop coupe), $3,074 (convertible coupe); Coronet R/T, 2,319, $3,442

(hardtop coupe), 296, $3,785 (convertible coupe). Polara production figures unavailable; prices as follows: Polara DeLuxe, $3,224 (hardtop coupe), $3,527 (convertible coupe); Polara Custom, $3,458 (hardtop coupe); Monaco, 3,522, $3,679 (hardtop coupe).

1970 Plymouth Barracuda, 'Cuda, Gran Coupe. Wb. 108 in., overall length 186.7 in. Engines: 340 cid, 275 bhp; 383 cid, 290 bhp; 383 cid, 330 bhp; 383 cid, 335 bhp (S); 'Cuda, 426-cid Hemi, 425 bhp, 440 cid, 375 bhp, 440 cid, 390 bhp. Production totals / base prices: Barracuda, 25,651, $2,764 (hardtop coupe), 1,554, $3,034 (convertible coupe); 'Cuda, 18,180, $3,164 (hardtop coupe), 635, $3,433 (convertible coupe); Gran Coupe, 8,183, $2,934 (hardtop coupe), 596, $3,160 (convertible coupe).

1970 Plymouth Valiant Duster 340. Wb. 108 in., overall length, 188.4 in. Engine: 340 cid, 275 bhp (S). Production total / base price: 24,817, $2,547 (hardtop coupe).

1970 Plymouth Road Runner. Wb. 116 in., overall length 204 in. Engines: 383 cid, 335 bhp; 426-cid Hemi, 425 bhp; 440 cid, 390 bhp. Production totals / base prices: 15,716, $2,896 (coupe), 24,944, $3,034 (hardtop coupe), 824, $3,289 (convertible coupe).

1970 Plymouth Road Runner Superbird. Wb. 116 in., overall length 218 in. Engines: 440 cid, 375 bhp; 426-cid Hemi, 425 bhp. (Note: Hemi V-8's horsepower rating was considered conservative by racers and engineers. True horsepower was more like 500/550 bhp). Production total / base price: 1,920, $4,298.

1970 Plymouth Belvedere, Satellite, GTX. Wb. 116 in., overall length, 204 in. Engines: 383 cid, 290 bhp; 383 cid, 330 bhp; 426-cid Hemi, 425 bhp; 440 cid, 375 bhp; 440 cid, 390 bhp. Production totals / base prices: Belvedere, 4,717, $2,603 (coupe); Satellite, 28,200, $2,765 (hardtop coupe); 701, $3,006 (convertible coupe); Sport Satellite, 8,749, $2,988 (hardtop coupe); GTX, 7,748, $3,535 (hardtop coupe).

1970 Plymouth Fury, Sport Fury. Wb. 120 in., overall length 215.3 in. Engines: 383 cid, 290 bhp; 383 cid, 330 bhp; 440 cid, 350 bhp, 440 cid, 390 bhp. Production totals / base prices: Fury III, 21,373, $3,091 (hardtop coupe), 1,952, $3,415 (convertible coupe); Sport Fury (hardtop coupe), S/23 (hardtop coupe), GT (hardtop coupe), 8,018, $3,313, $3,379, and $3,898 respectively.

1971 Dodge Demon 340. Wb. 108 in., overall length 192.5 in. Engine: 340 cid, 275 bhp. Production total / base price: 10,098, $2,721 (fastback coupe).

1971 Dodge Challenger R/T. Wb. 110 in., overall length 192 in. Engines: 340 cid, 275 bhp; 383 cid, 275 bhp; 383 cid, 300 bhp; 426-cid Hemi, 425 bhp; 440 cid, 385 bhp. Production total / base price: 4,630 (Challenger R/T only), $3,273. Note: 1971 was the final year for horsepower to be given in SAE gross measurements; from 1972 the figures would be calculated in SAE net measurements.

1971 Dodge Charger. Wb. 115 in., overall length 206 in.

Engines: 383 cid, 275 bhp; 383 cid, 300 bhp; 426-cid Hemi, 425 bhp; 440 cid, 370 bhp; 440 cid, 385 bhp. Production totals / base prices: 46,183, $2,707 and $2,975 (coupe/hardtop coupe); 500, 11,948, $3,223 (hardtop coupe); Super Bee, 5,054, $3,271 (hardtop coupe); SE, 15,811, $3,422 (hardtop coupe); R/T, 3,118, $3,777 (hardtop coupe).

1971 Plymouth Barracuda, 'Cuda, Gran Coupe. Wb. 108 in., overall length 186.6 in. Engines: 340 cid, 275 bhp; 383 cid, 300 bhp; 426-cid Hemi, 425 bhp; 440 cid, 385 bhp. Production totals / base prices: Barracuda, 9,459, $2,654 and $2,766 (coupe/hardtop coupe), 1,014, $3,023 (convertible); Gran Coupe, 1,615, $3,029 (hardtop coupe); 'Cuda, 6,228, $3,155 (hardtop coupe); 374, $3,412 (convertible).

1971 Plymouth Duster 340. Wb. 108 in., overall length 188.4 in. Engine: 340 cid, 275 bhp. Production total / base price: 12,886, $2,703.

1971 Plymouth Road Runner. Wb. 115 in., overall length 203.2 in. Engines: 383 cid, 275 bhp; 383 cid, 300 bhp; 426-cid Hemi, 350 bhp; 426 cid, 425 bhp; 440 cid, 370 bhp; 440 cid, 385 bhp. Production total / base price: 14,218, $3,147.

1971 Plymouth Satellite, GTX. Wb. 115 in., 203.2 in. Engines: 383 cid, 275 bhp; 383 cid, 300 bhp; 426-cid Hemi, 425 bhp; 440 cid, 385 bhp. Production totals (2-door hardtops only): Satellite and Sebring, 46,807, $2,663 and $2,931 (coupe/hardtop coupe); Satellite Sebring Plus, 16,253, $3,179 (hardtop coupe); GTX, 2,942, $3,733 (hardtop coupe). Note: After 1971 there would be no more Hemi V-8. Due to ever-mounting insurance costs and federal mandates, Chrysler wisely decided to retire this most fabulous engine while it was still ahead. Specifications from this point on will no longer include full-size Dodge/Plymouth cars like the Monaco or Fury, as they no longer had sporting appeal.

1972 Dodge Demon 340. Wb. 108 in., overall length 192.5 in. Engine: 340 cid, 240 bhp (SAE net). Production total / base price: 8,750, $2,759.

1972 Dodge Challenger Rallye. Wb. 110 in., overall length 192 in. Engine: 340 cid, 240 bhp (SAE net). Production total / base price: 8,123, $3,082.

1972 Dodge Charger Rallye. Wb. 115 in., overall length, 206 in. Engines: 340 cid, 240 bhp; 400 cid, 190 bhp; 400 cid, 255 bhp; 440 cid, 285 bhp; all engines SAE net and 440 offered only in Rallye series. Production totals / base prices: 7,803, $2,759 (2-door coupe); 45,361, $3,020 (2-door hardtop coupe); SE, 22,430 (2-door hardtop coupe), $3,249. Note: Rallye was a new, 1972 option package and the only Charger to have performance.

1972 Plymouth Barracuda, 'Cuda. Wb. 108 in., overall length 186.6 in. Engine: 340 cid, 240 bhp (SAE net). Production totals / base prices: Barracuda, 10,622, $2,808; 'Cuda, 7,828, $2,953. Note: This was the only high-performance engine option. There was a "Race Hemi" available only for competition use. A very few of

these engines might have found their way into private hands.

1972 Plymouth Duster 340. Wb. 108 in., overall length 188.4 in. Engine: 340 cid, 240 bhp (SAE net). Production total / base price: 15,681, $2,728.

1972 Plymouth Road Runner, Satellite. Wb. 115 in., overall length 203.2 in. Engines: 340 cid, 240 bhp (Std. Road Runner); 400 cid, 190 bhp; 400 cid, 225 bhp; 440 cid, 280 bhp; 440 cid, 330 bhp (Road Runner). Production totals / base prices: Road Runner, 7,628, $3,095 (2-door hardtop); Satellite Sebring, 34,353, $2,871 (2-door hardtop coupe); Satellite Sebring Plus, 21,399, $3,127 (2-door hardtop coupe).

1973 Dodge Dart Sport 340. Wb. 108 in., overall length 200 in. Engine: 340 cid, 240 bhp. Production total / base price: 11,315, $2,853. Note: Car had racy tape stripe that extended from front fender over the roof.

1973 Dodge Challenger. Wb. 110 in., overall length 199 in. Engine: 340 cid, 240 bhp (SAE net). Production total / base price: 32,596, $3,011.

1973 Dodge Charger. Wb. 115 in., overall length 213 in. Engines: 340 cid, 240 bhp; 400 cid, 175 bhp; 400 cid, 260 bhp; 440 cid, 280 bhp. Production totals / base price: 11,995, $2,810 (coupe); 45,415, $3,060 (hardtop coupe); SE, 61,908, $3,375 (hardtop coupe).

1973 Plymouth Duster 340. Wb. 108 in., overall length 195.8 in. Engine: 340 cid, 240 bhp (SAE net). Production total / base price: 15,731, $2,822.

1973 Plymouth Barracuda, 'Cuda. Wb. 108 in., overall length 193 in. Engine: 340 cid, 235 bhp (SAE net). Production totals / base prices: Barracuda, 11,587, $2,935 (hardtop coupe); 'Cuda, 10,626, $3,120 (hardtop coupe).

1973 Plymouth Road Runner, Satellite. 115 in., overall length 210.8 in. Engines: 400 cid, 175 bhp; 400 cid, 260 bhp; 440 cid, 280 bhp (SAE net). Production totals / base prices: Road Runner, 19,056, $3,115 (2-door hardtop coupe); Satellite Sebring, 51,575, $3,109 (2-door hardtop coupe); Satellite Plus, 43,628, $3,258 (2-door hardtop coupe).

1974 Dodge Dart Sport 360. Wb. 108 in., overall length 200 in. Engine: 360 cid, 4 bbl, 245 bhp. Production total / base price: 3,951, $3,320.

1974 Dodge Challenger. Wb. 110 in., overall length 199 in. Engine: 360 cid, 4 bbl, 245 bhp (SAE net). Production total / base price: 16,437, $3,143 (hardtop coupe).

1974 Dodge Charger. Wb. 115 in., overall length 213 in. Engines: 360 cid, 2 bbl, 180 bhp; 360 cid, 200 bhp; 360 cid, 4 bbl, 245 bhp; 400 cid, 185 bhp; 400 cid, 205 bhp; 400 cid, 250 bhp; 440 cid, 275 bhp (SAE net). Production totals / base prices: 8,876, $3,212 (2-door coupe), 29,101, $3,412 (2-door hardtop coupe); SE, 36,399, $3,742 (hardtop coupe).

1974 Plymouth Duster 360. Wb. 108 in., overall length 194.1 in. Engine: 360 bhp, 4 bbl, 245 bhp (SAE net). Production total / base price: 3,969, $3,288.

1974 Plymouth Barracuda, 'Cuda. Wb. 108 in., overall

length 195.6 in. Engine: 360, 4 bbl, 245 bhp. Production totals / base prices: Barracuda, 6,745, $3,067 (2-door hardtop coupe); 'Cuda, 4,989, $3,300 (2-door hardtop coupe).

1974 Plymouth Road Runner, Satellite. Wb. 115 in., overall length 212.4 in. Engines: 360 cid, 180 bhp; 360 cid, 245 bhp; 400 cid, 205 bhp; 400 cid, 250 bhp; 440 cid, 275 bhp (SAE net). Production totals / base prices: Road Runner, 11,555, $3,545 (2-door coupe); Satellite Sebring, 31,980, $3,468 (2-door hardtop coupe); Satellite Plus, 18,480 (2-door hardtop coupe). Note: 1974 was the final season for the Dodge Challenger (an emasculated Challenger would eventually appear as a Japanese captive import), Plymouth Barracuda and 'Cuda, and Satellite.

1975 Dodge Dart Sport 360. Wb. 108 in., overall length 201 in. Engine: 360 cid, 230 bhp. Production total / base price: 1,043, $4,014 (2-door fastback coupe).

1975 Dodge Charger SE. Wb. 115 in., overall length 216 in. Engines: 360 cid, 180 bhp; 360 cid, 190 bhp; 400 cid, 185 bhp; 400 cid, 235 bhp. Production total / base price: 30,812, $4,903 (hardtop coupe).

1975 Plymouth Duster 360. Wb. 108 in., overall length 197 in. Engine: 360 cid, 230 bhp. Production total / base price: 1,421, $3,979 (coupe).

1975 Plymouth Road Runner, Fury. Wb. 115 in., overall length 213.8 in. Engines: 360 cid, 180 bhp; 360 cid, 190 bhp; 400 cid, 165 bhp; 400 cid, 185 bhp; 400 cid, 190 bhp; 400 cid, 235 bhp. Production totals / base prices: Road Runner, 7,183, $3,973 (2-door hardtop coupe); Fury, 8,398, $3,672 (2-door hardtop coupe); 27,486, $3,840 (2-door custom hardtop); 17,782, $4,105 (2-door sport hardtop). Note: Fury replaced Satellite as Plymouth's intermediate line in 1975. Gran Fury was the only full-size offering. There were no high-performance models of any note over the next few years. Large engines had compression ratios cut back and were strangled by emissions controls. A truly unique period in motoring history had come to an end, never to return.

1983 Dodge Shelby Charger 2.2. Wb. 96.6 in., overall length 173.7 in. Engine: 135 cid (2.2 liter), OHC 4-cylinder, 107 bhp. Production total / base price: 8,251, $8,290.

1983 Plymouth Turismo 2.2 Coupe. Wb. 96.6 in., overall length 173.3 in. Engine: 135 cid (2.2 liter), OHC 4-cylinder, 100 bhp. Production total / base price: 9,538, $7,303.

1988 Dodge Daytona Shelby Z Hatchback Coupe. Wb. 97 in., overall length 175 in. Engine: 135 cid (2.2 liter), OHC, EFI Turbo II 4-cylinder, 174 bhp. Production total / base price: 7,850, $13,394. Note: Although under half the size of the big V-8s of a decade earlier, these turbocharged 4-cylinder engines could accelerate to 60 in 7 or 8 seconds with ease.

1992 Dodge Viper R/T 10 Roadster. Wb. 96.2 in., overall length 175.1 in. Engine: OHV, all-aluminum V-10, 488 cid (8 liters), 400 bhp (SAE net). Production total / base price: 3,000 (est.), $50,000.

1995 Dodge Viper GTS Coupe. Wb. 96.2 in., overall length 176.7 in. Engine: all-aluminum V-10, 488 cid (8 liters), 450 bhp. Production total / base price: n/a, $72,830.

1995 Chrysler Atlantic Concept Car. Wb. 126 in., overall length 199.5 in. Engine: DOHC, 4-liter I-8 (32 valves), 325 bhp. Production total / base price: 1, n/a.

1997 Plymouth Prowler. Wb. 113 in., overall length 165 in. Engine: SOHC V-6, 215 cid (3.5 liters), 214 bhp (SAE net). Production total / base price: 3,000 (est.), $35,000.

1998 Dodge Viper R/T 10 Roadster. Wb. 96.2 in., overall length 175.1 in. Engine: all-aluminum V-10, 488 cid (8 liters), 450 bhp. Production total / base price: n/a, $66,700.

AUSTRALIAN CHRYSLERS

1968 Chrysler Valiant 4-door sedan. Wb. 108 in., overall length 193 in. Engine: 273 cid, 195 bhp (SAE net). $3,650 (Australian) for VIP model. Valiant prices started at $2,490 and went up to $3,720 (Australian). Production for VE models, 68,688 (over an 18-month period).

1972 Chrysler Valiant Charger 770. Wb. 105 in., overall length 173.5 in. Engines: Hemi 215, OHV I-6 215 cid, 140 bhp; Hemi 245, 245 cid, 165 bhp, Hemi 265, 265 cid, 203 bhp; Hemi 265, 265 cid, 248 bhp; Hemi 265, 265 cid, 280 bhp; Hemi 265, 302 bhp; V-8 OHV, 318 cid, 230 bhp; 340 cid, 275 bhp. 31,857 Chargers built between 1971 and 1978. Base price: $2,970 (basic).

Index